SUFI MYSTICISM

SUFI MYSTICISM

Krishna P. Bahadur

Ess Ess Publications

4837/24, Ansari Road, Darya Ganj,
New Delhi-110002
✆ : 3260807
Fax: 3274173
E-mail: essess@del3.vsnl.net.in

First Published 1999

ISBN : 81-7000-250-8

Price : Rs.600/-

Published by :

Ess Ess Publications

4837/24, Ansari Road, Darya Ganj,
New Delhi - 110 002
Phone : 3260807

Laser Typesetting :

CINOGRAPHICS

E-41, New Multan Nagar
New Delhi
Phone : 5583866

Printed at :

Mehra Offset Press

Contents

Introduction 1

1. The Sufi Teaching 34
2. The Sufi Saints and Orders 69
3. Fundamental Beliefs 183
4. Growth and Evolution 237
5. Philosophy and Practice 248

Bibliography 264

ACKNOWLEDGEMENTS

The author gratefully acknowledges the assistance of the following books in this study of Sufism.

Four Sufi Classics London : The Sufi Trust. Octagon Press, 1980.

S.R. Sharda. *Sufi Thought* New Delhi : Munshiram Manoharlal, 1974.

Idries Shah. *The Sufis*. New York : Doubleday (Anchor Books) 1964.

The Sufi Message of Hazrat Inayat Khan London : Barrie and Rockliff vol. 1, 1960.

Quotations are acknowledge in the references (notes).

Dedication

To the memory of my beloved daughter
Sandhya
16 Oct. 1963 - 17 March 1979
and my beloved son
Sanjay
24 Feb. 1958 - 26 March 1980

Alas, that Spring should vanish with the Rose:
That Youth's sweet-scented Manuscript should close!
The Nighitingale that in the Branches sang,
Ah, whence, and wither flown again, who knows!

Fitzgerald.Omar Khayyām

Once the noble Ibrahim, as he sat on his throne,
Heard a clamour and noise of cries on the roof,
And also heavy footsteps on the roof of his palace.
He said to himself 'Whose heavy feet are these?'
He shouted from the window, 'Who goes there?'
The guards, filled with confusion, bowed their heads, saying,
'It is we, going the rounds in search'.
He said, 'What seek ye?' They said, 'Our camels'.
He said, 'Whoever searched for camels on a housetop?'
They said, 'We follow thy example,
Who seekest union with God, while sitting on a throne'.

JALALUDDIN RUMĪ (QUOTED ALDOUS HUXLEY).

PREFACE

> If you would be a pilgrim on the road of Love
>
> First make yourself humble as dust and ashes.
>
> *ANSARI OF HERAT*

A lot of misconception seems to exist about Sufism. One renowned scholar says that it 'gained an Oriental flavour from having been so long protected by Islam'*. In fact it was persecution by the orthodox Moslems of Arabia which gave rise to Sufism. The countries connected with Sufism were Iraq, Syria, Egypt, Persia, Khrossan, Balkh, Bukhara and Samarqand. After overrunning these, the Arab Moslems degraded the non-Arab Moslems of these countries even though, as R.A. Nicholson says in his *Literary History of the Arabs* (p., 248), 'these people were the backbone of the influential learned class and ardently prosecuted those studies, Divinity and Jurisprudence, which were then held in highest esteem'. Many Sufis were persecuted by the Abbasi Caliphs, as for instance Mansur al-Hallaj who was executed. Sarmad, a renowned Sufi saint, was beheaded by the command of Aurangazebe the Mogul emperor for failure to attend prayers at a mosque when asked to. Fariduddin Attar, another great Sufi, was slain by a Mongol when Jenghiz Khan invaded Persia. Another misconception is that the Sufis were strictly faithful to the precepts the Holy Quran and to the Prophet, peace be on him. They were doubtless Moslems, but they believed in the unity of religions, accepting all as embodiments of the truth, and did not believe, as the Holy Quran did, in the superiority of the people of the Book :' 'And

---

* (Introduction to Idries Shah. *The Sufis*. USA : Anchor Books, 1964, p., viii)

whoever desires a religion other than Islam, it shall not be accepted from him and in the hereafter he shall be one of the losers (Holy Quran 3 : 84 Trans.; Muhammad Ali). Hazrat Inayat Khan says : 'if being a Mohammedan means conforming to certain restrictions how can the Sufi be placed in that category, seeing that the Sufi is beyond limitations of this kind? ...The Sufi tolerates all [religions] and considers them all his; therefore he does not belong to a religion but all religions belong to him (*The Sufi Message of Hazrat Inayat Khan* vol.1, London : Barrie & Rockiff, 1960 pp., 53 and 56). Yet another misunderstanding is that 'several schools which had been considered to be the products of ancient Hindusim are revealed by scholars to have originated in Sufi teachings' (Idries Shah. *The Sufis* p., 401) and that Indian ascetics tend to 'burst into print to provide material for documentary photographers, to recruit disciples from abroad to try to spread their teaching as widely as possible' (pp., 405-6). As regards the first point, it is not mentioned who are these scholars who have 'revealed' it. The comparision of *shloks* to Aesop's fables, is laughable, as also is the outburst against Indian (read Hindu) mystics. For one thing, this is, if a cliche' be pardoned, like putting the cart before the horse, for the schools of ancient Hinduism like those of Shankarcharya, Ramanuja, Madhva and so forth were quite removed from Arabia and other Islamic countries from where Sufism started, and 'ancient Hinduism' goes back to the Upanishads and *Gita* and the Vedas, that is to say to a period when neither Islam, nor Sufism nor Christianity had taken birth. And as regards the Indian mystics, the example of Dandamis's retort to Alexander the Great, mentioned in the text of this book, will show the stuff Indian mystics were made of. In fact mysticism was one of the functions of Sufism itself. If some persons from abroad have become interested in Hindu cults like Krishnaism as evinced by the Hare-krishna and Krishna consciousness societies of the West, it does not show that these Hindu cults were advertising themselves, but that these Westerners were of themselves attracted to these cults. So is the case with the Osho philosophy of Acharya Rajneesh, or the transcendental meditation of Maharshi Yogi which is only a rehash of Pātanjali's Yoga Sutras. Having said what Sufism is not, let us see what it is. The early Sufis showed an ascetic and otherworldly tendency. As Maaz of Balkh said 'Ascetics renounce the pleasures of this world, but a Sufi ascetic renounces those of the next life also'. Secondly the Sufis were influenced by Greek philosophy mainly that of Plato, and Plotinus who is considered by some critics a Christian and Sufi mystic. Many of the Sufi ideas like the eternity of the soul, afterlife and reward and punishment in the next world came from the neo-Platonists. Sufism was not esoteric but it insisted on preparedness on the part of the seeker to receive the doctrine and the capacity to assimilate it. If necessary the teacher (Pīr Sheikh,or Murshīd) would test his capability before giving him the teaching. It involved, among some orders, like those of the Dervishes, certain rituals and secret practices also, but this was not a general characteristic. Sufism was also in essence spiritual. Love was the most essential emotion for the Sufis. Not carnal love, even though in it love is often expressed in the lover-Beloved metaphor, but love that brings attainment of the Divine and takes one to God. The teacher taught (*Murshīd-Murid*) bond was very strong in Sufism and the teaching was to be received without questioning. As Rumī said, 'You cannot teach by disagreement'. The Arabs acquired knowledge of Hindu philosophy as R.C. Majumdar comments in *The History and Culture of the Indian People* and Bertrand Russell in *History of Western Philosophy* (p., 444). Abu Yazid's interpretation of *tauhīd* shows the influence of Vedanta. Mansul al-Hallaj's an al-Haq is much like the *aham brahmasmi* of the Vedantists. Barring a few Sufis of the Ijadist school, the majority steered clear of religious shibboleths and adopted broadminded spiritual ideas shorn of all bigotism. Doubtless they were

Moslem and accepted the Holy Quran, but they did not agree to its admonitions against Kafirs and idol-worshippers. They adopted their own individual way of thinking and while avoiding religious conflicts and controversies, accepted that part of religions which relates to universal goodness. It appears necessary, therefore, to put Sufism in its proper perspective as a spiritual way of life beyond all religions, and a religion of all religions; avoiding giving it an Islamic twist as some writers on Sufism have given it.

The author is grateful to his publisher for bringing this book out in these difficult times and for the attractive format.

Introduction

zāhid sharab pīne de masjid mein baiṭhakar|
yā woh jageha batā de jahān khudā na ho||

['O pious priest, let me drink within the mosque, or tell me that place where God isn't present'].

Ghalib

Sūfīsm [pronounced as 'Soofeeism'] also known as Tasawwuf, is Islamic mysticism. There are various views about how the sūfīs [pronounced as 'Soofees'] got their name. According to one view they were sitters in the shrine (*ashabisafas*), another is that they were an Arab tribe of Suffa. Other views are — they are so called because they wore woollen garments (*soof* = 'wool'); or from *soof*, a 'row', as they will stand in the first row on the Day of Judgment; or from the Greek, *sophia*, meaning they were sophists. The most likely origin, however, seems to be from sāfa ('pure') implying that their hearts were pure. According to Professor E.G. Browne, however, it is certain that the term is derived from the word 'wool' and Sufi means 'wool-wearer'. Such a dress implied simple living and like the early Quakers in England, the Sufis wore it as a protest against luxury.[1] Yet another interpretation is that the old ascetics, who were among the earliest Sufis, were known as men of the *suffa* because, being homeless they slept on the terraces of mosques. They rely on the Holy Quran as the source of their faith but they give it a new interpretation, mystic union with God being the keystone of their doctrine. It is a hotchpotch of various beliefs like Vaishnavaism, Vedanta, Yoga and what may be termed Islamic liberalism. The Sufi is much like the bee which takes nectar from different flowers, not worrying about the kind of flower, so long as it has nectar to yield.

Despite the Sufis' acceptance of the Holy Quran as their scripture, there are vital differences between Islam and Sufism. Islam is rigid, Sufism is not, and has a more catholic attitude, showing greater tolerance. Moslems have zeal for *jihad* which is a kind of religious war, not for the establishment of righteousness (the *dharma-yuddha* of the *Mahabharata*) but to demonstrate the superiority of Islam; the kind of thing which Francis Bacon denounces, 'But we may not take up the third sword which is Mohammet's sword, or like unto it. That is to propagate religion by wars, or by sanguinary, persecution to force consciences.... [2]. The concept of *jihad* originates from the observation in the Holy Quran: 'Fight those who do not believe in God, nor in the latter day, nor do they prohibit what God and His Apostle have prohibited, nor follow the religion of truth out of those who have been given the Book, until they pay tax *in acknowledgment of superiority*, and they are in a state of subjection'.[3] Clearly, therefore, the Holy Quran considers Islam a crack above other religions, and Moslems 'to be the best community and raised up to guide and govern humanity as viceregents of God on earth, and Islam to be the chosen religion destrined to triumph over all other religions'.[4] But according to Schopenhauer, it is the *Upanishads* which get the pull over: 'They are the products of the highest wisdom', he says, 'They are destined sooner or later to become the faith of the people'. The Sufis had a broad outlook and believed in tolerance, not in the establishment of the superiority of a particular religion, resembling the idea contained in the *Gita* where Lord Krishna says 'I welcome all people, in whatever way the approach Me. All human beings are set upon My path',[5] and further, 'He who worships other gods with faith, he really worships Me even though contrary to the ancient injunction'.[6]

WHO IS A SUFT?

It is often believed that Sufis have links with the Orient only. That is not correct. They are spread all over the world, though mostly in Asian countries. Theirs is a classless society. One's next-door neighbour may be a Sufi, or the laundress who comes for the clothes, or one's family doctor. He may be rich or poor, high or low, an intellectual man or one who is illiterate, a lord or a commoner. Just *anyone*. The only requirement is he must follow the Sufi discipline, the elements of which will be given later in this book. Ambition, greed, pride, vanity, arrogance, blind obedience to people and customs — all these are shunned by the Sufis. Rather than being a theoretical philosophy (though there is much in it which is philosophical). Sufism is a way of life and conduct; in the words of Abu-Hafs, an authority on the Sufis, 'Sufism is wholly behaviour. There is a form of behaviour for every time and for every place and every state.[7] As we have said, they accept all sacred books, the Bible, the Quran or Torah or any other. They view Sufism as the cornerstone of all religions, and Ali el-Huzwiri, a Sufi writer, says that the Prophet Mohammed himself observed. 'He who hears the voice of the Sufi people and does not say *āmin* [Amen] is recorded in God's presence as one of the headless.'[8] The Sufis have no sect, religious dogmas, sacred cities like Benares and Mathura of the Hindus or Mecca of the Moslems, no monasteries or place of worship–mosque, church and the like. It can't be said with any degree of exactitude when the Sufi faith started and till when it lasted. It's thousands of years old and still exists, and according to Graves's estimate the number of Sufis is about fifty million. One of their striking ideals is to be of the world, yet not of it. As the sage Sri Ramakrishna said, 'Live in the world like a water-fowl. The water clings to the bird, but the bird shakes it off. Live in the world like a mudfish. The fish lives in the mud, but its skin is always bright and shiny'.[9]

Orthodox Moslems do not find anything worthwhile in Sufism because it does not have the bigotry of Islam. For example one Moslem writer raps Sufi mysticism, and not being content with that, also backcaps the most sacred scripture of the Hindus, the *Gita*, in a jawing quite out of the context:

> 'The Hindu looks on the absorption of the finite into the infinite as the culmination of happiness, and to attain that end he remains immovable in one spot and resigns himself to complete apathy. The sense of infinity makes it difficult for him to distinguish objectively between the priest and the God, or himself and the God; and eventually between the Deity and the different forms of nature in which he is supposed to be manifested. Gradually this train of contemplation leads to the formal conclusion as appears from the *Bhagvadgita* that creator and creation are identical. We see thus how curiously pantheism in its extreme manifestation, approaches to fetism, which preceded every other idea of the Divinity.'[10]

We will comment on this poppycockish notion presently, after we go on to quote another observation of this writer on Sufism:

'The responsibility for the present decadence of the Moslem nations must be shared by the formalism of the Asha'ri and the quietism of the Sufi Mystical teachings like the following:

> The man who looks on the beggar's bowl as a kingly crown
> And the present world a fleeting bubble,
> He alone traverseth the ocean of Truth
> Who looks upon life as a fairy tale.'[11]

As another writer, taking a more objective view, points out, 'there are in the Quran itself a few texts which lend themselves to a mystical interpretation, as, for instance, the words addressed to the Prophet concerning his victory over the heathen at the battle of Badr (Quran. viii, 171): "Thou didst shoot, but God shot". This on the face of it means no more than that God strengthened the arms of the Moslems against their foes; but it involves no great straining of the words to deduce therefrom that God is the Absolute Agent (*Fa 'al-i-Mutlag*) and man but "as the pen between the fingers of the scribe who turns it as he wills". However little critical examination of the oldest and most authentic records of the Prophet's life and teachings would warrant us in regarding him as a mystic or ascribing to him an esoteric doctrine, it must be avowed without reserve that such is the view taken by the more moderate Sufis, and even of such philosophically minded theologians as El-Ghazzali (A.D. IIII-2)'.[12]

Regarding the comment on the *Gita* it reminds one of Pope's observation about a little learning being a dangerous thing. Lord Krishna distinguishes between *parā prakriti* and *aparā prakriti*. From the Lord's *parā prakriti* – which consists of eight components, namely earth, water, fire air, ether, the mind, the intellect and the ego – follows creation. It is distinct from the other *prakriti* [primordial nature] which is the source of life and sustains the universe.[13] Thus creator and creation are not identical as the writer (S. Ameer Ali) thinks. As regards sitting 'at one spot' ('apathy' being the writer's own diatribe), the followers of all religions sit to remember God, the Moslem at the namaz, the Christian in the pews of the church and so forth. So why should the writer single out Hindus particularly? So also the Moslems have their qazis and the Hindus their pujaris and pundits. It is difficult to imagine how S. Ameer Ali gets the idea that Hinduism conceives God and the priest as one. In fact Lord Krishna clearly says, 'If a man offers Me a leaf, a flower, a fruit or water with devotion and a pure mind, I accept that offering given with love.'[14] It is quite evident therefore that the Hindus conceive God and the worshipper as separate. Islam spoke of the unity of God in almost the same sense as Christianity, both religions conceiving God as jealous and proclaiming himself as the God of the followers of that particular religion. The Holy Quran says 'Or have they taken gods besides Him. Say bring your proof.... And we did not send before any apostle, but we revealed to him that there is no God but Me, therefore serve Me'[15] So two in the Holy Bible, God says 'I am the Lord God of your (Moses's) fathers, the God of Abraham and the God of Jacob.'[16] And again to Moses '.... I the LORD thy God am a jealous God....'[17] The Sufis would never agree with such concepts.

THE NATURE OF THE SOUL

It was the Greeks among Europeans who made a systematic study of the soul. The Orphics believed it to be divine and immortal. The Pythagoreans adopted this view. Socrates was the first man in Europe to have a clear notion of the soul, and believed in its immortality. Plato developed this idea and concluded that God is the Soul. This divine Soul is immortal and continues to exist after the body's death till it has won final release form its chain of reincarnatious. Plotinus distinguished between the higher spiritual Soul and the lower which is attached to sensuality and worldliness. Man can pass from the narrowness of earthly life to the universality of the transcendent Soul and from there to take his place in the world of the Divine Mind. In rare cases the soul can achieve ecstatic union with the One in which Mind attains the highest state by leaving itself behind.

We can see in these views almost a repetition of what the Hindu sages of the Upanishads discovered thousands of years before the birth of Christ and long before European civilizations or the Islamic ones came into existence. Perhaps Hinduism is the only religion which so long ago analyzed the relation between God and the Soul, which Moslem writers contemptuously term 'mysticism;. And what is more it did not claim any superiority as Islam does. It was the only religion also which had room for both duality — God as Ishvara or Vasudeva — and the concept of the One Cosmic Absolute, *Brahman*, As the Christian, the Sufi also believed that the Kingdom of God was within. He called it the divine spark in all human beings. We will speak about this later in greater detail, here it would be sufficient to say that the Sufis unlike Moslems, believe in rebirth as Plato did, or as the poet says, the life's star, the soul, which comes on the earth, and sets somewhere else.[18] They [the Sufis] trace birth from somewhere before coming into the world and believe in returning into a cosmic realm. The only difference between the Hindu concept of rebirth and that of the Sufis is that the Sufis consider they have incarnated on earth for some particular objective, for they look on themselves as idealists to spread goodwill on earth. 'Remember why you are born in the world', says a Sufi message. Both the Hindu and the Sufi seek God in the heart or in the soul. The Hindu sees him as the Atman and Jalaluddin Rumī writes:

> 'I did not find him in church or temple
> Nor in a pagoda;
> I did not find him in the hill of Herat
> Nor in Kalandar or Kāf.
> I searched in Kaabaa too, he was not there,
> Nor could any holy man tell me the place
> My search was vain, because his abode
> Was nowhere but within my heart.'

An anecdote is related in which a deformed man whom Alexander the Great saw and remarked on his ugliness, replied to the emperor, 'This body is only like the scabbard for the sword-shaped soul inside. What matters is the soul, not the body'. Hakim Sanai also speaks of the soul and its relation to God: 'The fire shines and the water gleams from the Lord who is the Spirit of all nature. It is he whose strength and power dwells in the Soul'.[19] The obervation recalls the famous verse of the *Katha Upanishad*:

> The sun does not shine there
> Nor the moon and stars
> Nor the lightnings, much less the fires;
> When He shines then shines everything else
> By His Light all this is illumined.[20]

According to Hazrat Inayat Khan, the great Sufi mystic who gave talks on the Sufi creed in the West between 1910 to 1926, there existed before creation the Formless Absolute called *Zat*. From that came the consciousness of Existence called *Wahdat*, which gave rise to the first Ego termed *Wahdaniat*. The Absolute was concentrated at one point which was the Divine Spirit called *Arwah*. The concentrated *Arwah* divided itself into light, of two intensities, more light and less. Vibrations caused this light to give rise to forms known to the Sufi as *Asmaan*. In this way creation came and various bodies of beasts, men and all other creatures. Six steps towards such manifestation are said by the Sufis to have taken place. The first three are subtle (known as *Tanzi*) and the other three which are coarse and therefore visible (called *Tashbi*). All life consists of five elements, ether (*Nur*), air (*Baad*), fire (*Aetsh*), water (*Aab*), and *Khaak*, the earth. It will be seen that this Sufi doctrine is akin to the Hindu idea of bodies being formed from these five elements; only Hinduism calls them by different names – *samīrā*, *gagana*, *pāvak*, *jal* and *chit*. The Divine Spirit in these earthy bodies is the Soul.

The Hindu concept of the embodied soul also finds place in Sufism. According to Hinduism the unsullied immortal Soul known as the *Atman* is yoked to the body in which it is for the time being enmeshed, and it is then called the *jiva*. This *jiva* *seems* to take part in the pain and pleasure and other emotions of the body in which it is, but really it maintains its purity. It's like a transparent glass placed on a red cloth. Till the glass remains on it, it appears to be red (though all the time it retains its transparency), and when it is removed from the cloth the illusive 'redness' disappears. So too is the relation between the immortal Soul and the embodied one (the *Atman* and *jiva*). Another concept of Hinduism is that of sheaths (*koshas*) encasing the Soul. These are not actual covering but just veil the purity of the Soul metaphorically to various extents. The *Taittirya Upanishad* (2 : 2 - 5) mentions these are, from the outermost to the innermost, the *annamya* (of food, from *anna* ≐ 'food') the *pranamaya* (of the vital airs, from prana = 'breath'), *vijnanamaya kosha* (of bliss, from *ananda* = 'bliss'). Yet a third concept of Hinduism is that of overcoming the lower self which tends to take the individual to narrow selfish ends, by the higher Self which leads him to virtue, public service and selflessness. Both the *Upanishads* and the *Gita* speak of the higher self and the lower. If one subdues the lower one by the higher, the Self or Soul is one's friend. But when the lower predominates it results in the fall of the man.

The Sufis imbided all these three elements of Hindusim. The Sufi initiation consists of taking the 'lesser and the greater pledges'. The lesser one is merely preparatory to the greater pledge. The Sufi rejects the lower appetites 'by choice', as the term is. This implies a kind of change of attitude to things and resistance to temptations. The *koshas* are also recognised by Sufis as the Soul's veils and their endeavour is to remove them for they are impediments in the vision of the divine. This view is similar to the descent of the *Atman* to the *jiva*. The Sufi belief is that the human soul descended to the earth from its divine origin. As the light of the sun dazzles the eyes if a man looks at it directly but it doesn't if viewed through a smoked glass, so too this Soul of divine origin had to be veiled in order to fit into the worldly environment. Expressing this, the Sufi says 'Those Souls which knew one another, come to know one another again, to recognize one another on earth'. This leads us to the similarity of the Sufi concept of emancipation, again much like that of *moksha* or *mukti* of the Hindus. The Sufi initiate is made to realize by the teacher that his home is 'beyond the stars'. Thus, as we have already said, incarnation in overtly accepted by the Sufis and they relate the pre-birth state with that of after-death. The object to strive for is, therefore, immortality, which is the same as *mõksha* and the Sufi expression of 'Dying before one dies' implies just this.

THE SUFI CONCEPT OF GOD

The Sufi believes in one God. He may have different names -- Allah, Khuda, Gott, Dieu, Bhagavana, Ishvara and so forth. He exists in all the different forms of the universe and yet he is beyond all forms. Here again a parallel may be drawn between the Sufi doctrine and Lord Krishna's words to Arjuan: 'Whatever belongs to the states of purity [or goodness], activity, or dullness is from Me, but I am not in them. I stand quite apart from them, supreme and external'.[21] The Sufi believes God to be the highest ideal the mind can conceive. Jalaluddin Rumī says 'I become whatever God makes me – a cup, a dagger, a fountain, or fire. If he makes me a friend I extend friendship; I am his instrument like a pen in the hands of a writer; I do as he wills, who am I to obey or not to obey'.

However in the *Mishkat* of El - Ghazzali a very ancient treatise on Sufism, we find stet observation that God might not be actual Identity but something resembling Identity, in other words there could be duality too which is mistaken for Unity which, (i.e., unity) incidentally is one of main principles of orthodox Islam. 'I am He' says El-Ghazzali, and 'He whom I love is I; two spirits in one body'. He gives the example of a man looking into a mirror and thinking itself, i.e., believing that the two, the mirror and his own reflection are really one. Again El-Ghazzali gives another example to illustrate this duality in identity. One may see wine in a wine-glass and though they are two separate things – the wine-glass and the clear wine in it – he may field they are not separate, as they really are, but one, either the wine without the wine-glass or the wine-glass without wine in it.[22] In another passage we have the following observation of his:

> '.... you must further know that those endowed with this Insight [Relation of Lights to Allah] never saw a single object without seeing Allah along with it. It may be that one of them went further than this and said "I have never seen a single object, but I first saw Allah", for some of them only see objects through and in Allah, while others see objects and then see Allah in and through those objects. It is to the first class that the Koran alludes to in the words "Doth it not suffice that the Lord seeth all?" and to the second in the words, "We shall show them our signs in all the worlds and in themselves". For the first class have the direct intuition of Allah, and the second infer Him from His works'.[23]

Thus Sufism is not so rigid in its stand on monism as the Holy Quran is. God, for the Sufi is perfection and he is even beyond the reach of man. As the Lord says in the *Gita* 'Thousands try to know *Brahman*, but of those hardly any succeeds in knowing him.'[24]

It is wrongly thought that Vaishnavism was inspired by Sufism. It is the other way around. The *Upanishads* conceive the union of the Soul with *Brahman* (the Absolute) in erotic terms which have a Vaishnava ring 'In this highest state the soul in free from desires evils and fears. As a man clasping his wife limb to limb is immersed completely in bliss and is unaware of everything else, the individual soul enfolded by the supreme soul, knows neither inside nor outside'.[25] This *Upanishad* dates back to the eight century B.C. It will be seen that the Vaishnvava symbolism of the *mādhuryabhava* (the love of a beloved and her lover), is much older than the similar

Sufi thought Sufi poetry often express the spiritual longing of the soul in terms of human love. In the allegory '*Salaman and Absal*, Jami wrote: 'Balkis nursed a secret in her bosom. She said 'No day ever passes when I see the lovely youth go by without my heart longing for him' The poet speaks of heaven (represented by Asman a woman) as a place of security from evil (this security being allegorically represented by Salman), in the form of love between them from childhood to youth. Salman's nurse Absal becomes fond of him. Absal's beauty is narrated in the Oriental style, breast as roses and a face as the moon. Jami writes: 'When childhood passed and Asman became a young man, she still pursued him.' A lover sits in a garden raving for his beloved but speaking of the stars, moon and the flowers. He is asked, It's okay you are madly in love with your beloved but what have the stars, moon and flowers to do with that lover? Jami makes the youth answer 'In the language of lovers the stars and the moon are likened to my beloved's body, her hair is like the hyacinth flower and her cheeks like the roses in this garden. I sit here pining for her as the weeds in the shade of the cypress tree.' Relating the love of Zulaika for Yusuf, Jami gives a graphic description which would put any Vaishnava utterance in the shade: 'Burning with love Zulaika got a huge hall built and got hold of a man who by clever device made her own form reflected in every part of it, walls and ceiling [the idea recalls Shah Jahan's hall of mirrors in which he disported with lovely girls]. Then she invited Yusuf there. At first he was a little embarrassed, but soon passion drove out all temerity and in Jami's flowery language [translated beautifully by the renowned Edward Fitzgerald]:

'.... a Hand from Darkness
Touch'd; and ere a living Lap
Through the mirage of bewilder'd
Eyes seduced him, he recoil'd
And let the skirt of danger slip'.[26]

Then there is the oft-quoted allegorical anecdote of Jalaluddin Rumi depicting the identity of the Soul and God, expressed again in Vaishnava terminology:

'A man went to the door of the Beloved and knocked.

A voice asked, "Who is there?"

He answered, "It is I".

The voice said, "There is no room for Me and Thee".

The door was shut.

After a year of solitude and deprivation he returned and knocked.

A voice from within asked. "Who is there?"

The man said, "It is Thee".

The door was opened for him'.

Thus there is no differnece between *Brahman* and the *Atman*. Lover and Beloved are not two, but one. The Sufi concept of the relation between. God and man is very much like the love of the Lord depicted by the Alvars, one of whose sages, Namm 'alvar was intoxicated with God's love as a bride for her husband who has gone away:

'Day and night she knows no sleep
In flood of tears her eyes do swim,
Lotus-like eyes! she weeps and reels,
Ah! how without Thee can I bear
She pants and feels all earth for Him?[27]

The Sufi symbolism of lover and beloved is very much akin to that of the Vaishnavas. When the beloved one of God reaches the exalted *mādhurya* state then to him 'Every sound conveys the message from the Lord. Every form and sense points to the Divine Presence and every touch to the warmth of the Divine Contact. The devotee attains to the state of divine frenzy. The rustling of the wind is taken as indicating his approach. The dark blue sky, the sea and the landscape are symbolic of the Divine Presence'.[28]

The divine frenzy of the Vaishnava *ma dhurya* state also finds expression in the Sufi dervishes and their symbolic dance much as in the *sankirtan* of Chaitanya.

This dance of the dervishes, an esoteric ritual, was seen by Dr. Selima Infandiari. The Dancing Dervishes are encountered mostly in Turkey, and some in Jordan. The dancers wear loose white robes with hoods tied to their waists with white rope girdles, and the dance was presided over by a Sheikh, accompanied by haunting music, the dancers being barefooted and cries of Yaa-hoo! and Yaaa-hooo! increasing in tempo in consonance with the music and the speed of the dancers who kept turning their heads from left to right. The writer goes on to describe the culmination of this dance of the Dancing Dervishes thus:

> 'The tempo of the music increased as the whole circle of men started to move clasping each others' hands, while the others closed the circle, leaving him outside.... Every half-minute or so, it seemed, the pace grew and the music seemed louder.... The circle whirled like a top. The men seemed to have no feet.
>
> 'Suddenly the circle broke up, and each started to twirl on his own axis.... The solitary turners [some having left] held their arms outstretched, eyes closed, breathing deeply now.
>
> 'This could hardly have lasted more than twenty minutes. The cheeks of the flute-players were puffed out fit to burst. The drummner-boys

> seemed as if under a spell, their eyes popping. The dancers continued their cry of hooo!...
>
> 'Suddenly they stopped spinning. Without the slighest sign of giddiness, They bowed to the Sheikh and filed away'.[29]

In this way divine frenzy which recalls Chaitanya or the votaries of the Hare-Krishna order, creates a state which brings the devotee near to God.

A CREED OF LOVE

Almost all religions preach devotion to God through love and fear The *Gita* speaks of three paths to God, namely wisdom or knowledge, desireless works and *bhakti*, i.e., single-minded love of God. Of these it counts love as supreme.

Christianity too emphasizes love. Although Sufism is more a creed and a way of life, than religion, love is rated the highest. The *Sari al-lbad ila'l Maad* of Hakim Sanai explains the Way to God by an allegory. The seeker reaches the abode of saints who had been completely freed from the bonds of matter, form, duality and opposites. These were the men of light whom worldliness could no longer touch. The seeker wished to join them, but one of the Saints stayed him and said 'Go back, you aren't yet fit for this place for you are still tied to the world of forms contrariety and attachment'. Continuing the saint said that no one could know the Way by himself. 'It is shown only to those whom God wills and who are sincere in their pursuit.' It was the same thought as is expressed in the Holy Bible 'The wind bloweth where it listeth, and thou hearest the sound there of, but canst not tell whence it cometh and wither it goeth'.[30] The *Gita* also teaches detachment and absence of all desires. Lord Krishna says 'As rivers enter the sea and disappear into it, yet the sea remains constant, so too that man is worthy of praise in whom all desires are extinct, not one who clings to them'.[31] These are only quoted as showing similarity of thought. Sufism is really not a religion at all. There can only ba a Sufi who chances to be a Hindu, Moslem or Christian or of any other religion. And those who try to bend Sufism towards any religious creed do not really grasp the spirit of Sufism at all. What the Sufi firmly believes in is love; love for God and love for all human beings. The West often gives only one interpretation of love — the human aspect concerning sex. But as Tomlin says, 'Possibly the Orient was wiser to permit the open parade of such tendencies within the sphere of religious ritual than their covert parade through the dream-world as in our Western consciousness.... "obscenity" might rather be a attributed to the tendency found almost universally in the Occident, namely to associate sexual operations with other purely automatic activities'.[32] So when Rumī, the renowned Sufi Master says 'Wherever you are, whatever your condition is, always try to be a lover,[33] he speaks of the spiritual aspect of love, not its human connotation. *In his Masnad Rumī says*:

Bitter things appear sweet
Copper, gold
Stings are like honey
Lions harmles as mice
Illness is comforting
Anger turns to liking
King's are enslaved
And even the dying revive
When there is love in the heart.

The Sufi makes a distinction between Ordinary love and Special love. This is mainly on the basis of difference in love's intensity. Ordinary love views only outward beauty of grace (called *baraka*). Special love goes deeper and feels their essence.

The concept is much like that of *ananya bhakti* [*bhaktyā ananyaya*: *Gita* 11.58] of which Krishna speaks, meaning thereby unswerving or single-minded love (devotion of God). Perhaps the Sufi concept of special love is reflected in King Lear:

'Love is not love
When it is mingled with regards that stand
Aloof from the entire point'.[34]

This is illustrated by the story of the man who saw a lovely woman and going to her swore he was madly in love with her. The woman said, 'See here is my sister beside me who is much more beautiful then me'. The man shifted his attention to that woman, seeing which the woman he had approached said 'When I saw you from a distance I took you to be a man of wisdom. When you accosted me, I took you to be a lover. But now I know you are neither'.[35] Ordinary love is steeped in egoism and in it the lover is more concerned in himself than in his beloved while in special love the lover thinks nothing of himself and is thoughtful only of the woman he loves. Love whether, ordinary or special, is of course only in the spiritual plane, i.e., love of man for God, not in the human one of lust or sex.

Since the Sufi believes that there is the Divine Spark in every human being, love of God presupposes for him service – not only of his teacher but also of all people. In the *Gita* Shri Krishna says 'Both the ignorant man and the wise work, but while the ignorant one works selfishly, the wise works for the world's welfare'.[36] The relation between the Sufi teacher and his disciple is very close. This will be treated in detail in a separate chapter. Here it would be enough to say that according to Sufi belief there is no enlightenment without service. A Sufi teacher advised his followers to 'live in society and bear the blows and the buffets of the people'.[37] Sheikh Nizam-ud-din Aulia said that there were two kinds of devotion God expected his devotees to have. The first, called *laazmi*, is confined to the devotee alone; the second, *mutaa'adi*, is aimed at helping all human beings. The reward of the first kind is to the devotee alone. The reward of the other kind is endless and limitless.[38] The Sufi was asked to attend to the poor and the miserable.

To continue with the Sufi concept of love, the general idea is of its being a spiritual force, a bond between God and man. Abdullah Ansari says that love is like an engulfing stream. Another sage likened it to union after separation. There is no delight, he said than giving oneself to love with a pure heart. Poet Rashiddudin Wathvath wrote about love, 'My beloved dwells in my eyes always so that they seem to be one. My eyes have become my beloved and the beloved has become my eyes. Jami say's the Loved and the lover are both from God and likens him [God] to a veiled Bride who can be seen only by the true lover. Quite often Jami uses erotic imagery to speak of this love, as for example kissing each other and tasting the 'forbidden vintage of the lips' or lovers embracing each other and coming closer and closer like two almonds in one shell, the space between them gradually vanishing.[39] Another poet, Khyali, blames the beloved for tormenting her lovers by keeping away from them! Thus we see that the terminology of the Vaishnavas dominates the Sufis too when they speak about love. Indeed at times, though rarely, the symbolism loses its objective and gets lost in the erotic, as in the following tale from the *Baharistan* of Jami:

> 'A famous beauty began to lose her looks, and her former admirers no longer sought her company. I said to one of them 'After all she is the same person as before.... How can you desert her?
> 'Have a care what you say' he replied 'that which enraptured my heart and captivated my reason was a spirit which breathed in the harmonious form of her limbs, the litheness of her body, the firmness of her skin, the delicacy of her voice. Note that this spirit has left them, how should I love those dead forms?[40]

But then religions, which are the cradle of spirituality sometimes inexplicady take a turn to the erotic as the narration of procreation ceremonies in the *Brihadaranyaka Upanishad*, which Max Müller found so obscene that he left that part untranslated, and in the Holy Bible we have the beautiful Song of Solomon which, though by no means erotic, yet describes the loveliness of women in what Hindi poets would call a *nakh-shikh varnan* [narration of the beauty of a women from head to feet].

Although Sufis respect the rituals of all religions, they believe in actual experience of the truth. He knows what a thing is like who tastes it. Philosophy and arguments are not enough, what is required is actual experience, and the keynote of all experience is love. Ibn El-Arabi says 'My religion is love. I have three beloveds, yet they are only me. They *appear* as three, but are in reality only one. Similarly the Sufi mystic, Hazrat Inayat Khan, emphasizes the sacredness of love. Love, he says, is God, and so it is sacrilege to speak of it repeatedly in vain. The person who has love in his heart does not need to speak it out. It is like an earthen jar which one fills with water. When the water keeps dropping into it, it makes a gurgling noise. But when the jar is nearing fullness, the gurgling ceases. Love is a revelation, it does not need to be taught. It cannot be defined. Love is the divine spark within the heart, which, when fanned becomes a conflagration. The true import of love is to be gentle, kind, humble, modest and tolerant. It implies sacrifice, endurance, universal love and the spirit of service. It is what Abou Ben Adhem told the angel, 'Put me down as one who loved his fellow men'.

The Sufi concept of love is much like the *bhakti* (devotion) of the Hindus. Although God cannot be known as he is beyond everything that can be conceived by the human mind, he can be thought of as concrete too. He is *Jamal* in his absolute beauty and *Hum* when seen as the phenomenal. Like the *advaitist* and the *dvaitist* of the Hindu faith, the Sufi too believes in the Formless Absolute as well as God as Self-revelation. This is one of the many points of departure of Sufism from orthodox Islam.

SIMILARITIES BETWEEN SUFISM AND HINDUISM

Though it wouldn't be right to identify Sufism with any religion, it does have some similarities with Hinduism. We have already pointed out the Vaishnava strain in it. The belief of *Brahman* being a state of external bliss *ananda* is shared by the Sufis. True living means not mere momentary peace, but everlasing bliss. A Sufi mystic says:

> 'Even if the whole universe were within our grasp it would be impossible fully to satisfy our life's demands. It [true life] does not work for momentary peace, but for one that is everlasing. It does not desire to love a beloved held in the arms of mortality. It needs a beloved to be always before it. It does not want to be loved only for today and perhaps not tomorrow. It wishes to float in the ocean of love.
>
> 'It is therefore that the Sufi seeks God as his love, lover and beloved, his treasure, his possession, his honour, his joy, his peace; and this attainment in its perfection alone fulfils all demands of life both here and hereafter.[41]

There are vital differences between the orthodox Moslem viewpoint and that of the Sufis, even though both accept the Holy Quran as their basic scripture. The Moslems depend on external behaviour only, good deeds and absolute obedience to religious observances. The Sufis emphasize love of God, purity of the heart and mind. Eschewing the bigotry of Islam, Sufism was not averse to other faiths. A Sufi wrote:

> 'O you who sneer at the idolatry of the Hindu
> Learn also from him how worship is done.[42]

Indeed some observations of the Sufi mystics would be heresy and sacrilege for the followers of Islam. Abu Sa'id ibn Abi'l Khair, a Persian mystic wrote

'Not until every mosque beneath the sun
Is ruined, will our holy work be done,
And never will true Moslem appear
Till faith and infidelity are one'.

Al-Wasiti said, 'Ritual acts are only impurities'. 'I am the Truth', said Hallaaj And Abu Yazeed al Bistaamee explained 'Praise be to Me!'

There are some differences between the Vedanta doctrine of Hinduism and Sufi philosophy. Sufis generally are not celibates, though some are. They believe in being of the world yet not of it, like a lotus growing in a dirty pond, yet rearing its head above the waters. Sufis do not believe in avatars, only in a Paigambar who is a Guiding Spirit on earth sent by God to redeem mankind. They do not worship God on the form of an image or portrait, though they may worship Pirs by meditating open them. The Sufis express their devotion through emotion while the Vedantic seeks inner calm and non-attachment.

The similarities, however, are far more striking. The Sufis are not like orthodox Moslems, strict monists. Their faith is a kind of qualified monism. As Hindus believe in the unmanifest (the cosmic Absolute or *Brahman*) the Sufis too call the two Utter darkness and *Tayyunal*.[43] Other common beliefs between Vedantists and Sufis are: The practise of breath-control, meditation, fasts and penance, recitation of *mantras* (sacred formulae), counting the rosary, *moksha* (union with the Supreme Being), toleration, love and devotion and submission to the teacher (guru or pir).

The *Gita* advocates rituals, but when the yogi goes beyond them to a higher spiritual state, their performance is no longer necessary. So too the Sufi. When the rituals have been practised continually for long, a point of saturation is reached. The aspirant then reaches a higher spiritual understanding and rituals fall off from him like the ripe fruit from the branches of a tree. Those who keep on practising rituals remain at the lower level of understanding. This is analogous to the teaching of Shri Krishna in the *Gita*: 'But that man has no duty to perform [*kāryam na vidyate*] who rejoices in the soul and is content and satisfied with it alone. That man has nothing to gain or achieve by and work. It is all the same for him whether he works or does not work. He has no ambition for any object in this whole created universe'.[44] The Sufis too are remarkably free from ambition. A Catholic, Father F.K. O'Halloran who moved among Sufis noted that though they excel in whatever work they undertake, they do not pride themselves on it. It seemed to Father O'Halloran that they believed they had been naturally endowed with a more than average capability and so there was nothing for them to brag about.[45]

We find traces of the Tantra, Samkhya and Yoga in Sufism. One of the rites practised by Sufis is the 'embrace' in which signs are made signifying a five-pointed star. These are believed to be five vital centres unside the body which are very senstive to spiritual illumination known in Sufism as *baraka*. These are activated under stimulus. There is evident similarity between this and the Tantra doctrine of the *chakras*. Sufis believe in regulation of the breath which Pātanjali called *pranayama*. Yoga is a very ancient school in the Six Systems of Hindu philosophy and certainly much older than Sufism. The Sufi believes in External Reality which is the essence of knowledge and beauty. This Reality is reflected in creation. The world of creatures is its outward manifestation. As we have pointed out Sufism believes in love being a way to God just as the Hindu believes *bhaktī* (devotion) to be. Yahya says 'The person who sees anything apart from God [the Beloved], cannot really see him'. God is *Jamal* when considered as

Absolute Beauty and Husn in his phenomenal aspect. Pātanjali's Yoga prescribed a preminary discipline in the form of *yama* and *niyama*. The Sufis also formulate such a code of ethics:

1. A Sufi must resign God completely which, as we have said before, is the same as the Hindu concept of *ananya bhakti* (single-minded devotion). The Sufi gives great importance to a guru or teacher (we will speak about this in greater detail later), particularly to the choice of one. But once having chosen him, he is enjoined to give him the atmost respect and unquestioned obedience. Thus the relation of guru and disciple is much like the one prevailing in the *gurukuls* and tols of ancient India.

2. Devotion and sincerity of purpose (*ikhlas*) means unswervingly moving towards God, and ridding oneself of all hypocrisy and pretence.

3. Repentance (*tauba*) which finds a parallel in the Hindu (*prashchita*) signifies giving up of evil and turning the mind from worldly things to the divine. When one repents, he shows remorse for the feelings of jealousy, enmity, anger and so forth which may have arisen in him. This helps him to remove pollution from his soul and restore its pristine purity.

4. A concept which is shared not only between Sufism and Hinduism but with Islam too is the fear of God. Fuzail, a Sufi saint of Mev, says 'All things are subordinate to the devotee who fears God'. The idea of fear of God [or *Brahman*], finds place in the Upanishads.

'From fear of *Brahman*, the wind blows and the sun rises.

From fear of him Agni and Indra do their appointed tasks,

and death's god goes about gathering the souls of the dead.[46]

The fear of God is emphasized in the Holy Quran at many places: 'O men, fear your Lord, and dread the day when a father shall not atone for his son, nor shall a son atone for his father in anything. Verily the promise of God is true. Therefore let not the life of this world deceive you in respect of Allah[47]. 'And We will set up a just balance on the day of judgment, so no soul shall be dealt with unjustly in the least; and though there be the weight of a grain of mustard seed, yet will We bring it up and sufficient are We to take account.'[48] The Holy Bible also charges men to fear God: 'Fear God and keep his commandment: for this is the whole duty of man. For God shall bring every work into judgment with every secret thing. Whether it be good or whether it be evil.[49] However, it should be remembered that more than fear, love of God is the dominant feature of Sufi philosophy. What really is implied by fear is respect or reverence.

5. A liberal attitude is the main element in Sufism. We have already remarked on this. Latif, a Sufi of Sindh said, 'When the truth is one, why should people quarrel about the way of reaching it?' This recalls what the *Rigveda* says 'The truth is one, but sages call it by different names.[50] Yahya, son of Ma'az also a native of Balkh said 'A Sufi gives up all worldly pleasures. He only desires union with his Beloved (God). He cannot see anything other than God? Another Sufi, Bayazid of Khorassan says, 'There's nothing apart from God The cup, the wine and the drinker of wine are one and the same. Sufis abjure the world's pleasures and patiently accept suffering. According to Junaid of Nehawand, a Sufi

> philosopher, a Sufi should detach himself from everything that is 'non-God'.

There are other common beliefs between Sufis and Hindus. We have mentioned the rosary. This has a special significance for the Sufis. The *misbah* (as the rosary is called by them) is said to have a special power which is communicated to one who counts its beads. But if one holds the *misbah* while having impure thoughts in his mind, it may do harm instead of good. Hinduism believes in *mantras*, which are sacred formulae which if uttered correctly, as communicated by the guru to the disciple, can achieve results which may seem magical and to defy rational explanation. These *mantras* contain in them the power of the teacher, which makes them effective, just as a banknote is a mere slip of paper, but is made valuable because of the undertaking on it denoting that it is worth so and so dollars or rupees, or whatever currency prevails in the country to which it belongs. In the same way Sufis believe in *zikr*. When *zikr* is endowed with the power of the chief of the Sufis [analogous to the Hindu sage or guru], it becomes charged with power, but if it isn't, and is vainly it may bring great harm, and even drive the person who utters it, mad. The *janeu* or *yajnopaveeta* is the sacred thread which caste Hindus wear, and is considered to be an important rite as circumcision for the Moslems. The Sufis similarly wear the *zunnar*. They believe that if this thread or sash is not correctly worn, the person concerned can fall sick or come to harm if his mind goes towards the divine. Thus we find there are many beliefs and rituals of Sufis resembling Hindusim. One if the most authorative Sufi mystics was Al-Ghazzali who wrote the *Mishkat* from which we have already quoted earlier. In the introduction to this, the writer [of the introduction] comments:

> 'It contains much in the first place which on the face of it reads like naked pantheism.... there is

open eulogy of the formula *la¯huwa illa¯Huwa*, 'here is no it but He' which is declared to be more expressive of real, absolute truth than the Mohammedan creed itself *lā ilāha ill-Allāh* "there is no god but God". This would seem to be as unreserved an assertion of pantheism as could be found in philosophic Hinduism itself'.[51]

Moslem writers tend to underplay the Hindu element in Sufism They bring out that firstly, it was Hindusim and more especially Vaishnavism that took its inspiration from Sufism and the 'spirituality of the East is a mere derivative of the Sufi Schools'; and secondly this moribund Hindusim has fascinated 'Western students, anxious to find spirituality in action in the East'.[52] The writer, who seems to place his trust in tales and legends, goes on to relate how Sufi saints like Moinuddin Chisti performed miracles to defeat the persecution of Hindu chieftains like Jayapal and Prithvi Raj. It has already been pointed out that the distinguishing feature of Sufism, the creed of love, was taught by Shri Krishna to Arjuna centuries before Sufism took its birth, and as to the Vaishnava element, the Upanishadic passage depicting the Soul's search and union with God (*Brahman*) comparing it to a wife and her husband clasping each other limb to limb, has been quoted. Thus the Sufi symbolism of Beloved and Lover which is one of the props of Sufism (as the off repated, example, of the Beloved knocking at the door of the Lover of Jalaluddin Rumī) was used in the Aryan age when both Islam and Sufism or for that matter Christianity had not taken birth. Later Vaishnavism was a development of the worship of Vishnu, the Bhagavata religion, the Upanishads, *Narada Bhakti-sutras* and the love of Radha and the *gopis* (cowherd maids) for Krishna. However, to hassle about periods and dates in much like the 'which came first, the chicken or the egg?' kind of questioning. Different sages and wise men keep hitting on the same truths at different times and periods and that does not mean they are all imposters emulating one another, for truth is no one's copyright. It could be possible that the Vaishnavas like Sri Chaitanya, Ramananda and others discovered the truth which the Sufis spoke of and the two schools of thought independently evolved a philosophy which happened to have many elements in common. As regards the fascination of Western students for the spiritualism of the East, the enthusiasm for cults like Krishnaism as evinced in the Hare-Krishna movement still exist and seems to have taken permanent root. This is not an unnreasoned bug, but because Western materialism in the shape of affluenza, sex, and so forth have made the people of the West turn to the East.

Another similarity between Sufism and Hinduism, is the expression of wise sayings in a brief pithy manner. This is like the Sanskrit *sutras* (pronounced 'sootra'), not *shlokas* [meaning a couplet in verse] as one writer says. It seems Moslem interpreters of Sufism belonging to the Christian tradition are eager to reconcile the two, and they interpret parts of the Holy Quran to suit their notions. Chapter 112, really the concluding one of the Holy Quran runs as follows '*In the name of God, the Beneficent and merciful.* 1. Say: He, God, is One. 2. God is He on Whom all depend. 3. He begets not, nor is He begotten; 4. And none is like Him'.[53] It is to urged that this was the answer given by Prophet Mohammed to a group of Bedouin Arabs who asked him to what Allah could be compared with. Idries Shah interprets this as follows: ".... Allah may not be compared to anything. There is no analogy possible between this being (Allah – that which is to be worshipped) and anything familiar to humanity. Allah is the word used to denote the final objectivity, uniqueness, something that has no relation with numbering, anything in time anything which propagates in a sense familiar to man'.[54] And this, the writer believes, is the 'common ground between Moslems and Christians'. But is it? In the Book of Exodus of the Old Testament of the Holy Bible, God appeared to Moses in the burning bush and said, 'I am the God of the father, the God of Abraham, the God of Isac, and the God of Jacob'.[55] We are further told that 'Moses hid his face for he was afraid to look upon God'. This is not to imply that Moses was face to face with a God having form, for he never looked at him. But it certainly limits God to an inner circle. Further on in the same book the Lord tells Moses, '....I the Lord thy God am a jealous God', and 'Thou shalt have no other gods before me'.[56] Now if the Holy Quran says, God is One and is He on Whom all depend, how could there be a Christian and a jealous God [jealousy is certainly not a divine attribute] and one limited to Prophets mentioned by him. A comparison between religions is just not possible, if the object is to identify one religion with another. We may point out the similarities only, for each faith stands on its own pedestal, and any comparison to establish the oneness of one with the other is a futile exercise, for thereby one may reach absurd conclusions as shown by a parable related by Swami Ramakrishna: 'There was blind man who wanted to know what milk looked like. He was told it was white as a crane. He asked what a crane looked like and was told it was like a sickle. When he asked what a sickle looked like, the blind man's friend bent his own forearm and asked him to feel it. 'Ah!' the blind man said, after he had felt his friend's forearm. 'it's quite clear now. Milk is something like a bent forearm'! Religions are a matter of faith and though, as Robert Burton says, 'One religion is as true as another', Thomas Browne's observation in Urne-Buriall is equally so, 'The religion of one seems madness unto another'. And ironically if one at all gives an analogy to the aforesaid observation of the Holy Quran, it could be to the concept of *Brahman* most, as contained in the religion of those whom Moslems slew as kafirs and whose idols they broke and embedded in the steps of mosques, and whose temples they razed to the ground. Krishna says is the *Gita*.

'Those persons, however, who worship the Imperishable, beyond the reach of words, and Unmanifest, Omnipresent and Unfathomable, Immutable, Immovable and Constant: those who restraining the senses and in every way remaining even-minded, are engaged in the welfare of all beings: doubtlessly attain Me'.[57] That perhaps, is closer to the One God on Whom all depend, and at any rate would be closer to the Sufi ideal. In fact the Sufi is not much concerned with similarities or differences between religions. All that he insists upon is that the person, of whatever religion he may be, ought to act according to the Sufi doctrine and follow the Sufi way. A Sheikh teaching his disciple said, 'Essentially all ritual, symbolism and so on is a reflection of a truth. It may have been concocted, adapted, diverted to other ends, but it represents the truth – the inner truth of what we call the Sufi Way'.[58]

The Sufis do not have a particular scripture in the way the Hindus have the Vedanta, Christians the Bible and Moslems the Holy Quran. Though they accept the Quran they give it an interpretation which is different. The most significant departure is in their liberal attitude. They would certainly not subscribe, for example to the Quranic observation which condemns all who are not those who have been given the Book, i.e., followers of Islam. The Holy Quran says:

> 'Fight those who do not believe in God nor in the latter day, nor do they prohibit what God and His Apostle have prohibited, nor follow the religion of truth, out of those who have been given the Book, until they pay the tax *in acknowledgment of superiority* and they are in a state of subjection. And the Jews say: Ezra is the son of God; and the Christians say: The Messiah is the son of God. These are the words of their mouths; they initate the saying of those who disbelieved before; may God curse them'.[59]

It is clear, therefore, that the *jizyah* (poll tax) is required by the Holy Quran to be paid by those who do not accept the superiority of Islam to their own religion. Every religion parades its superiority, but none so openly as Islam. It is also evident that, according to the aforesaid Quranic passage, Islam regards Christians too as idolators. The footnote of the translator of the aforesaid passage says, 'The doctrine of the sonship of the Messiah is here plainly stated to be an imitation of earlier idolatrous systems, and this is now an established fact'.[60] In view of this scriptural testimony, it is difficult to agree with Idries Shah that common ground exists between Moslems and Christians, for the belief that Christ is the son of God is fundamental to Christianity. To the Sufi a *fatwa* would be a derogatory act for he respects all religions and would hardly show any concern for criticism of his own beliefs even though he rigidly sticks to them. To such denunciation the Sufi will maintain patient silence, for his language is that of humility not of egotistic vanity. Jami, the renowned Sufi says: 'I hope of the noble character of my readers that if they find a fault in my work, they will cover it with the hem of the robe of pardon and indulgence and not strive to divulge it with the tongue of denigration and malice'.[61] That aptly sums up the Sufi attitude.

REFERENCES

1. *The Sufi Mystery*. ed. Nathaniel R. Archer London: The Octagon Press, 1980. PD., 165-66.
2. Francis Bacon. *Essays*. *Of Vanity in Religion*. London: Oxford University Press.
3. Translation of the Holy Quran by Muhammad Ali. Lahore: Anjuman I-Ishaat-I-Islam, 1928. The Immunity. Ch. 9, Sectioon 4.29. Islam Shall Triumph (italics, author of this book).
4. Harsh Narain. *Jizyah and the Spread of Islam*. New Delhi: Voice of India Press, 1990, p.1 [Quoting Āe 'Imriān. (3) 19,85

and al-Mā' idah (5)3; and Al - Tawbah (9) 33, al-Fath (98) 28, ds - Saff(61) 9}.

5. *Bhagavadgita*. 4 : 11.
6. Jibid, 9 : 23.
7. *Four Sufi Classic*. England: The Sufi Trust. Octagon Press 1980. P., Vii.
8. Idris Shah. *The Sufis*, New York: Anchor Books. Doubleday, 1964. Introduction, Robert Graves, p., vii. The Introduction is very illuminating.
9. *The Gospel of Sri Ramakrishna.*
10. *The Sufi Mystery* ed. Nathaniel P. Archer. London: The Octagon Press 1980, p., 192.
11. ibid, p., 208.
12. ibid, p., 167
13. *Bhagavadgita* 7 : 4 - 5.
14. ibid, 7 : 21.
15. The Holy Quran. Trans. Muhammad Ali. Lahore: Ahmzdiyya Anjaman - I - Ishart - I - Islam, 1928, p., 328.
16. Exodus iii, 15.
17. ibid. 20 4.
18. 'Our birth is but a sleep and a forgetting;
The Soul that rises with us, our life's Star
bath had eleswhere its setting.
And cometh from afar.
Wordsworth. *Ode, Intimations of Immortality*.
19. *The Sair ul lbadilah* of Hakim Sanai. Adapted from *Four Sufi Classics*. Kent: Sufi Trust, 1980.
20. *Katha Upanishad*. Ch. 5, verse 15.
21. *Bhagavadgita* 7 : 12 - 13.
22. *Four Sufi Classics*. The Sufi Trust Kent: The Octagon Press, 1980, The *Niche for Lights trans*. W.H.T. Gairdner, p., 122.
23. ibid. p., 128.
24. *Bhagavadgita* 7 : 2.

25. *The Brihadarānyaka Upanishad*, section 4.
26. *Four Sufi Classics*. Sufi Trust. Octangon Press 1980, p., 31.
27. Dasgupta. *A History of Indian Indian Philosophy*, vol. 3.
28. Sen, D.C. *Chaitanya and his age*.
29. *The Sufi Mystery*. Ed. Nathaniel P. Archer London: The Octagon Press. Withnessing a Sacred Dance. Dr Selima Isfandiari, pp., 55-56.
30. St John 3 : 8.
31. *Gita* 2 : 70.
32. Tomlin, E.W.F. *Great Philosophies of the East* London: Arrow Books, 1959, p. 229.
33. Idres Shah. *The Sufis*. New York: Doubleday, *1964 The Creed of Love, p. 357.*
34. Shakespeare. *King Lear*. 1. 1. 241.
35. *Idris Shah. The Sufis*. The Book of the Dervishes. New York: Doubleday; 1994, p., 317.
36. *Bhagavadgita*. 3 : 25.
37. *Siyar-ul-Aulia*, p., 237.
38. ibid. p., 411.
39. This is contained in Jami's *Salaman and Absal*
40. *Four Sufi Classics*. Ths Sufi Trust Kent Octagon Press, 1980. pp., 211-212. [On Love].
41. *The Sufi Message of Hazrat Inayat Khan*. London: Barrie and Rockliff. 1960, vol. 1, p., 24.
42. K.A. Nizami *Aspects of Religion and Politics in India During the Thirteenth Century. Asia,* 1961, p., 263.
43. *The Sufi Mystery* ed. N.P. Archer.
44. *Bhagavadgita* 3 : 17-18.
45. *The Sufi Mystery*. ed. N.P. Archer, London: Octagon Press, 1980, pp. 35-36.
46. *Taittireya Upanishad* 8(1) Agni is god of Fire and Indra of the firmament.

47. Sirdar Ikbal Ali Shah. *Islamic Sufism* Delhi: Idarah-l. Adabiat-I Delhi, 1933, p., 69 (xxx : 33).
48. ibid, (xxx : 47).
49. *Ecclesiastes*. 13.
50. *ekam sad vipra bahudha vadanti.*
51. *Four Sufi Classics* The Sufi Trust. London: Octagon Press, 1980, p., 97.
52. *The Sufis*. Idries Shah, New York : Doubleday Anchor Books, 1964, p., 402 et seq.
53. Trans. Muhammad Ali. Lahore: Ahmadiyya Anjuman I-Ishaat-I Islam, 1928, p., 622.
54. *The Sufis*. Idries Shah. New York: Doubleday, pp., 413-414.
55. Exodus 3 : 6
56. ibid. 20 : 5 and 3.
57. *Bhagvadgita*. 12 : 3-4.
58. *The Sufis*. Idries Shah. Seeker after Knowledge p., 350.
59. The Holy Quran. Trans. Muhammad Ali. Lahore: Ahmadiyya Anyuman - I-Ishaat-I-Islam, 1928, p., 195.
60. ibid, fn.
61. *Four Sufi Classics*. The Sufi Trust.
    London: Octagon Press, 1980,p., 222.

1

The Sufi Teaching

If you have eyes to see
I will be your friend:
If you have feet for travelling
I will take your hand.

Hakim Sanai: Sair Al-Ibad Ila"l Maad

DIFFERENT INTERPRETATIONS OF THE UNKNOWN

All religions are an excursion into the Unknown and if they have any one thing in common, it is dogma. The Unknown has never been fathomed, nor will it ever be, for no one can say with any real authority what lies before birth and after. In the final analysis all religion in mere speculation. The only beliefs essential to all religions are God and the soul. Without God religion becomes atheism, and without the concept of a soul the phenomenon of death would be inexplicable. But thereafter the similarity ends. One religion believes in transmigration of the soul from one body to another and consequently rebirth. Another doesn't. Though religions generally believe in divine judgment and consequently in the good and evil of works, they disagree about how and when such judgment will be given. Christians believe in the Day of the Last Judgment and Moslems have a similar belief the *yaumula qiyaamah* [the day of the great rising or resurrection] on which those dead and buried will rise up and be judged for their deeds. According to Raghib, the well-known lexicologist of the Quran, there are three *as-saa'* ahs (another popular term for resurrection), the *kubraa*, the rising for being judged; *wuslaa* which comes somewhere in the middle, after the passing away of one generation; and thirdly the *sughraa*, the hour of death of the human being. Thus the rising is a rather long-drawn-out process. According to Hinduism there is no rising or resurrection. The soul departs and goes to Chiragupta who reads out from a great register called Agrasandhani the account of the deeds done in life when the soul was in the man's body. The judgment follows immediately and if it is rebirth in a different body [not necessarily human] the soul enters that body after a wait. Modern research into the Unknown, comprising the experiences of those declared clinically dead and who later revived, of which the most remarkable perhaps is of Dr Raymond A. Moody Jr. [*Life after Life*], concludes that there is no God such as religions conceive but a being of light, of which the writer says.

> `Despite the light's unusual manifestation [an indescribable brilliance which however does not dazzle] however not one person has experienced any doubt whatever that it was a being, a being of light. Not only that, it is a personal being. It has a very definite personality'.

Dr Moody goes on to relate in the words of a woman's out-of-the-body experience what happens when the being of light finds the Soul before it:

> When the light appeared, the first thing he said to me was "What go you have to show that you've done with your life?" or something to this effect. [Then followed a flashback of the entire life of the woman with the images vivid, three-dimensional and in colour]. Now I didn't actually see the light as I was going through the flashbacks.... yet I knew he was there with me the whole time that he

carried me back through the flashbacks, because I felt his presence and because he made comments here and there. He was trying to show me something in each of these flashbacks. *It's not like he was trying to see what I had done — he knew already* — but he was picking out these certain flashbacks of my life and putting them in front of me so that I would have to recall them.

All through this he kept stressing the importance of love — He showed me some instances when I had been selfish with my sister, but then as many times when I had really shown love to her and had shared with her. He pointed out that I should do things to other people, to try my best. There wasn't any accusation in any of this though. When he came across times when I had been selfish, his attitude was only that I had been learning from them too.

'He seemed very interested in things concerning knowledge too. He kept on pointing out things that had to do with learning, and he did say that I was to continue learning, and he said that even when he comes back for me (because by this time he had told me that I was going back) that there will always be a quest for knowledge. He said it was a continuous process, so I got the feeling that it goes on after death. I think he was trying to teach me as me went through those flashbacks'.[1]

WHO IS A CANDIDATE FOR SUFISM?

While religions are speculative and doctrinal, even dictatorial, the findings of Dr Moody are to a large extent based on research, and beyond that one cannot have a peep into the Unknown. We can see how Sufism, comes nearest to the conclusions of these researches. Love is the most prized and essential element in it – love of God and universal love of mankind. Knowledge is also extolled. We are told that a Sheikh said to a disciple who approached for enlightenment, `While you live you are learning'.[2] The Sufi guru is a man of wisdom. He guides the disciple till the teaching is inculcated in him and thereafter withdraws. The teacher has a very especial place in Sufism, just as among the Hindus or the Sikhs, if not indeed more. He has to be chosen with care but once he is chosen, the disciple must put his full trust in him. The importance of a teacher is very great in Sufism because it has many esoteric rites. Shri Krishna says in the *Gita* that works like sacrifices and oblation, charity and austerity should not be given up. It is enough if they are performed desirelessly. One who lives in the world cannot abandon works but he can and should abandon the fruits of works. Besides, if they are done in this manner they purify the doer.[3] The ancient seers of the *Upanishads* used to test the worthiness of the disciple and if he wasn't worthy he was asked to go back and come again after a certain period of time. It is practically the same with the Sufis except that while the Upanishadic sages were persons with indisputable repute, there happened to be many false teachers of Sufism. The Sufi was, therefore, asked to make sure of the genuineness of the teacher. One way was to beware of those who showed particular eagerness to teach. The genuine teacher gives instruction and then leaves the disciple on his own. The teaching takes the form of exercise (*zikr*) and these vary according the nature and constitution of the seeker. Teachers who provide it ready-made and the teaching same for every aspirant come within the category of false ones.

In quite a few cases, because of the ritualistic nature of the teaching, the disciple may be puzzled by it. But he must determine to persist and serve the teacher in whatever way he indicates. Thus the relation between teacher and disciple is very close indeed, much as that between the *shishya* (student, or disciple) and guru of the ancient *gurukuls* (schools) of India. The Sufi believes that real enlightenment can only be obtained by such sincere and loving service. Once the disciple accepts a teacher he should entirely rely on him. It is only he [the teacher] who can know what the disciple has to imbibe, the disciple cannot himself know. A Sufi saying is that it's better to entrust oneself for discipleship to a cat than to try to teach himself on his own! Another is that the weight of the burden the teacher carries in undertaking the responsibility to teach is so great that if the disciple takes it on, he would be crushed beneath it!

Having chosen the teacher, the Sufi pledges to obey him and be guided by him in every way. This undertaking called the Lesser Pledge is much like the complete submission of the disciples of the Upanishads to the ancient seers, though not so exacting. We are told in the *Chhāndogya Upanishad* that Upakosha lived as a religious student with Satyakāma Jābala `tending his teacher's fire for twelve years'. Other teachers made their pupils practise austerities for years before they accepted them. The Sufi teacher is not so fastidious. Called by various names such as *arif* (`sage'), *Murshīd* (`guide') Pīr (`Elder'), or Sheikh (`chief'), he ascertains the worthiness of the would-be disciple by instructing him for a thousand and one days, the period being open to extension in case the disciple shows promise. If the disciple can't imbibe the teaching even then, the discipleship ends. There may be some aspirants, however, who are more capable of absorbing the teaching and these do not have to undergo such preliminary instruction. They are trained independently of the others. The Indian sage Shri Ramakrishan could recognize a person fit for discipleship intuitively and by merely touching him. He could see through a person and evaluate the extent of his receptivity. The Sufi teachers were endowed with much the same kind of intuition, and disciples were drawn to them just as Shri Ramakrishna's disciples were, as his biographer Romain

Roeland records: `From all direction, without understanding what command or what power constrained them, they felt themselves drawn as if caught by an invisible thread; they circled, they approached and soon one after another they arrived'.[4] There were yet the third category of Sufi disciples who were treated much like a general doctor referring some patient to a specialist; inasmuch as he was formally accepted but sent to another teacher who specialized in the kind of teaching which was required for that seeker. Some Sufi organizations like the Naqshbanidis have a kind of combined course of instruction to a few chosen aspirants (the *markaz* group) who are given the teaching in a series of sessions (*majlis*). Sufism cannot be taught or received in isolation, perhaps because a large part of it is mystic ritual. Besides, anyone eager to learn about it ought to have implicit faith in the teacher for which he takes what is known as the Greater Pledge. There are many persons who are out to know about Sufism only to satisfy their curiosity. This attitude is deprecated and discouraged by Sufi teachers. Of these they say `If they do not know where to look they are not yet worthy of finding for the Teaching is now expressed everywhere in the world'. A certian foreign student approached a Sheikh with this kind of questioning attitude. The Sheikh assured him that he himself would be an enlightened Sufi and asked him to keep on having faith in the doctrine. When he had gone, doubtless puffed up with confidence regarding his ability to be a Sufi leader, the Sheikh turned to his disciples and said `Look, I told him what he wanted to hear. Do you refuse a child a sweet or tell a madman he's mad? We don't teach those whom we know they can't be taught. If someone asks you whether you like his coat and the way it fits him, you don't tell him that its unsightly and that he should dress better. There are some people who just can't be taught'.[5] Thus the Sufi aspirant ought to beware of false teachers, and one prominent quality of such a guide is that he is eager to teach. Rumī warns the disciple not to judge the teacher by what he sees in him externally `Do not concentrate your attention on a jar' he says, 'but on the water that's in it; not on the wineglass but on the wine it contains'. We should look at the whole, not the part. Rumī givẹs the example of several people making tent. Some weave the cloth of which it is made, others prepare the ropes, and so on. But together they are engaged in the task of making the tent. Life should be looked as a whole, says the Sufi, as Browning says:

> `Our times are in His hands
> Who saith "A whole I planned,
> Youth shows but half; trust God.
> see all, nor be afraid!"'[6]

The Sufi quest is sometimes likened to a journey both in the literal sense as well as the metaphorical. We find Sufis and their teachers spread through many lands, and the gathering of experience is one of the aspects of the Sufi way. The other journey is that of the mind. The metaphorical journey has been spoken of by Hakim Sanai in his *Sair-al-lbad ila'l Maad*. The person descends from the summit of a high abode to a city attractive on the outside but smelling horribly with everything upside-down, the trees their roots above and branches below (cf. *Gita* 15 : 2 `Nourished by the qualities the branches of this *peepul* tree spread out both below and above. Its twigs are sense-objects, and the roots which run down below are the bonds of works in the world of human beings'). There the man meet an two-faced angel whose exterior is of fire and interior of light, obviously representing good and evil in the world. Thereafter he goes to where there are beasts of insatiable appetite representing the hunger for material things. But at times he has `intuition of a superior state', the spiritual, which while it lasts, brings peace. Thus he remains suspended between the two. An old man `gentle and serene, modẹst and subtle' becomes his guide. He tells him that mere argument is useless for 'words are from the kingdom of ignorance' and they have no use in the bosom of knowledge'. A similar idea finds place in the *Isha Upanishad* which deprecates mere theoretical knowledge shorn of virtuous works: 'Those who are devoted to mere rituals enter into blinding darkness and those who delight in ritualistic philosophy without doing good works fall into darkness which is even greater'.[7] The seeker's guide promises to lead him to the right path. They go to a place where there is a huge poisonous serpent, but the guide takes the seeker through without harm and they reach a valley of demons and then to a rocky desert full of smoke where live ignorant and bewildered people caring only for each other, i.e., lacking universal love. After crossing the desert they reach a huge ocean which the aspirant is afraid to enter, but his guide says it will purify him. From there the two — teacher and disciple – reach a world full of young men, all mad, but not with love, perplexed, and not having any desire for true knowledge. After leaving the waters of the ocean and the land of ignorant youths, the seeker finds himself in the air and is filled with misgiving 'How can I be here' he says, 'I have no wings to fly?' But the guide chides him for harbouring doubt. The doubting mind can achieve nothing and the man with such a mind is like an arrow soaked in water with bends and turns into a bow. One should have a firm and single resolve and be like an arrow which cannot ever be bent.[8] Their journey then leads them to a magic castle where people are worshipping gold and silver as though they were gods and where there is a monster whose head is turned towards lust and its tail towards passion, i.e., a castle of greed, lust and lascivousness. Then they reach a valley full of scorpions snakes and such evil creatures. Prompted by his guide, the seeker devours all these creatures. They reach a mountain of fumes with bottomless abysses from which come voices, 'This well is mine!' 'This path is mine!' 'This paradise like garden is mine!' and so forth, i.e., those people are assailed by egotism. The seeker is now tired and says, `haven't we travelled enough now?' to which the guide gives a pertinently forceful answer, typical of a Sufi teacher: `This journey is not for the weak-willed. The lover must travel light with no baggage but noble poverty'. Thus the journey of one who wishes to learn about Sufism is an arduous one. But the guide assures the traveller that they are nearing the goal. The seeker is happy that night has fled and the dawn has come `Time stands still here' the old man explains, `You have got salvation and release from the world'. However, the guide warns him that it isn't the end. `The people who you see here' he says, `are fascinated by mere knowledge. Do not linger here. Leave this small rivulet and turn to the ocean. You are about to enter into the Divine Presence of the Supreme Being'. But thereafter the guide suddenly vanishes leaving the seeker all by himself. The disciple begins to flounder, rising and falling by turns, for the veils have not yet been removed from the Divine. When he does manage to get past them, he finds himself in the land of the exalted who are basking in God's glory. But as the teacher is no more there to guide him, the traveller cannot enter the way and join these liberated souls for he is still `tied to the world of forms' and `sunk in the poison of attachment'. The conclusion is that no one can know the way by his mere effort. It reveals itself only to certain people who are qualified for it. The teacher, says Hakim Sanai,

> `will liberate your thought
> and awaken your creative Self
> Hold to him till you attain
> sincerity and vision....
> He is the traveller in this world;
> He is the one whose eyes are open'.[9]

Who is this old man of gentle manner who, Hakim Sanai say, guides the Sufi seeker? In a sense he is a messenger of God? According to Hazrat Inayat Khan, creation exists in cycles called *Uruj Kemal* and *Zeval*. Each cycle is in the control of a Master with many guides under him. There have been numerous Masters since the beginning of creation under different names, but they are all representatives of the One Master of eternity, and they all speak the same truth. But the vanity of religions is such that this oneness is seen as many, as sometimes one shape and image is seen distorted in cleverly arranged trick-mirrors. Followers of these various religions are shortsighted enough to proclaim their own scriptures and prophets to the exclusion of others, as for Christians there is only Christ (believed by them to be the Son of God), for the Moslems the Prophet Mohammed, for Hindus Krishna, Rama Shiva and other gods and avatars. The Sufi does no suffer from such religious myopia, and so he recognizes all religions as expressions of the same truth and all gods and prophets as its propagators. The great emperor Akbar is sometimes said to have the Sufi touch in seeking a synthesis of religions in his Din-l-Ilahi, but had he been a true Sufi he wouldn't have tried, for the Sufi is unconcerned about the disparity of religions. He thinks all such separatist tendencies to be an impediment to the Sufi teaching. The mind of the seeker must be free of all preconceived notions, as a jar must be clean of all impurities before pure water is poured in it. The search is not for dogmas but for the truth and the Sufi disciple is called a seeker of truth (*salik-al-haq*). What truth is, is itself a very vexed question, as difficult to explain as to understand. Questioned by Pilate Jesus said, `To this end was I born, and for this cause came I into the world that I should bear witness to the truth. Every one that is of the truth heareth my voice'. Pilate asked Jesus `What is truth?' and then walked away and later told the waiting Jews `I find in him no fault at all'.[10] There can't be any absolute truth according to the Sufi, but only relative truth. In the Sufi chronicle, *The Subtleties of the Incomparable Nasrudin*, we have a tale about this. There was a king who complained to Maulana Nasrudin that his subjects never spoke the truth. Nasrudin said `there is truth and truth. People must practise real truth before they can use relative truth. They always try the can use relative truth. They always try the other way round. The result is that they take liberties with their man-made truth because they know instinctively that it is only an invention'. This was too complicated for the king who thought that truth was just truth and that was quite clear, so he decided to force his subjects to speak the truth. The gallows were put up for a offenders. When Nasrudin entered the kingdom, the captain said `where are you going? Tell me truly or you'll be hanged' 'I'm going' said the Maulana 'to be hanged on the gallows.' `I don't believe you' the captain said. `Well then, I've told a lie' Nasrudin said, `hang me' `But that would make it the truth!' `Exactly' said Nasrudin, `your truth'.[11] Thus as Bacon says `Truth may perhaps come to the price of a pearl, that showeth best by day. But it will not rise to the price of a diamond or carbuncle that shows best in varied lights'.[12]

The Sufi teacher would like to have such preconceived notions removed and begin on a new slate. The first and most essential requirement in the prospective disciple in humility. Self-pride is ruinous to understanding. As the Sufi, Abu Hashim says, pride is very difficult to get rid of, for it is as difficult to spot it as the faint print of an ant's foot or a black stone in the pitch dark of night. It is easier to uproot a mountain with a needle, he says than to wrench away pride from one's heart. The idea is very much like that of Shankaracharya in the *Vivekachuramani*, `The great *ahankara* (ego) even though apparently cut down to the roots, will, if excited even for a moment by the mind, come to life again and cause a hundred distractions, just as during the rain clouds are scattered about in the storm'. Every man thinks he is in possession of the truth and so complete receptivity is hindered. The Sufi teaching is not merely theoretical. It is a way of living and constant effort and the aspirant ought to have complete resignation before he can be instructed. False knowledge, which the seeker has and mistakes for the true, creates a barrier between himself and his teacher. This barrier has to be removed. Like the teaching in the *Gita*, the Sufi emphasizes the importance of work. Rumī says that work should not be given up. Indeed what the seeker is seeking is to a large extent derived from work. All Sufis are engaged in some occupation. Because of the expertness of the worker, says Rumī, wool can be woven into a beautiful carpet, Reason is of course of importance. But it has its own place. Rumī gives the example of a man who wants to have a suit made. He buys the cloth and selects his tailor. But once having done so he places complete reliance on his tailor for the stitching of the suit. So is the case with the Sufi teacher and his disciple. There should be complete confidence of the teacher's ability on the seeker's part. Once the teaching begins, the aspirant must not expect any miraculous transformation. The learner must give full attention, for unless he does so, he will not learn. The teaching has to be given gradually bit by bit. If one is taken from a dark room suddenly into sunlight, he will be dazzled and not see anything at all. To a large extent the Sufi is close to nature. Hazrat Inayat Khan says that `the sacred manuscript of nature is the only scripture which can enlighten the reader'.[13] The disciple is at first one who scoffs at ideas other than his own. The teacher corrects this attitude slowly by prescribing meditations The teacher brings about the change gradually, as we see nature working. The seed grows into a tree, the tree bears buds which gradually burst into a flower. It all happens slowly, imperceptibly but with surety. So too is the way of the Sufi teacher. He sows the seed of knowledge in the mind which he thinks fertile enough. Thereafter he allows it to sprout and grow, and to some he may appear to be doing nothing as a tree gathering nutriment before bursting into bloom when spring comes. The seeker yearns for something, but he does not know really what it is and so his mind is confused. The Sufi teacher knows this, and his endeavour is to remove this confusion. For example, people are used to think in fixed patterns. Some of the Nasirudin stories illustrate this.

There is no absolute logic, as for example because there is smoke there must be fire, for many things in the world are illogical like the distribution of wealth and suffering. So too one can't jump to conclusions as regards cause and effect. The Maulana was walking in a lane when a man fell off a roof on to him. The man who fell was not hurt, but Nasrudin was, and he was hospitalized. 'What do you infer from this?' he was asked by his disciple, and he said. `Nothing is absolute certainty, like "if a man falls off the roof he will break his neck". See it was that man who fell, but my neck broke'. The man with a one-track mind finds himself unable to take a different point of view. He sticks to his own and can't see another. This often causes deception. This is illustrated by the tale of the smuggler. The Maulana used to take his donkey often across the check-post with a load of straw on it. He admitted that he was a smuggler, but whenever a search was made nothing incriminating could be found in the straw or on his own person, but he accumulated a great deal of wealth, obviously by just these visits. Sometime after when he had given up taking his donkey across, a puzzled customs officer met him and wanted to know what he was sumuggling when nothing could be found on him. `Donkeys' said Nasnidin. The Sufi aspirant should also realize that `good' and `bad' are only relative terms. What might appear right to one may seem wrong to another. A person who hates killing living creatures may not like shikar. Another who is an enthusiastic hunter may delight in it. A king who was nuts on hunting and also paley with Nasrudin asked him to accompany him on a hunt. Though he was reluctant, the Mulla had no choice but to go. When he returned someone asked him how the hunt went. `Fine', said Nasrudin `How many animals did you see?' the man asked. `None' he said. `Then how could the hunt have gone well?' he was asked. `Well, I think it is wonderful when you are out to hunt beasts' the Mulla said, `and you see none at all'.

We have mentioned that the essential quality of an aspirant is complete resignation and humility to his teacher. This has been wrongly characterized as an Oriental mentality, but it is not really so.[14] The Christian has the same mentality when he approaches the priest for confessing his sins and the Moslem for the qazi and Imam. The communication of a Sufi teacher is of an esoteric type, which, though Moslem writers on Sufism are at pains to deny, is very much like the Tantra practice. For a clear understanding of this we have to see what knowledge and reality mean to the Sufi preceptor. The intelligence of the common man is of the worldly kind. It is confined to the daily experiences of life. That of the man of religion tries to scan the other-worldly phenemena, as for example out-of-the body experiences. Sometimes a threefold division is made. The first is ordinary knowledge of which the distinguishing factor is piety; the second the inner knowledge which encompasses the divine. The third is that of theology which lays down the do's and don'ts for human beings. The wise Sufi (known as Arif) is one who can instinctively understand what lies behind some event or act. Inward knowledge is expressed in contemplation. The Sufi who has it believes that the past is gone and beyond recall, the future is not in our hands for it has not yet come and we know not what it will be. The only thing we have is the present, and that too is slipping away from us each moment:

`Out of Eternity
 This new day is born;
Into Eternity
 At night, will return'.[15]

For the Dervish order of the Sufi, it is the essence of a thing which is of the utmost importance. First comes the inner essence (*dhat*) and the reality (*haqikat*). Then there is *baraka*, the individual quality of the man. The essential knowledge is to know one's own self which is veiled by desire, selfishness, hypocrisy, self-praise and self-love, greed, avarice, irresponsibility, hurry and regligence, The Tantric element can be seen in the practice of the dervishes who believe in there being spots of illumination (*lataif*). The Sheikh teacher gives illumination to the aspirant by activating the *lataif* which are five in number, through exercises. Although some writers are loath to compare the *latiaif* with the *chakras* (centres) of Tantra, the likeness is too close to be ignored. We have already mentioned this while speaking of the similarities between Hindu and Sufi beliefs. The five *lataifas* are the heart, spirit, secret, mysterious and deeply hidden. Another centre apart from these is the overall personality of the person. Yet another, the seventh, subtlety, is found in the real sage who gives these exercises to the disciple. The parts of the body which are activated are the Self, the portion under the navel, the heart, the part of the body adjacent to the heart, the portion above the heart, the forehead and the brain.[16] The likeness of this to the Tantric centres from the *muladhara* to the *sahastrara* can't be denied. The significance of these centres is realized when they are activated. This awakening of the *lataif* is a mystic rite much like the awakening of the *kundalini* in Tantra, and has to be practised only under the expert guidance of a Sheikh or dervish. Without a teacher the discriminatory power of the *lataif* is not woken, and self-pride may lead the aspirant astray causing a setback in his progress. He may then be misled by false teachers, who may cause him to experience false `release', and even to join derogatory cults. The object of genuine Sufism, which is to develop the man in whom there is perfect goodness (*insan-i-kamil*), is defeated. Many cults degenerate because they depend more on the teachers than the teaching. They depend on reasoning, not practical training and experience. For example we have that of the Osho of Acharya Rajneesh which was very much bound by his own personality. Sufism guards against this by making mystical experience, living and behaviour more precious than knowledge or theoretical arguments. One of the Nasrudin stories brings this out. The Maulana was taking a scholar across a river. He said something to the scholar which was grammatically faulty, on which the man, proud of his learning, said `Have you never studied grammar?' Nasrudin admitted he hadn't. 'Then you have waste half your life' the scholar said. After a little while the Maulana asked him `Have you ever learnt how to swim?' The scholar said he hadn't. `Then you have wasted your *entire* life' Nasrudin said, `we are about to sink'! The Sufi himself is never censorious even when others, not understanding the Sufi doctrine, condemn or criticize it. This is illustrated by another Nasrudin story. He went to a moneyed man to ask for charity. A servant came out and told him `My master is out'. `All right' said Nasrudin, `even though your master could not give anything, when he returns please give him this advice from my side' Next time you are away from home, don't leave your face at the window. Someone might steal it'! The Sufi believes that intelligence has two aspects — intellect and wisdom. The former is the cognizance of the external world of names and forms. This is what we call learning'. One just sees the world around him and while it is perception, it does not bring him any internal peace. Knowledge, on the contrary looks within. It centres on the soul and tries to grasp the similarities of human beings. This is analogous to the Gita's ideal of the universality of all life `He who sees the same Supreme Lord dwelling in all that exists, the Indestructible amid that which perishes, he indeed sees with the eyes of truth.'[17]

The Sufis believe that there are messengers of truth known as Wali, Ghauth, Qutub, Nabi and Rasul. They penetrate into the inner world of the unseen in different degrees and come at certain periods of time. Nabi, for example guides a community, while Rasul is the messenger for entire humanity. The Qutub is one round whom all worldly activities revolve. He is not known by anyone for he never reveals himself, and if anyone claims to be a Qutub, he would be an imposter. Revelation is the knowledge of the inner Self. When consciousness is directed within, the unseen is disclosed. This unseen world is called the *Chouda-tabaq*, the fourteen planes comprising the seven earths and the seven heavens. This revelation is expressed in the Holy Quran which says `The veil shall be lifted from thine eyes and thy sight shall be keen'.[18]

The Sufi disciple has to go through many stages in the teaching. These are mentioned in various books written at different times for the guidance of various communities. Hujwiri wrote the one meant for India, Attar for Persia, Rumī for Turkey, Ibn El-Arabi for Mecca. Thus there are different guide books for various times, but all contain the Sufi doctrine in some form or other. Other writers on Sufism belonging to more recent times have more or less adapted their interpretations of the Sufi beliefs from these Masters. Sufi training centres have sprung up in various parts of the world – North Africa, Central Asia, Spain, India and the near East. When a belief which is not dogmatic spreads, it also gives rise to false teachers who claim to know all about it and are quick to take credit their phony utterances. This is brought out in one of the remarkable Nasrudin fables. One day a relation of the Mulla brought him a duck as a present. The Mulla was delighted and got its meat cooked and gave the relation too some of it so that both had a hearty meal. Soon after, men came, each claiming to be the friend of the man who had brought the duck and expecting to fork out a meal from the Mulla. Nasrudin was quite fussed up when a visitor said `I am the friend of the friend of the friend of the kinsman who brought you the duck', and he thought he was going to get a meal like the others. Nasrudin put a bowl of hot water before him. `What is this?' the surprised stranger said. `This' said the Mulla, `is the soup of the soup of the duck my relation brought'! People who put their trust in such imposters believe mistakenly that they can get enlightenment from them and they go on seeking truth at the wrong place from the wrong person. This again is illustrated by a Nasrudin story. A neighbour saw the Maulana searching for something in the lane on which they lived and asked him what he was looking for `My key' the Maulana said. `Where did you lose it?' his neighbour asked. `In my house' said Nasrudin. `Then why are you searching for it here?' `Because answered the Maulana `here there's more light'! The disciple who does not fully trust the teacher, by taking a rational stand, cannot really benefit by the Sufi teacher. It's like giving colours to someone who thinks he can paint, but instead of executing a beautiful painting with them merely draws triangles and geometrical diagrams. To such a disciple the teacher is loath to give the teaching, for he can hardly absorb it. A neighbour wanted to borrow Nasrudin's clothesline, but was told by the Maulana it was not available because he had hung flour on it to dry. `But how can you dry flour by hanging it like clothes?' the amazed neighbour said. `Maybe you can't', said Nasrudin `but it's a good enough excuse for not lending it'!

The Sufi teachers believe that goodness and truth will of themselves draw people to Sufism. People will come where there is sweet and wholesome water, they will not be attracted to a place where there is viciousness. The teacher prescribes exercises (*zikr*) but these ought not to be constant. They should have variety, and repetition is a sign of degeneration. A Nasirudin story brings this out. The Mulla fell into pool, but a passerby managed to save him by holding him up. Thereafter every time the man would see him, he would remind him about it. At last the Mulla got fed up and taking his friend to the pool, deliberately jumped into it and when the water was his neck [the full depth of that shallow pool], he shouted out to his friend `That's as far as the water would have been had you not steadied me up. *Now* will you go and stop bothering me'.[19] The goal of all teaching is to create a restless pursuit of the divine. Mansur al Hallaj says. `I made haste to be one with you, crossing land, sea and deserts and turned away from everything else, till I reached you'. The Sufi teacher gives instruction to the disciple according to his receptivity. He also protects him from harm by his spiritual power (*baraka*). Thus the responsibility cast on the Sufi teacher is tremendous. As regards the capability of the Sufi teacher, that is considered to be beyond all doubt, provided the correct teacher is approached. And it is not difficult to find such a teacher. The Sufi will forthwith say about this `If they do not know where to look for such a teacher it means they aren't fit enough for the teaching, for now there is no dearth of such teachers, who can be found the world over.'

As has been pointed out, the Sufi believes that he has a special mission in the world and his origins go back to some life before their present life. Rumī says that man comes from the heavens and goes back to them. A cryptic saying of Sufis for a Sufi is `Have you forgotten why you are here?' A Sufi aspirant is sponsored by a man who is expert in judging the capability of would-be students and who enumerates their peculiarities, presumably so that the teacher or guide may decide on the kind of instruction required. The sponsor is called the `Translator'. The actual esoteric teaching is something peculiar to Sufism and runs as follows:[20]

The disciple comes bare-breasted to the guide asking to be admitted to the teaching calling himself the `negligent one' who has come to `make amends'. If he begs forgiveness for his lapse he gets permission. We have remarked that the aspirant must show complete humility and eschew all self-pride. Most probably the idea of such an approach is to make sure that there isn't an iota of conceit in the aspirant. After this he is given a cotton cap bearing a design on it, an interlinked triangle or some other such pattern. This is to point out that the Sufis' origin is beyond the stars. He is taught the epithet `near and far' signifying that though the Sufis' origin is after off, it is also near and the space separating these is really of no consequence. It means that this distance is no hindrance in achieving eternal life. The Sufi must obey the orders the guide gives to the fullest extent and without questioning. There are four degrees of enlightenment, but they are reached step by step, gradually. Indeed some may not go beyond the first stage at all. The aspirants continue their discipleship, according to a mysterious Sufi belief, even after death. There they meet a Sufi who by his powers saves him from the terrors of hell. How this comes about is not very clear. The Sufis are believed to have miraculous powers such as walking on water, healing by touch, changing one object into another and so forth. They can stay in extreme cold with only an ordinary sheet as covering. Even it the sheet is wet they can make it evaporate and turn dry! They can cast their words and pictures miles off, heal by mere spittle, teach by telepathy, make objects disappear and throw them long distances, emit a greenish glow and do such other wonders. If they are asked why they don't exercise these powers if they have them, they say that they do, but imperceptively. They claim that the world would be in much worse condition if they didn't. All this would seem rather far-fetched to a non-Sufi, quite irrational and certainly militating against the concept of humility and the eradication of self-pride on which they place such great emphasis, but then it should be remembered that Sufism is an esoteric cult and though the stress is on mystical enlightenment, rituals too play a major role. The Sufi may lay claim to such powers when his attention is drawn to some mysterious happening, but he almost never talks about them. It is also significant that these rites and beliefs are confined to the Dervish Orders and are not universal, for Sufism is essentially spiritual.

The Sufis engage themselves in work, but they are entirely free from ambition. They have no desire for achieving prominence, power, or worldly success. They know the art of doing things well, but do not attach any significance to their success, believing that it is the natural consequence of their superior ability. They neither claim nor expect any credit for their achievement. They believe that the entrance to Immortality has four gates namely Justice, Order, Knowledge and Truth. He who can successfully pass through these is emancipated. After a certain period of teaching on the spiritual plane (*tawajjuh*) illumination (*tajalli*) comes to the disciple. If however false teachers undertake the task of training, evil consequences come about which may lead to many ills and vices. Thus the Sufi is repeatedly cautioned to be wary of such self-appointed teachers who are really imposters.

The Sufi seeker's final quest is detachment. Emancipation is achieved when one completely turns away from the world and all worldly things and desires. We have related how in his *Sair ul Ibad ilal Maad* Hakim Sanai concludes that the seeker cannot be liberated unless he frees himself from `the prison of attachment' and `the world of forms'. In the *Parliament of Birds* Fariduddin Attar the Chemist depicts the various stages a disciple goes through. The birds represent humans and their leader, the hoopoe asks them to set out on the quest of finding the mysterious king of the birds. Each bird thinks,`this is a very rewarding task, why shouldn't I go by myself'. Guessing their thoughts the hoopoe explains to them that they should not have such self-seeking and rather do what's right. The seeker, he says, will have to go through seven valleys respectively of the Quest where he will be faced with the impediment of desire which he has to overcome; the valley of Love where he will experience deep longing for the Beloved; the Valley of Instuitive Knowledge where he will have direct realization of Truth; then going through three other valleys, he arrives finally at the valley of Detachment where he finally abandons all desires. We see in this a parallel to Shri Krishna's teaching in the *Gita* in which he gives various ways in which God can be reached and thereafter concludes that the most effective of them all is doing works without desire of reward : `You can reach Me by fixing your mind and understanding on Me alone. If you can't do that try to reach Me by constant concentration through yoga; failing that by loving service. And if you are incapable of that too, then resort to controlling your mind and relinquishing the fruit of works. For knowledge is better than aimles effort, better than knowledge is meditation, and even better than meditation is the renunciation of the fruits of works, because it brings instant peace'.[21] Love of the first kind (which we have elsewhere classified as `ordinary') is transient, for it loves the form of outward beauty which is perishable. So in the Valley of love the seeker grasps the difference between mere outward attraction to forms and the essence of love which permeates every part of the man's being and makes him perfect. From the valley of Love the aspirant goes to the Valley of Unification where he learns that what he thought as diverse is really the One, as the poet Shelley says:

> `The One remains, the many change and pass;
> Heaven's light forever shines, Earth's shadows fly;
> Life like a dome of many coloured glass,
> Stains the white radiance of Eternity'.[22]

After thus realizing the unity of existence in the Valley of Unification, the seeker moves on to the Valley of Astonishment. Here he is surprised to discover that there is nothing that he took to be knowledge. There is only love, and nothing but love. The final valley is that of Death. Here he understands that even when merged with the ocean the drop remains a drop. It cannot become the ocean. This is slightly different from the Hindu concept of the *Atman* and *Brahman* which are believed to be identical and the one (*Atman*) merges into the other when emancipation is obtained,

The Sufi teacher, Hazrat Inayat Khan, also speaks of such a journey of the soul from its divine source to its manifestion in bodies and then ultimately back to the source; but the terminology used by him is different. Every soul, according to him orginates in the Omnipotent Light (which Hindus call *chaitanya*). This light passes first to the angelic heaven (the term for `angel' being *malak*), and of those whom it touches a few become human beings on earth. So man is only an imperfected angel, the baby and child being the purest expression of this angelic spirit. Voicing this same sentiment Jesus says in the Holy Bible `Suffer the little children to come unto me and forbid them not: for of such is the kingdom of God'.[23] The Sufi idea of angels is also borne out by the Holy Quran according to which while men are engaged in violence and killing, angels are free of such animosities and engaged in prayer : `And when the Lord said to the angels, I am going to place in the earth one who shall rule (in it), [i.e., a *khalifah*], they said What! wilt Thou place in it such as shall make mischief in it and shed blood, and we celebrate Thy praise and extol Thy holiness?'[24] But according to the Holy Quran these angels descend only on those who follow Islam : `When [at Badr] thou didst say to the believers : Does it not suffice you that your Lord should assist you with three thousand of the angels sent down?'[25] As regards the shedding of blood for which God's angels deprecated men, it is ironical that the same holy book which speaks about it, should itself sanction such bloodshed, `So when the sacred months have passed away, `slay the idolaters wherever you find them .... for God is Forgiving and Merciful'.[26] The entire history of the Moslem domination of India from Mahmud Ghazni to Aurangzebe gives evidence of this bloodshed in the name of Islam, which the angels are said to disapprove!

To go on with Hazrat Inayat Khan's narration of the journey of the seeker's soul, he says the Hindus call angels *sura*, which is a misconception for *surā* really means `wine', though the conclusion about angelic persons being men of pure lives is the same as the Hindi *daivya purusha* or spiritually endowed persons.[27] Similarly the Sufi teacher's interpretation of the Hindi *asura* as `lifeless' is mistaken, for it means `a demon' or a `demoniac person'.[28] The spiritual man is on a higher plane than others. The Guardian Angel is one who protects good people from dangers. Another belief of Hazrat Sahib is that the angels record the good and evil deeds of people on earth. These angels are respectively the angels of *Khair* and *Khat* [this approximates to the Hindu belief of Chitragupta, but they (the Hindus) take him to be a god]. When a person dies two angels called *Munkir* and *Nakir* come to his grave to ask questions and judge the deeds of the person. Some angels are believed to live in heaven who are given the name *Nūr*, and others in a place opposed, called *Nāar*. Another division is between the angels of power, known as *Jelal* and those of beauty, called the *Jemal* angels. In the angelic heavens the angels live as breath or a current which in a worldly concept may be likened to electricity. In acquiring a body, which differs in its constitution while in the angelic heavens from the physical, the soul forgets its heavenly nature and is made captive.

After leaving the heavens, the soul goes to the sphere of the jinns which is the mind-world. The mind is not like the human intelligence, but more illuminated and pure. However, it is closer to that of men than of angels. The angelic heaven (known in Hinduism as *Indraloka* or *swarga*) is higher than the jinn-world and the soul may stay on here (even as certain souls stay on in the angelic heaven) or choose to descend on the earth. Those who encounter the jinn-sphere are men of knowledge, musicians, philosopher, thinkers, scientists etc.; those of whom poet Browning speaks:

> `Each sufferer says his say, his scheme of the
> we al and woe:
> But God has a few of us whom he whispers in the ear;
> The rest may reason and welcome:
> It is we musicians know'.[29]

Thus from the Eternal Being the Soul descends into the world of knowledge. This concept is also found in the Vedanta in the *Mundaka Upanishad* where Shaunaka, the great householder asks the sage Angiras, `By knowing what, sir, is all this known?' The sage tells him `The knowers of *Brahman* declare that two kinds of knowledge are to be known – the higher and the lower. Of these the lower is the *Vedas*, phonetics, ritual grammar, etymology, metrics and astrology. And the higher is that by which the undecaying is known'. The *Brahma Sutras* distinguish between the knower of *saguna* (qualified) and *nirguna* (Cosmic Absolute) *Brahman*. The souls of the former go to the *Brahmaloka* (anagous to the Sufi angelic world) and the latter merge with *Brahman*. In the same way does the Sufi draw a distinciton between the Soul which is the Divine Spark of the Eternal Light and the one that finds its place in the jinn - world.

After passing through the sphere of the jinns the soul arrives in the physical plane. Hazrat Inayat Khan believes that this coming is expressed in a cry, for the soul finds itself in a new place which is the state of captivity. The Sufi teacher believes also in five spheres of consciousness on decent of the soul on earth — that of *Nasut*, *Malakut*, *Jabarut*, the sphere of dreams, the *Malakut*, and *Lahut* that of deep sleep. The *Nasut* is the state of physical limitation, as the Holy Quran puts it `God alone is rich and all souls living on earth are poor'.[31] The next sphere, the *Malakut* is that of thought and imagination and gives greater freedom to the soul than before. The third sphere is that of *Jabarut* which is that when, while being in the waking state, the soul is not conscious of the waking condition as in a reverie, when one is ther but unconscious of the surroundings because his mind is elsewhere. The fourth sphere is the soul when the person is asleep and dreaming and is known as *Malakut* and the fifth, the *Lahut*, of deep sleep. A sixth state is that of *Hahut* when the soul shorn of all distractions rests in itself. This analysis of the soul's states is very much akin to the Hindu concept of the four states of the soul ù the waking, the dream, the dreamless sleep and the *turiya* which comprises the first three and is the Eternal Witness of them all. The *Hahut* state of Sufism is analogous to the Pātanjali's *chitta vritti nirodha* [the suspension of the thought process] known by the familiar term `*samadhi*'. Though these spheres are indicated separately, they may, from the general point of view, be classified as three — *Nasut* of the plane of the world, *Malkut* of the world of jinns and *Jabarut* of the angelic world.

A Sufi belief expressed by Hazrat Inayat Khan is that there are four types of persons on this earth. The highest kind is the dreamer, the idealist and refined person, one whom the poet william Morris speaks of:

> `Thou shalt do the deed and abide it, and sit
> on thy throne on high
> And look on today and tomorrow as those
> who never die'.[32]

The second kind of persons are the artists and people of nature loving, tender elusive and detached. The other two kinds are of the lower categories. The one has no eye for beauty and is materialistic in outlook seeking only wordly gain, while the other, the fourth and most degraded kind thinks of only food and drink, momentary pleasures, sex and bodily comforts. He is a hedonist or what is known in Hindusim as a Chāravāka. What is the purpose of this world of existence of various kinds of souls? Why creation at all? The Greeks believed that the gods are cruel in bringing about suffering and death, as Shakespeare expresses:

> `As flies to wanton boys, are we to the gods;
>
> They kill us for their sport'.[33]

The idea of sport persisted with the Hindus but it was *lila* (*leelaa*), divine sport, not one whose object was cruelty, rather for the unfolding of the play of existence from the imperfect to the perfect for `in the pure crystal of Non-being, being itself is the only flaw'. When the director or producer has an idea he expresses it in a movie. An artist expresses himself in a painting, a musician in notes a troubadour or singer in song, a poet in his poetry. In the same way God expresses himself in his creation. The perfection is reached by man through his own dharma (duty) and through self-realization:

> `This above all: to thine own self be true
> And it must follows as the night the day
> Thou canst not then be false to any man'.[34]

After its sojourn on the earth in some body, when death comes the soul is released. It goes back the same way as it came – from the materialistic earthly life to the world of jinns and thence to the angelic word and finally attains the same perfection it had before its downward journey. In that state no desire remains, for it has shaken off all ambition. As Hazrat Inayat Khan concludes: It is I who was, if there were any. What I had thought to be myself was not myself, but was my experience. I am all there is and it is myself who will be, whoever there will be It is I who am the source, the traveller and the goal of existence. Verily truth is all the religion there is, and it is truth which will save'.[35]

Thus the Sufi teaching has been metaphorically explained by a journey which the disciple undertakes, and by the various conditions of the soul from perfection through imperfection to perfection again. Most religions explain creation as emanating from God. Christianity goes on to narrate the fall of man from the perfect state to the imperfect. Except for the interpolation of the two worlds of angels and of jinns specifically, the idea is the same. Paradise may be likened to the angelic world in which Adam and Eve were placed by God, and from where they were driven out to the earth for disobeying the Lord:

`Of Man's first disobedience, and the fruit
Of that forbidden tree, whose mortal taste
Brought death into the world and all our woes
With loss of Eden'.[36]

The Sufi Journey set forth by these two Sufi saints, Hakim Sanai and Hazrat Inayat Khan depics an almost similar fall.

What then is the Sufi way and teaching, and how is it different from others? Its first notable feature is that it is free from the dogmas of religion. Even though it accepts both the Holy Quran and the Prophet, it does not have the Islamic opposition of the Quran to other faiths it does not divide people into believers and non-believers. Though believing in the one Divine Spark it does not have a vicious sting against idolatory. In fact it accepts both non-dualism and dualism. The second aspect of Sufism is that it gives various ways of acquiring the teaching, being a combination of rituals, esoteric observances, practical instructions and an exposition of proper conduct and behaviour. In this respect it could to likened to the training given to pupils in the ancient *gurukuls* of India, a kind of composite training comprising all aspects, theoretical as well as practical. If we were to give parallels we may quote the following respectively from the famous Christian prayer and an Upanishad:

1. `Lord, make me an instrument of your peace. Where there is hatred let me sow love; where there is injury, pardon; where there is doubt, faith; where there is despair, hope; where there is darkness, light; where there is sadness, joy.

   O Divine Master, grant that I may not so much seek to be consoled, as console; to be understood as to understand; to be loved as to love; for it is in giving that we receive; it is in pardoning that we are pardoned; and it is in dying that we are born to eternal life'.[37]

2. `Speak the truth, practise virtue. Do not neglect your studies, nor be indifferent to your own welfare. Make the offerings due to the gods and the manes. Revere your parents and your teacher

   `Whatever deeds are blameless and whatever good works have been performed by us, those only should be performed by you, not others. Honour those who are learned by offering them a seat and show obedience to them and be eager to learn. Give with sympathy, humility and abundance. Give gladly and willingly. Never give a gift for which you are not completely willing. If you are in doubt regarding any acts or conduct of yours, you should shape them according to the acts and conduct of men of wisdom who can judge well but not harshly, who love virtue, and who are themselves devoted to good deeds, not urged to them by others. And as to those whom people may malign, you are not to take them at their word, but behave towards them as those aforesaid wise men behave'.[38]

According to the Sufi saint, Abu-Said ibn Abil-Khair, Sufism means to forget whatever one has in his mind, to give whatever one possesses and to put up with whatever fate brings to him. Another essential constituent of Sufi teaching is that it is imparted by a guru. The teacher occupies a very conspicuous and exalted position in Sufi teaching and is much more than a priest or pundit. The Sufi teacher, Abdullah Ansari, asked his disciples to imbibe every observation of a sage and if they could not do that, at least remember the sage's name, for he is the reservoir of love. The resignation of the disciple to his teacher, who is often a Sheikh, ought to be complete. Complete faith, obedience, submission of the will, respect, confidence and secrecy on the part of the disciple, are essential. The aim of the teacher is to get rid of the veils which hide the truth from the aspirant. These veils are of desire arising from ignorance, self-centredness, self-pride self-love and adulation of oneself, doubt, greed for more and more, irresponsible behaviour, lack of perseverance, laziness and sloth which takes away alertness from the disciple [what the Hindu would classify as *tāmasa*]. The Sufi teachers are not preachers in the sense of missionaries or those who try to get converts by imposing themselves on people of other faiths. They endorse the view that `a religion that requires persecution is of the devil's propagation'.[39] Since there are no preachers or preaching, the nature of the Sufi teacher and his teaching can be defined only by what the taught say about it. One thing they say is that once a Sufi decides on a teacher, he should go to him with full confidence and accept all he says without dispute. It's like a patient and his doctor. The patient decides in whose medicare he should place himself, but having done so he must have complete faith in him and take whatever medicines he prescribes without questioning. From what Sufi disciples say about their experiences, it seems the call to seek a teacher comes form within. It is a kind of intuitive urge. The Sufi aspirant may hear an inner voice which tells him to go to a teacher for instruction, and if he tries to find his own way without such instruction, he is likely to destroy himself. By himself a man is subject to many different ways and he will not know what path to take. It is the teacher who shows him the right path. It is like a soldier whom the police train to become a commando. The soldier then acquires a skill he could not acquire by himself. Rumī says that learning is not so simple as people may take it to be. It is got by words, practice, detachment and companionship. But once having got it, what was an ordinary stone becomes a gem. The would-be disciple has certain assumptions to which he sticks fast. He does not have an open mind. Thus true understanding is not possible.

The teacher makes the disciple's mind responsive to the right way of thought. The interaction between the Sufi teacher and his disciple is of a special kind which changes the whole way of the latter's teaching. Ironically enough, the ascetic or the man who is detached and ever constant cannot prove to be a competent Sufi teacher, for then he has nothing to communicate and Sufism is more a kind of communication than teaching. The teacher covers a wide compass, a kind of one-counter for many purposes. This is because living itself, particularly good living, is a complex process and so the Sufi teacher must have a many-sided approach. Besides, he will not be one having a worldwide reputation, for it is only the aspirant who is worthy who recognizes and seeks him out; as the Sufis say, the bat can see in dim light, but if a brilliant one shines on him, he is dazzled and cannot find the way. The person who wishes to be initiated into Sufism must have eagerness to find truth and still more the capacity to recognize it where it exists. How is one to recognize a genuine Sufi teacher. It is not easy; in fact the real master's appearance is as unpredictable as that of Shankaracharya's description of the knower of *Brahman*. The Sufi sage, guide, elder or Sheikh, may be dressed in ordinary clothes or in one of patchwork and he may be of any age. Hujwiri, in his account, tells us of a young man who was a Sufi teacher and had a bottle of ink dangling from his waist. A would-be disciple saw him, and taking him to be an imposter thought he would test him by a question. He asked him what Sufism was. `Sufism' said the teacher in reply `is not thinking that a man is not a teacher just because he carries a bottle of ink'.[40] Sometimes the robe worn by a Sheikh may, in addition to being patch work, be intricately embroidered and he may have a horn, belt, cap, bowl and a rug of sheep's skin. Before he can start teaching, the Sufi teacher must get the `Robe of Permission' from his own preceptor. After that he can start his teaching and, as we have said, he adopts different types of instruction for various pupils according to their natures and capabilities. Thus teacher, taught and the teaching is a composite process. Jalaluddin Rumī expressed this by observing that the adept cannot teach if there be disagreement In other words the aspirant has got to be receptive.

Yet another aspect of Sufi teaching is the vast variety it involves. Indeed to the uninitiated observer, much of it may even sound contradictory. The ancient Sufis who lived in the period of the Prophet — the first four Khalifas, Salman, Abuzar, Miqdad, Ammar, Maaz and others — were ascetics of great piety having zeal for Islam who devotedly read the Holy Quran and lived simple lives in poverty. Yet ascetism is not an essential quality of Sufi teaching, which teaches more how to live wisely, well and to be of rightful conduct and behaviour than to keep oneself in isolation. The Sufi ideal, as we have said elsewhere, is to be in the world, but not of it, and to free oneself of ambition, pride, greed and blind faith. A number of Sufis following these ascetics, taught in Iran. We shall speak of them in a later chapter. Of the Sufi creed a large part consists of rituals which are aimed firstly in creating a certain mystic and ecstatic atmosphere and secondly to signify thereby the ever-changing and evanescent nature of existence. We have given an account of a sacred dance of Dervishes witnessed by Dr Selima Isfandiari. Major Desmond Martin has given another account of such an esoteric rite in which 'yoga-like exercises were performed to special music', the devotees going round and round a tall pillar of lapiz lazuli with their hands touching it. Major Martin mentions a mystic symbol, a ninefold emblem known as *No-koonja*, and saw the 'Ceremony of the Key'. The Key was used to open an ornate door which slid down and showed a procession of men carrying candles and singing a drirge in honour of the teachers. The wooden enclosure on which they were, revolved, changing into various panels depicting orchards, gardens, birds and other motifs made from wood and painted cloth. The significance, as explained to Major Martin, was that all teaching is, like the wooden box, `unnatural' and `institutionalized' and it is the `Key of the Real Man' that conveys real bliss and meaning to life.[41] Apart from rites and coremonies, the Sufi teachers use other means of teaching the doctrine by *zikr* (mystic formulas), miracles, and also by anecdotes like those of Mulla Nasrudin (some of which we have given) and others, sayings of the Masters and so forth. Thus the Sufi teaching may be likened to the colours of the rainbow. The Light of the Spirit is the white light of which these colours are formed and this Light is the Sufi teaching which takes many forms as the white light is constituted of various colours. But when this varicoloured spindle is rotated all these different forms become the one light of Sufism. Or we may liken the teaching to a kaleidoscope which when turned ever so little braks into different patterns rearranging in lovely order. The variety of the Sufi ways of teaching gives it a resilience not found in other rigid systems and religious orders.

REFERENCES

1. Dr Raymond Moody. *Life after Life*. Bantam Books, 1975, pp., 65-68 (italics mine)
2. *The Sufis*. Idries Shah, p., 348.
3. *Bhagavadgita* 18 : 5 and 11.
4. Romain Rolland. *Prophets of New India*. London. Cassell, 1930
5. Fom Idries Shah. *The Sufis* p., 400.
6. Robert Browning *Rabbi Ben Ezra*
7. *andham tamah pravishanti ye avidyaa mupasate*/tato bhuya iva tetamo yau vidyah yamarath||–ISHA UPANISHAD. 9.
8. The *Gita* (2.41) `Those of resolute minds, Arjuna, resolve wisely and with singleness of purpose, but they who waver, vex themselves, frittering away their thoughts in indecision'.

9. *Four Sufi Classics*. The Sufi Trust 1980 (Octagon Press) p., 182. The account of the Way of the Seeker Trans. David Pendlebury has been adapted from pp., 163 - 183 (sumarized).
10. *St John* (the Holy Bible) 18 : 37 - 39.
11. *The Sufis*. Idries Shah. New York: Double day 1964, pp., 97-68.
12. *Essays*. Francis Bacon. London: Oxford University Press On Truth. According to the great Sufi master, Hazrat. Inayat Khan `There is one truth, the true knowledge of our being within and without, which is the very essence of all wisdom'.
13. *The Sufi Message of Hazrat Inayat Khan*. London : Barrie and Rockchif, 1960. vol. 1, p., 15.
14. As for instance Idries Shah in *The Sufis*, The Teacher, the Teaching, the Taught. p., 389.
15. Thomas Carlyle.
16. Idries Shah. *The Sufis*, p., 333.
17. *Bhagavadgita*. 13 : 27.
18. *The Sufi Message of Hazrat Inayat Khan*. The Sufi Movement, Geneva. London: Barrie and Rockliff, 1960, vol. 1., p., 39.
19. These Nasirudin stories have been complied and related by Idries Shah. The subtleties of Mulla Nasirudin. The author expresses his gratitude for using them.
20. For this account the author is indebted to Father F.X. O `Halloran's, `Among the Sufis' in *The Sufi Mystery* ed. N.P. Archer London : The Octagon Press. Sufi Trust, 1980.
21. *Bhagavadgita* 12 : 8 - 12.
22. P.B. Shelley *Adonais* L 11.
23. St Mark. 10. 14.
24. The Holy Quran. Trans. Muhamad Ali. Lahore : Ahmadiyya An-Juman-I-Islam, 1928, 2.30, pp., 8-9.
25. ibid. 3 : 123. This relates to the battle of Uhud when Abu Sufyan marched agaist the Muslims who were outnumbered and faced defeat. The angels came to help them. So the angels, according to the Holy Quran are only to help believers of Islam.

26. Holy Quran 9 : 5 (Tran.;) Muhammad Ali.
27. *The Sufi Message of Hazrat Inayat Khan*. Geneva: Barrie and Rockliff, 1960, vol. 1, pp., 115-116.
28. ibid, p., 116
29. Robert Browning. *Abt Vogler*.
30. *Mundaka Upanishad*. 1 : 1 : 3-5.
31. *The Sufi Message of Hazrat Inayat Khan*. Barie and Rockcliffe, 1960, p., 141 op. cit.
32. William Morris. *The Wisdom of Brynhild*.
33. *King Lear*, Act 4, scene 1.
34. Shakespheare. *Hamlet* Act 1, scene 3.
35. *The Sufi Message of Hazrat Inayat Khan* London: Barrie and Rocklife, 1960, p., 185.
36. John Milton. *Paradise Lost* Book 1.1.1
37. Christian prayer attributed to St Francis of Assisi
38. *Taittirya Uparishad* 1. 11. 1-4. The word `brahmins' has been taken as meaning `men of wisdom'.
39. Hosea Ballou
40. Idries Shah. *The Sufis*. New York : Doubleday, 1964, pp., 397 - 98.
41. *The Sufi Mystery*, ed. N.P. Archer. Sufi Trust. London: Octagon Press. An Afghan Community'. Major Desmond Martin, pp., 40 - 43.

2

The Sufi Saints and Orders

'From where does that light come?' I asked a child who was walking with a candle held in his hand.

The child blew it out at once. 'Tell me where the light has gone' he said, 'then I'll tell you where it came from'

Hasan of Basra

TIE SAINTS

Sufism is often likened to the Vedanta philosophy and sometimes it is mistakenly thought that the Vedantists were contemporaries of the ancient Sufi saints.[1]

It by the Vedantists is meant only Shankaracharya, this assumption could be correct for Shankara lived in the eighth-ninth century. But he was only an exponent of the Vedanta's non-dual aspect. The Vedanta comprises the Vedas the *Upanishads*, the *Bhagavadgita* and the *Brahma-sutras*. Of these the *Gita* is perhaps thousands of years old. Shri Krishna says in it that the yoga teaching he is giving to Arjuna was given by him to the Sun-god (Vivasvan) who thereafter gave it to Manu, the Father of mankind and Manu gave it to Iskvaku, king of the earth. Calculating in terms of the *yugas* of Hindu cosmogony. Manu taught the yoga of the *Gita* to Iksvaku some 2,005,000 years ago. The age of the present Manu is reckoned as 305,300,000 years, of which we have crossed about 120,400,018 years. Thus the yoga of the *Gita* must have been first taught by Krishna to Vivasvan more than 120,400,020 years ago!

The *Upanishads* date back to 800 B.C. and the *Brahma-sutras* find mention in the *Gita* - *brahmasūtrapadaishava hetumadbhirvinishitaih* (*Gita*, 13: 4). Thus the sages (*rishis*) of the *Upanishads* lived long before either Islam or Sufism or Christianity was even heard of. However, the main exponents of the Vedanta could be said to living near about the period of the ancient Sufis (Shankaracharya 788-820). The Sufi mystics lived between the eighth and the fifteenth centuries. The earliest Sufis were the first four Khalifas, Salman the Iranian, Abuzar, Miqdad, Ammar Maaz and others who were pious, homeless, devout faithful followers of Islam and devoted to the Prophet. The Iranian Sufis were of very ancient origin. Prominent among them were the following: Hasan Basri who was directly instructed by Ali, the fourth Khalifa. He was very devout. Someone told him that he could reach God only by passing a thousand year in the flames of hell. He wept and said 'I would like to be that man'[2]

Habib Ajami who died in A.D. 738 was a money-lender, who renounced the world and became and ascetic. He used to say that he spent his time in purifying his heart and left others to pursue bookish knowledge and arguments. He was a disciple of Hasan Basri (also known as Hasan of Basra), and built a monastery on the bank of the Euphrates.

Ibrahim Adham, who died in 875, was a nobleman of Balk who left the comforts of worldly life and became an ascetic. he used to say that two loves, i.e., the love of God and that of the world could not exist in the same heart. The idea was taken up by Jalaluddin Rumī in his example of the lover knocking at the door of the Beloved which we have already quoted in speaking about love in Sufism. Here it may be mentioned that this ancient creed of love was only love in the spiritual sense. Later, the Sufi Masters introduced erotic imagery to narrate the Soul's experience on earth as in *Salman and Absal* of the saint, Jami, from whom we have quoted before. Finally the spiritual element was completely lost in the sensual as in the anecdote in which when a woman on ageing began to lose her physical beauty, her admirers ceased to come to her. When questioned why, one of her lovers said that it was because she had lost the beauty of her limbs, the litheness of her body, the delicateness of her smooth skin and the sweetness of her voice![3] The spiritual had, with the decline of Sufism, been driven away as clouds before the wind. But to go on with our account, when someone asked Ibrahim Adham to take him to the nearest dwelling, he pointed to the cemetery. Self-control was greatly prized by him and used to say that it was better to control and restrain oneself than to rule over an empire.

Fuzail, son of Ayaz, who died in the year 803, lived in Merv. Emphasized the love and fear of God. He was fond of solitude. Ahmad, son of Khazruvait, was a native of Balkh (Afghanistan) who died in A.D. 854, used to say 'It you want to give your soul life, kill it. God can be seen and if one can't see him, he must be blind'. Two other Sufi sages also belonged to Balkh. One was Abu Ali Saqiq who died in A.D. 812. He had no covetedness. If I earn anything he would say 'I use it to help the needful and if I don't, I thank God'. Another saint of Balkh was Hatam Asam who died in A.D. 871. He believed that a Sufi patiently bears hunger and suffering, controls his passion and wears clothes made of coarse cloth. A disciple of the eighth Shiah Imam, Imam Reza, Maruf Kharkhi of Khorassan (d. A.D. 821) used to say that a Sufi is a guest of God. He has the right to be served but not to demand anything. He believed that love of God was a gift. The Sufi should strive to know the real and distinguish it from the unreal. Also belonging to Khorassan lived Abul Husain Nuri (d. A.D. 907), who was of the view that knowledge and reasoning are of no avail in reaching God, for he reveals himself to whomever he wills. 'I looked at his light' he said, 'till I became light myself. A Sufi's soul ought to be pure and he should be detached, not hankering after wealth or worldly comforts'. He believed that Sufism does not involve knowledge of science or philosophy, or the performing of rituals. It means morality, purity, desirelessness, self-sacrifice and turning away from worldliness. Another saint of Khorassan Bashar-e-Hafi, (d. A.D. 841) believed that one should know God and he was indeed unfortunate who did not know him. Bayazid of Bistam, also of Khorassan (d. A.D. 874) was one of the early Sufi authors. He taught the going away of consciousness when mystic union with God (*fana*) took place. It is said he was on his way to Mecca when he was stopped by the high-priest who said that he needn't proceed to Mecca, rather take him (the high-priest) to be the embodiment of the divine. He was a theologian, poet and philosopher, but his works are not extant. He said that a Sufi did not care for comfort and accepted suffering, he loved God and practised humility. He used to say 'I am the cup-bearer, the wine and the drinker. Beneath my cloak there is nothing but God. I went from God to God till I heard from within "O thou I"[if, Rumi's lover knocking at the Beloved's door]. Pride of self is the worst vice'.[4] A saint of Balkh, Yahya, son of Ma' az (d. A.D. 867) said much the same as Rumī and Bayazid about love of God. He who sees anything apart from his Beloved, he said, cannot see the Beloved. Love is unaffected by either the Beloved's kindness or cruelty. Ascetics renounce the world but do not spurn the pleasures of paradise, but the Sufi renounces both. Sirri al-Saqti (d. A.D. 867) emphasized piety. The wise man is detached and seeks truth. The Sufi saint Sahl, son of Abdulla of Tustar (d. A.D. 896) was a firm votary of Sufism. One may not understand its value in the beginning, he said, but once imbibing it, he would be devoted all his life to Sufism. Junaid of Nehawand (d. A.D. 910) was disciple of the aforesaid saint. Sirri al-Saqti. He declined to lecture on Sufism so long as his teacher was alive but the Prophet directed him in a dream to do so and, with the consent of his teacher, he began to give talks on Sufism. He held that one got the greatest delight in meditating on God's unity. One should live in God and die in him. A Sufi must live a detached life. He should be humble and equate himself with the ground which is trodden underfoot or like a cloud which falls as rain on the earth. Unlike the earlier Sufis, he gave importance to wisdom and used to say 'It is better to sink ecstasy in wisdom than to sink wisdom in ecstasy.' Abu Bakr Shibli of Khorassan who was in the same school and class as Mansur-e-Hallaj exhorted Sufis to love truth. Like Shankaracharya, the Hindu sage, he found the world unreal, and so asked Sufis not to be worldly. He also believed in breath-control [cf, Pātanjali's *Yoga-sutras* and *Gita* 5:27-28] and said that the Sufi should love his fellow-men and all creatures.

These early Sufis were more inclined towards the inculcation of good behaviour and conduct, piety, love of God, kindness to all living beings and in showing how one should live by living noble lives themselves. Though they were not against the acquisition of knowledge they believed in the intuitive realization of truth. It was only rarely that they showed any desire to proselytizing such as that of Shibli of whom it is said that once when he was ill the Caliph sent a Christian doctor to cure him. Shibli told the doctor that he would automatically get cured if the doc got converted from Christianity to Islam. On the doctor agreeing Shibli left his bed completely cured and the doctor embraced Islam.[5] Whatever authenticity may be given to this story, one thing is certain, that it does not represent the spirit of Sufism which, while accepting the Holy Quran, was never in favour of conversions in any manner whatever. Gradually the Sufi saints began to preach the doctrine of Sufism and with them we enter the stage of theoretical knowledge. With this was combined subtle observations which have a Zen-like meaning, as for example the tales of Mulla Nasirudin, some of which we have related. These saying try to drive home the truth by mysterious, often contradictory maxims, sometimes having wit and humour. For example there was a blind man walking with a jar on his shoulders and a lamp in his hand. Someone asked him of what use would the lamp be, seeing that he was blind. The man said 'I do not carry it for myself but for those who have eyes, lest they bump into me and break my jar'. Bahlul, was in he presence of Harun al Rashid, when he was told by a minister who wanted to ridicule him that the king had appointed him (Bahlul) to be in charge of pigs and monkeys. 'All right' said Bahlul. 'Then pay heed to my orders and carry them out'. Such anecdotes were compiled by Nuruddin Abdurrahaman whose pen name was Jami (b. A.D. 1414, d. A.D. 1492), in his work *Baharistan*, which he wrote for his fourth son.

With Hallaj, the carder, also known as Husain son of Mansur (B. A.D. 858) we enter the age of the Sufi philosophers and writers. While the earlier Sufis did not believe in putting their beliefs in teaching and talks, the ones coming after them, did. Hallaj, who belonged to South Iran, was a great traveller and visited Gujarat (in India), Central Asia and Baghdad. He was much misunderstood and suffered a fate analogous to Jesus Christ who was crucified for speaking of the way of Truth. In the same manner Islamic fanaticism could not stomach his observation *an - al - Haq* ('I am the truth') though he was speaking thereby of the divinity of the Soul, an essential concept of Sufism. Owing to this and partly because of court intrigue, he was made to undergo great suffering and finally executed in Baghdad in A.D. 922 when he was sixty-four years old. Hallaj was thus one of the earliest martyrs to

Sufism, and his tragic end depicts vividly the dogmatic and hard-shell attitude of Moslem orthodoxy, which is not only uncompromising but also inmical to non-Moslems. Some prominent Western writers have tried to define the Islamic attitude and have observed that according to Ali el–Hujwiri, the Prophet said that one who hears a Sufi and does not say '*amin*' 'amen' [i.e. agree with what the Sufi says] should be considered to be heedless, and that 'it was in Sufi Style that he [the Prophet] ordered his followers to respect all People of a Book, meaning those who respected their own sacred scriptures – a term later used to include Zoroastrians'.[6] However, the Sufis never themselves cared whether people paid heed to them or not, for they weren't really preachers of any religious doctrine. In the Aneclotes of the Wise contained in the *Baharistan* of Jami, it is said that it's better to eat the vegetables grown in one's own garden than roasted lamb offered by another[7]. In other words indoctrination is not favoured by Sufis, and when they have no desire to preach not listening to them could never be condemnable so far as they were concerned. In another part of the *Baharistan* we are told that the Prophet Mohammed is believed to have said that the believer is full of spirits and talks pleasantly while the hypocrite is 'sullen and frowning'. It follows that he who is a non-believer, i.e., not a Moslem is a hypocrite. As regards the aforesaid, the observation of respecting the People of a Book,' of the Prophet, what the Holy Quran says repeatedly is 'those who have been given *the* Book.[8] '*The* Book'could therefore only mean the Holy Quran, and the assumption that refers to all scriptures seems to be mistaken and endows Islam with the kind of eclectism which it doesn't really possess. But to go on with Hallaj's doctrines, the one which seemed most obnoxious to those who ordered his execution, was that good works were more significant than prayer. This was quite possibly taken to mean the negation of the traditional *namaj* performed by Moslems as a sacred duty. Those who judged him failed to understand that prayer really meant communion with God, the virtue of which no religion could deny; not even Islam, Hallaj's other beliefs were, 1. When associated with the body (which he called the 'animal soul'), the immortal and divine spirit becomes limited. This concept is much like that of the Hindu idea of *jiva*. The Soul, they believe (the *atman*) is really of the nature of *Brahman*, the Eternal Being, but when embodied, it becomes the *jiva*, and as such has to take part in the physical and mental states of the body in which, for the time being it remains, recovering its pure and divine nature when it is released from that body. 2. The Supreme Being cannot be compared with any other thing or thought of a another. It is beyond reasoning and argument. This too, is much like the Hindu concept of *Brahman* which conceives God in the non-dual aspect as *na iti, na iti*, i.e. 'not this, not this', and as immovable, dwelling everywhere, beyond thought ever constant, inexpressible and as Shri Krishna say in the *Gita - aksharam anirdeshyam avyaktam sarvatrgam achintyam kutastham achalam dhruvam*[9] 3. Hallaj also believed that suffering brings one close to God and one should patiently bear it. This is indeed very true. When one of joyful and experiences the pleasures of the world, he also remains involved in the world. People flock to one who has power and wealth and so long as they have these they do not bother about God or the other world. Christ said that it was easier for a camel to pass through the eye of a needle than for a rich man to enter the kingdom of God and in the Sermon on the Mount Jesus blessed those who were poor, meek and humble. Aeschylus says that wisdom is gained by pain[10] and in the *Katha Upanishad* Naciketas says to the god of Death:

> 'Knowing that life ends, however long its span
> And pleasures of the senses last but a moment
> Who is the mortal who can expect joy from these?

To turn toward God one has to turn away from the world, for both can't exist together in the mind. And it is suffering, and thereafter the realization that the world is no sharer in one's suffering, that makes the sufferer turn away from he world to God; for as the goldsmith tests the purity of gold by putting it through the fire, so does God test man's faith through suffering. But the rigidity of Islam could not pardon Hallaj for these elevated and innocuous doctrines. A Sufi sage Zun-nun who was not of Iran, was a Nubian living in Egypt. (A.D. 860). According to him spiritual insight derived from wisdom (ma'rfat) brought one nearer to God. When one became a spiritualist (*aref*) he was on the way to godliness. Some of the saints of this middle period of Sufism were renowned masters of Sufism, such as jami, whom we have mentioned, El-Ghazzali, Hakim Sanai, Sheikh Saadi, Farididdin, Jalaluddin Rumī, Ibn El-Arabi, Omar Khyyam and others. We go on to speak about these

El-Ghazzali, Hakim Sanai and jami lived in the period beginning with 1058 (the date of the birth of Ghazzali, and ending 1492, the year of Jami's death). These Sufi saints were exceptions to the theoretical and erudite trend that the middle school of Sufism adopted, and their legacy gave rise to some exceptions among the later Sufis who followed them, like the great teacher Jalaluddin Rumī. The ancient Sufi, Fushanji, realized that the spirit of Sufism was its essence, not the outward form of it. Hujwiri who wrote *Revelation of the Veiled* a millenium before the aforesaid saints, was also of the same view. These Sufis did not consider bookish knowledge of much account. Instead they emphasized the acquiring of detachment and spirituality.

According to them Sufism could not be made to fit any preconceived notion, any name or form. The Sufi sage, Nuri, considered Sufism to be a characteristic idea rather than learning or ritual. The effect of the Sufi teaching and the Sufi way was, they said, primarily to preclude indifferent or negative behaviour patterns and transform conduct and behaviour. It is for this reason that the Sufis cannot be said to mean a specific category of people conforming to a particular religion or cult. They are neither Hindus, not Moslems, nor Christians, nor Buddhists, nor distinguished by any other rigid belief, though as we have said earlier, any person belonging to any faith conforming to the Sufi way would be called a Sufi. From this it also follows that no one aspirant can expect to fit in with a stereotype readymade pattern of Sufism. For example, when one goes to a holy place, like a temple or mosque, he puts off his slippers before entering. Now supposing when the congregation leave and the slippers are somehow switched, each person will have a footwear, but he will have one which does not fit. So too if the same Sufi teaching is imparted to all seekers without distinction, the Sufis it turns out will all be out of tune. This explains why the ancient Sufi masters did not reproduce their teachings in scholastic tomes or rigid scriptures. It also shows how difficult the Sufi teacher's job was, and the ancient teachers like Abu-Hafs the blacksmith, and Nishapur, Hujwiri stressed that the form of behaviour which had to be inculcated in the Sufi disciple varies with place and time. And this is quite obvious. If someone going to condole a person's death, for example, were to appear with a smiling face and start laughing and cracking jokes, he would invite frowns and looks of disapproval. He would not be behaving properly in accordance with the place and occasion. And if a person who is hurrying to catch a plane were to be stopped by someone who insists on telling him about how he lost his watch (doubtless of consequence to the loser, but not for the hearer for whom the second and final call has come to board the plane) that would be ill-timed behaviour, and completely taboo for a Sufi. It's much like the wedding guest and the Ancient Mariner:

'He holds him with his glittering eye-
The Wedding-Guest stood still,
And listens like a three years'child:
The Mariner hath his will.[12]

A Sufi wouldn't have thus stopped a man keen to attend a marriage! Many persons lay a false claim to be Sufis, but it is only the perfected aspirant to can be called a Sufi, as Hujiwiri says (a *kasf*). The person still not an adept is known as a *mutasawwif* ('one who tries'). The third type, far more numerous, are the pretenders. Hujwiri calls them respectively, the men of union, of principles and of superfluities.

Jami, of whom we have spoken before, had his early schooling at Herat and at a school started by Tīmur at Samarcand. He outstripped his other fellow-students and learnt Persian, logics, astronomy and theology, amazing his teachers by his precocity. It is said that he had a vision of the renowned Sufi Sheikh, Mohammed Sa'aduddin Kaashghari, who asked him to come to him. So Jami returned to Herat from Samarcand, as commanded by the Sheikh. He was taken as a disciple and attentively learnt the Sufi teaching, on the completion of which, he retired into solitude. It was only long after that, on the death of his Master, he began to preach Sufism at the mosque where his teacher had taught. He began to express Sufism in poetry and his verses were greatly appreciated by everyone including royal princes and potentates. In A.D. 1477 Jami set out on a pilgrimage to Mecca which Moslems were required to visit once in a lifetime, along with a number of his followers. The caravan proceeded to Baghdad where one of Jami's companions who was reproved by him for misquoting a verse, fell out with him and brought a charge against him before the tribunal. He was acquitted honorable, and his accuser was pilloried at the marketplace. Jami stayed four months at Baghadad and thereafter went on to Medina and then to his destination, Mecca, where he performed all the ceremonies required to be gone through by

Moslems. From here he turned homeward and stayed for forty days at Damascus and from there to Amida, the capital of Mesopotamia. He found that war had broken out there, and so with the help of an escort provided to him by the kindness of the king, proceeded with speed to Tabriz. The *diwan* of that place urged him to stay there for some time, but Jami was eager to go back home to see his aged mother, so he went on, and reached Herat in the year A.D. 1473 after about a year's absence. The poet, saint and philosopher died in 1492 at the age of 81 years. He left behind his wife, for his four sons had died before, three in infancy, and one in young age. He is said to have written ninty-nine books of grammar, poetry and theology, one of which *Baharistan* has been preserved in an English library. That, along with *Yusuf and Zulaikha* and *Salaman and Absal*, are his most prominent works.

We have already spoken of the enigmatic Mulla Nasrudin. His anecdotes are well-known and off repeated. Though they are mysterious and often seem to be jokes or sayings which on the surface make little sense, they are pregnant with suble meaning and each one tries to emphasize some trait of Sufism. It is not known if a person of that name ever lived and if so, when, or whether he is a mythical character to serve as a medium through which these tales are told. We have narrated some of these sayings, but it is worthwhile adding to them for they convey in a subtle manner the niceties of Sufism. We shall call him just 'Mulla' in relating these.

The Sufi believes that the truth of many things cannot be arrived at by mere reason and logic, for the truth may conceal something that may not be true. In other words the truth may not be the whole truth. The Mulla said he had been taught that the man who had not been wronged should resent it just as much as the man who *had* been. After a pause he said such resentment should not be shown till one is sure the wrong is really a wrong. On the contrary the so-called wrong may really be of some advantage. This is illustrated by another tale which has nothing to do with the Mulla, but justifies his conclusion. A man was journeying on a lonely road infested by robbers. By his ill-luck he fell a victim to them. They took away his money and in the process chopped of a bit of his little finger. The man bandaged it and stopping the bleeding proceeded on. Unfortunately he was spotted by some evil tantriks who were on the lookout of someone whom they could offer as a human sacrifice. They pounced on the man and were about to carry out their fell design, when the noticed the chopped finger, 'We can't offer this man as a sacrifice' one of them pointed out, 'as his limbs are not whole'. So the unbound him and set him free. Thus the chopped finger, doubtless bemoaned by that man, turned out to be a blessing in disguise, for it saved his life. Even an untruth might turn out to be an advantage to someone. Kahlil Gibran told a story to bring this out. He said once he was discussing spiritual matters with a saint when a highwayman came along limping and said to the saint that he had come to him to atone for many wrongdoings done by him. He confessed to have been guilty of theft, plunder and even murder. The saint gave him the surprising reply. I too am guilty of all these crimes. The highwayman thought when such a faultless man as this saint has also done all this, what need is there for me to lament? He was comforted by this thought and went away a happier man, singing a song, a thing he had never, with his troubled conscience, done before. Gibran asked the saint why he had owned up all this, which really he hadn't done. The saint said 'It never did me any harm, but it certainly served to bring peace to that disturbed man.' It is often said there is truth which hurts and falsehood which comforts – *apriya satya and priya asatya* (*apriya* meaning 'unloving', *priya* 'loving'; *satya* truth, *asatya* 'untruth). Of truth, the Sufi would say 'Truth is that which cannot be fully spoken, and that which can be spoken is not necessarily the truth'.[13] Speaking about non-violence and Satyagraha M.K. Gandhi said 'For what appears truth to the one may appear to be error to the other.' Roger Bacon says, 'There are four chief obstacles in grasping truth, which hinder every man, however learned, and scarcely allow any one to win a clear title to learning, namely, submission to faulty and unworthy authority, influence of custom, popular prejudice, and concealment of our own ignorance accompanied by an ostentatious display of our knowledge'.[14]

The question what truth really is arose when Jesus Christ was brought before Pilate, the Roman governor about which have already spoken before, and Pilate's enigmatic observation about it by which be made it known in one and the same breath that he understood truth and yet refused to understand it[15]. But as the fourth century Roman historian, Marcellinus Ammianus says, 'The language of truth is unadorned and always simple'. This is also the Sufi viewpoint:

'Truth is simple. But for the very reason that it is simple, people will not take it; because our life on earth is such that for everything we value, we have to pay a great price and one wonders, if truth is the most precious of all things, then how can truth be attained simply? It is this illusion that makes everyone deny simple truth and seek for complexity. Tell people something that makes their heads whirl round and round. Even if they do not understand it, they are most pleased to think "It is something substantial; it is something solid; for it is an idea we cannot understand; it must be something lofty." But something which every soul knows, proving what is divine in every soul and which it cannot help but know, that appears to be too cheap, for the soul already knows it. There are two things; knowing and being. It is easy to *know* truth but most difficult to be truth. It is not in *knowing* truth that life's purpose is accomplished; life's purpose is accomplished in *being* truth'[16]

In the same strain the poet Robert Browing says in *Paracelsus*:

> 'Truth lies in ourselves; it takes no rise
> From outward things; whatever you may believe,
> There is an inmost centre in us all
> Where Truth abides in fullness; and to *know*
> Rather consists in opening out a way
> Whence the imprisoned splendour may escape,
> Than in effecting entry for a light
> Supposed to be without'.

In both knowing truth and being truth, the judge is the man's conscience (*antahkaraṇa*) which as a thermometer registers fever, the barometer weather and the blood-pressure instrument, the blood pressure; registers instantly whether an action is right or wrong (though if persistently disregarded it may then be blunted and cease doing so. As Karl Barth the Swiss theologian says, 'Conscience is the perfect interpreter of life'[17] and Emmanuel Swedenborg, the Swedish scientist and theologian, 'Conscience is God's presence in man'.[18] In the *Bhagavadgita* Shri Krishna says that only the truth exists: 'Of the non-existent there is no coming to be and of the existent there is no ceasing. The reality of both has been realized by the seers of truth who have known them thus'.[19]

To continue with the Mulla Nasiruddin's anecdotes there is one which emphasizes the world's imperfections. Someone asked the Mulla what the relation between things worldly and of the other world was. The Mulla got hold of an apple that was half-rotten, saying it was one from paradise. 'How can that be so?' said someone. 'it's rotten on one side' 'Well' said the Mulla 'that's how near to a heavenly one you'll be able to get in this corrupt world.' The Hindu concept of the world is much the same. In chapter 9, verse 33 of the *Bhagavadgita* Shri Krishna tells Arjuna: *anityam asukham imam prāpya bhajasva mām* 'Having come to this fleeting world which is devoid of happiness, worship Me'. The world is called *mrytuloka*, i.e., transitory existence the end of which is death. The Buddhists also consider this world of corruption or evil and suffering as one far from paradise. The *Samyutta Nikāya*, a Buddhist scripture says:

> 'What do you think monks'. [the Buddha said] which may be more, the flow of tears your have shed on this long way, running again and again to new birth and new death, united to the disliked, separated from he liked, complaining and weeping, or the waters of the four great oceans?....... But how is this possible? Without beginning or end, O monks, is this round of rebirths. There cannot be discerned the first beginning of beings, who sunk in ignorance and bound by thirst, are incessantly transmigrating and again and again run to a new birth. And thus, O monks, through a long time you have experienced suffering, pain and misery, and enlarged the burying ground; truly enough to be disgusted with every kind of existence, long enough to turn away from every kind of existence, long enough to deliver yourself from it.[20]

Suffering, Buddhism believes, is not however a brute force of nature. If it was so one could never get rid of it. One must reject secular values and search for the spiritual. Worldly remedies only make a man stick to worldly ties like attachment, ties which are ephemeral. Besides that which is pleasure-giving for some time is also not happiness, as the poet Robert Burns wrote:

> 'But pleasures are like poppies spread-
> You seize the flow'r, its bloom is shed;
> Or like the snow falls in a river —
> One moment white–then melts for ever'.[21]

What exactly is the spiritual path? It is most certainly one that impels a man to goodness. In the *Kaṭha Upanishad* we are told story of Nachiketas. In those days wealth was counted by the number of cows one had. Vājashravasa a brahmin was gifting away cows when performing a ritual Sacrifice known as the Vishvajit. His son, Nachiketas, noticed the cows were old and decrepit and unworthy of being gifted. so his asked his father repeatedly 'to whom will you gift me?' When he repeated his question a third time, his father, losing his temper said 'I give you to Death.' The boy was spiritually minded so he thought his father's words must be obeyed and hurried off to the abode of Yama, the (Hindu Death-God). But Yama had gone away and came back only after three days. So the boy had to wait at Death's doorstep. When Yama returned, he was aghast to find that a brahmin boy had remained without food and water so long and to atone for this fault, he offered Nachiketas three boons. As his first boon the boy asked that his father, Vājashravasa, may not be worried about him. Yama promised that it would be so and Nachiketas would go back to a happy reunion. As his second boon the boy wished to know the mode of a sacrifice which would enable him to attain heaven. The third boon asked, however, stumped Yama, for Nachiketas said 'When man dies some say "He exists", some again, "He does not". I would like to know the truth about this'. Yama tried to wriggle out by promising untold wealth and every thing material to be desired, even the kingship of the earth in lieu of this boon. But Nachiketas persisted, saying 'All these things are most transient. They wear out the vigour of the senses. The whole life-span is short. So keep your horses, dance and song to yourself'. Thus cornered Yama taught the wisdom of spiritualism to Nachiketas, as contained in the second chapter onwards of this *Upanishad*. The good, said Yama, is one thing, the pleasant quite another. 'Both of these approach man; he who is wise prefers the good to the pleasant but the fool sticks to the pleasant because of greed and attachment'.

By his story about the half-rotten apple, Mulla Nasrudin was bringing out this difference between spiritualism and materialism, that which is imperfect and worldly and that which is heavenly and untouched by the world. As poet Robert Browing says:

> 'On the earth the broken arcs; in the
> heaven a perfect round'.[23]

Another Nasrudin anecdote also emphasizes the value of goodness in life as well as the significance of the Sufi teacher in imparting the teaching to the learner. Nasrudin took a bag of salt on his donkey to sell the salt in the market. As he crossed a shallow stream with it, the salt dissolved in the water, much to the donkey's relief, as its burden was lightened. But the Mulla could not buy the much needed provisions for his meals. Next day he loaded the donkey with a bale of wool. This time because of the wool being soaked with the stream's water, the donkey's burden greatly increased and became hard to carry. But because the wool's weight was considerably more, the Mulla gained by getting more money for it. Here the salt stands for goodness or wisdom and the wool for the Sufi (teacher). The import is that when man forsakes the path of goodness he loses and when he listens to the words of the wise he gains thereby.

The Sufi insists on a receptive mind. Unless that is not there, one gains no advantage. Aldous Huxley says:

> 'To be clearly and constantly aware of the divine guidance is given only to those who are already far advanced in the life of the spirit. In its earlier stages we have to work not by the direct perception of God's successive graces, but by faith in their existence. We have to accept as a working hypothesis that the events of our lives are not merely fortituitous but deliberate tests of intelligence and character. specially devised occasions (if properly used) for spiritual advance.

> Acting upon this working hypothesis, we shall treat no occurrence as intrinsically unimportant. We shall never make a response that is inconsiderate, or a mere automatic expression of our self-will, but always give ourselves time to consider what course of behaviour would seem to be more in accord with the will of God, most charitable, most conclusive to the achievement of our final end. When such becomes our habitual response to events, we shall discover, from the nature of their effects, that some at least of these occurrences were divine graces in the disguise sometimes of trivialities, sometimes of inconveniences or even of pains and trials. But if we fail to act upon the working hypothesis that grace exists, grace will in effect be non-existent so far as we are concerned. We shall prove by a life of accident at the best, at the worst of downright evil, that God does not help human beings, unless they first permit themselves to be helped'[24]

Sufism is a kind of mysticism, and this implies what is beyond the perception of the senses. Evelyn Underhill says, 'Mysticism then, is not an opinion: it is not a philosophy. It has nothing in common with the pursuit of occult knowledge. On the one hand it is not merely the power of contemplating Eternity: on the other, it is not to be identified with any kind of religious queerness. It is the name of that organic process which involves the perfect consummation of the love of God; the achievement here and now of the immortal heritage of man. Or if you like it better–for this means exactly the same thing–it is the art of establishing his conscious relation with the Absolute'[25]

Mysticism is all that reason is unable to explain. Even science and mathematics have to take fundamental things for granted, for example geometry starts with an axiom which we are told is a self-evident truth. There are certain basic things which stand no reasoning, like a note in music, a figure in painting and a word in speech. Such thing like life and death, dreams and unconsciousness and time, have ever been and still remain, mysteries. Some lucky man understands and grasps them now and then; a lover intoxicated with love, a devotee drunk with faith, or a hermit whose eyes are turned to things which others can't see. When he does so it is an experience beyond the commonplace, and to that one may apply the term 'mysticism'.

In the Nasrudin stories we find an illustration of the in sufficiency of reasoning and logic in arriving at conclusions. What is necessary is that the deduction must be right, not the way of coming to it. The Mulla is portrayed as a magistrate. Two persons came to him, one charging the other of biting his ear. The other said 'I didn't bite it, he did it himself'. The Mulla asked them to wait and retiring to his chamber tried to bite his own ear. Of course he couldn't and every time he made the attempt, he fell down and bruised his forehand. Then coming out he examined the foreheads of the two men and seeing one of them with the bruises he declared he had done it himself! although he compensated the other man. The giving of compensation was the right settlement, but saying that the man with bruised forehead had bitten it was illogical. In another such tale someone came to the Mulla with a closed fist and asked him what was there in it. On the Mulla's asking for a clue the man told him that it was egg-shaped and laid by a hen. 'Ah! I know' the Mulla said 'It's most probably a cake'! Two points made by Sufism is firstly that all actions are interrelated and that self-help is life's principle. To bring out the first, Nasrudin was walking on a lonely road when a troop of horsemen came his way. In panic, lest they rob him or press him into military service, he went and hid himself in a graveyard. The soldiers saw him doing so and greatly wondering went to him and offered to assist him if he was in some kind of trouble. The Mulla realizing his error said 'Well it's a little complicated, for *I* am here because of *you*, and *you* are here because of *me*'! The theory of self-help is illustrated by a Nasrudin tale in which the Mulla went into a general merchant's shop and asked the shopkeeper if he had leather, nails and dye. The man had all these. 'Then', said the Mulla 'why don't you make yourself a shoe'. The Sufi belief in self-help was once brought home to me forcefully, though by a military officer who might or might not have been a Sufi. That year there was a very great flood in Lucknow which affected about two third of the entire capital so much so that boats began to ply on most of the city's roads. Many people whose houses had been submerged in the flooded waters took shelter in the outskirts of the city. Temporary camps came up to provide them with food and other essential facilities. One of these needs was for toilets and the possibility there was only having trench-latrines. A military officer was also deputed there for whatever assistance was needed. I had been put in charge of one of these camps. Thinking that the military would have been faced by many such problems I approached him and requested to be helped in it. The military man just smiled and said, 'Well you ask some of these men working with you to take hold of spades and pickaxes and dig a trench. That's all there is to it'. It was my lesson in self-help much in the Nasrudin manner!

A Nasrudin tale brings out the nature of the Sufi teaching. No instruction is to be given to those completely ignorant because they will not be able to grasp it, and so too to those who already know, for they don't need to be taught, The Mulla was giving a talk on Sufism. 'Do you know what I'm going to tell you? ' he began. Some people shouted 'No'. In such a case I shall not venture to teach people so ignorant', the Mulla said. A week after the people persuaded him again to give his talk. 'Do you know what I am going to say?' he asked. There was a chorus of 'yes'. 'This being so' the Mulla said 'there's nothing for me to tell', and he went away. Anyway, he was prevailed on to give them a third opportunity to listen. Again he began by saying 'Do you all know what I am about to tell?' The people gathered there said 'Some of us know and some don't'. 'Then' said Nasrudin 'Let those who know tell those who don't'!

The Sufi mystic does not go anywhere to be enlightened. He believes mysticism is the link between all beings. The Mulla had come back to his village from the capital of the kingdom and the fellow villagers were all agog to hear of his visit.

'The king' said Nasrudin 'spoke to me'. The villagers were impressed. 'Just imagine the king actually spoke to one of us!' they remarked. Some, however, who were more inquisitive asked him what the king had said, 'What he said' the Mulla told them was very clear and loud enough for all to hear. He said "Get out of my way!" '

The usual attitude of religious scriptures is that wealth is evil and must not be sought. The Holy Bible says 'It is easier for a camel to go through the eye of a needle, than for a rich man to enter into the kingdom of God'. So too the *Katha Upanishad* says: "You have not gone into this path of wealth, Nachiketas, in which many men perish........ To the ignorant foolish person befooled by the delusion of wealth, the path of the hereafter never appears. "This is the only world" he thinks and no other, and so thinking he falls into the control of Death again and again'. The Sufi does not so despise wealth, but he emphasizes that money should be in the hands of those who need it, deserve it and use it well. Nasrudin asked a rich man for some money telling him that he wanted it to buy an elephant. The man said that if he didn't have money enough to buy one, how could he maintain it, for maintaining an elephant was a costly. 'I asked you for money' the Mulla said, not advice'! Money, the Sufi believes, is necessary for maintaining smooth relationship between people just as oiling a machine makes it smoother in working and more lasting. But the money ought to be spent for some useful purpose, even as the Sufi teaching is to be given only to the deserving, not to ignorant persons or those prejudiced against it. The Sufi teaching is an esoteric one and it would be futile to learn it by half-hearted attempts. There are two Nasrudin tales to illustrate the difficulty of imbibing the teaching and about the attitude of Sufism to money. The Mulla was sitting by the side of a lake dropping curd into the water. When questioned why he was doing so, he said 'I am trying to make yogurt'. 'But how can you make yogurt this way?' the questioner said, 'the curd has to be put in milk not water'. 'Well' said Nasrudin, 'it's anyway worth a try'. This absurdity brings home the futility of those who think Sufism can be learnt the easy way. On another occasion a man, seeing the Mulla throwing money into a pool of water asked him why he was doing so. Nasrudin said he and the donkey he was riding was about to slip down into the water and had they gone down he'd be drowned. Just then the frogs in the pool began to croak. The donkey was frightened and reared up. Thus both I and he were saved. 'I am rewarding the frogs by throwing them the money'! Obviously for the frogs the money had no significance. So too money in the hands of those who can't use it properly or to the best advantage, is useless and its giving it to them unwarranted. The general attitude towards wealth and money, however, is quite different. We have quoted what Christ said in regard to the impossibility of a rich man entering heaven. And again 'No servant can serve two masters: for either he will hate the one and love the other; or else he will hold to one, and despise the other . Ye cannot serve God and mammon'[28]. In the *Gita* when Arjuna wished to know from Lord Krishna the characteristics of those who transcend the qualities (the *guṇātitas*) the Lord mentioned, among others 'that person to whom a clod of earth, or a stone or gold, is the same' [*sama-Ioshtāma kanchanah*].[29] Kabir, who is sometimes spoken of as akin to a Sufi says:

ustati nindā doū bibarajita, tajahu mānu abhimānā
lohā kanchana sama kari jānahi, te mūrati bhagavānā

['The man who is indifferent to both praise and blame, who is free from vanity and arrogance, and to whom iron and gold are the same; is the very image of God'].[30] Ovid speaks of 'The criminal love of riches'.[31]

The jokes, stories and anecdotes of Mulla Nasrudin greatly resemble the sayings and anecdotes of the Zen masters. Zen is one of the products of the Chinese mind after its contact with Indian thought, which was introduced into China in the 1st century A.D. through the medium of Buddhist teaching. When a Zen master was asked what his future life would be, he said 'Let me be a donkey or a horse and work for the villagers'. While crossing a bridge one monk asked another 'How deep is the river of Zen?' The other answered 'Find out for yourself' and was about to throw the man in the river. However he was restrained from doing to by others. A Zen master held up his staff and said 'If you have one I give you mine; if you have none, I will take it away from you'! Another, was giving a talk on Zen, and holding up his staff said 'When you know what this is you have finished the study of Zen'. Saying that he walked out of the room! One of the earliest masters of the T'ang dynasty declared that Tao is merely one's everyday life-experience. When asked to elaborate, he said 'When you are hungry you eat, when you are thirsty you drink, when you meet a friend you greet him'. Someone asked 'What is Zen?' 'I do not understand? the master said. 'What is Zen? he repeated. The answer was 'This silk fan gives me much cooling breeze'. Puzzled, he asked again 'What is Zen?' 'Zen', said the master.

The object of Zen is to make one realize that it is nothing external, but one's own daily experience. Dogo, a Tao master, had a disciple of the name of Soshin whom he gave no teaching as the novice expected, for long. When he asked the master why, the teacher said 'I have been giving you lessons on Zen ever since you came'. 'What lessons?' asked the bewildered lad. The master said 'When you bring me a cup of tea, I take it, when you serve me a meal I take it also, when you bow to me I nod. In what other manner do you expect to taught Zen?' Soshin began ponder over this puzzling statement. The master said 'If you want to see, see immediately. If you are lost in thought you will miss the point.'

The Zen teacher Goso Hyen (Wu-tsu Fa-yen) of the Sung dynasty illustrated the teaching much in the manner of a Mulla Nasrudin story. A burglar's son seeing his father ageing, thought, if he is not able at any time to burgle how shall the family carry on without a breadwinner. So he went to his father and asked him to teach him how to do it. One night the father broke the fence of a house, got inside the house and opening a large chest told his son to get in and remove all the costly clothes inside. As soon as his son got into it the father shut the box and locked it from the outside. Then he went outside, knocked on the door loudly waking up the entire family, and quietly slipped away through an opening of the fence. The startled family members lighted candles and went round everywhere. Finding everything in order they concluded that the burglar had gone. Meanwhile the trapped lad inside started cursing his father silently for playing such a dirty trick on him. He began to consider how he could escape. Then an idea struck him. He began to make a noise like the gnawing of a rat. The mistress heard it and calling the maid asked her to take a candle and examine the chest. As soon as the maid opened the lock the lad jumped out, blew away the light, pushed the astonished maid away and fled, the family members in hot pursuit. Seeing a well by the roadside, the burglar's son picked up a large stone and threw it in the well. While his pursuers crowded round it, he made his escape. On reaching home he began to upbraid his father saying that he had left him locked in the chest and he had a narrow escape. His father asked him to tell all about it. When he had heard him he said 'There, you have learnt by this the way of burglary and you'll be able to do it expertly after me.'[32] It was of course like teaching a child swimming. The best and surest way is to just cast him into the river water near its bank.

Another renowned Sufi was Fariduddin Attar, the Chemist, about whom we have also mentioned before. We have narrated his account of 'The Parliament of Birds' and the quest of a mysterious king, Simurgh, living in the mountains of Kaf which the hoopee initiates. Fariduddin was born near Nishapur, a village associated with Omar Khayyam, His father had a medical store which Farid took over. Hence his appelation 'the chemist'. he said that it is folly to give up something just because others have misused it. Although rituals rules and regulations are contained in Sufism, he said, the creed is not fettered by them. He wrote one hundred and fourteen works on Sufism the most prominent being the 'Parliament of Birds' of which we have spoken, in which seven valleys which have to be traversed are mentioned, being respectively those of the Quest, of Love, Intuitive Knowledge, Detachment, Unification, Astonishment and finally of Death in which the seeker realizes that even after being 'merged with the ocean a drop yet remains meaningful'. This is different from the Hindu concept of *moksha* according to which the Soul merges with the Absolute. The denial of this belief is one of the reasons for the marked admiration of Sufism in the West, for the Westerner is aghast at the concept of losing his 'personality'. That is why though Sufism spread in India, its origin lies outside, Iraq, Syria, Egypt, Persia, Khurasan, Balkh, Bukhara and Samarqand. The Moslem of Arabia overran these countries and those of the Sufi belief were given the usual

Islamic alternatives of Islam or the sword. Many preferred death, but many others either accepted Islam thrust on them with horrible vengence or agreed to pay the poll tax (*jizyah*) to live on ignominously. There could be no compromise for the Moslem scripture the Holy Quran itself enforces such persecution:

> 'Fight those who do not believe in God, nor in the latter day, not do they prohibit what God and His Apostle have prohibited, not follow the religion of truth, out of those who have been given the Book, [i.e., the followers of Islam] until they pay the tax in *acknowledgement of superiority* and they are in a state of subjection ..... So when the sacred months [of Ramadan] have passed, slay the idolaters wherever you find them, and take them captives and besiege them and lie in wait for them in every ambush; but if they repent and keep up prayer and pay the poor-rate, leave their way free to them; *for God is forgiving, Merciful*.'[33]

Despite all prevarications and hair-splitting justifications the message of the Holy Quran is clear. Nobody but a Moslem has the right to live in the world, and therefore one who professes any other creed must be slain or forced to accept Islam. It was this exactly what the Turkish invaders of India did to Hindu non-believers right from Mahmud Ghazni to Aurangzebe. The surprising thing, however, was that the Arab Moslems did not spare even Sufis who most certainly believed in the Holy Quran! The reason seems to be that though they did believe in the Book (as Moslems called it) they were more moderate in their views. In fact much of Sufism in nearer to Hinduism than to Islam. Idries Shah denies that the *bhakti* movement in Hinduism which produced such great names as Madhva, Ramanand and Kabir are based to a great extent upon Sufi thought and practice introduced into India after the Islamic conquest.'[34] It is quite apparent that this author has missed the implication of the *bhakti* movement the origin of which is much earlier either than the birth of Christianity or of Islam. In the *Bhagavadgita*, Lord Krishna says that his devotee never comes to grief. He can never perish–*pratījānīhi na me bhaktah pranashyati*, and 'I am in those who worship Me with devotion and they are in Me - *tu mām bhaktyā mayi te teshu cā 'py aham*. At the end of his discourse to his disciple, Arjuna the Lord says 'Fix your mind on Me, be My devotee, worship Me with folded hands; thus you will certainly attain Me. This I truly promise ..... The *bhakti* poets and saints never took inspiration from the Sufis and the roots of the *bhakti* movement lie in treatise of much earlier times, as we have said before the advent of either Sufism or even Christianity or Islam. It is the *Narada Bhakti Sutras* which are the source of the creed of devotion expounded by the *bhakti* poets. It is said that at one time Maharshi Vedavyasa was staying in his hermitage Badarikasharama. Narada the royal sage of the gods (*devarshi*) happened to visit him and when the sage had taken his seat, Vedavyasa questioned him as follows: 'Reverend sir, the soul seeks to free itself from the bonds of pleasure and seeks deliverance from the rounds of births and deaths, Works do not help it to achieve the goal. Knowledge without devotion is of no avail. Devotion is the only way and all others are subordinate to it. Therefore I humbly beseech you to explain the doctrine of devotion'. Then Narada delivered his discourse on *bhakti* (devotion) in eighty-four aphorisms. Thus the *Narada Bhakti-sutras* go back to about 2000 B.C. and the view of Idries Shah aforesaid is absolutely incorrect. It could however be that the Sufis were in some measure inspired by the *bhakti* cult, particularly *Vaishnavism*, if at all they were inspired by any faith. In fact the Sufi is one who accepts no religion and yet is not an atheist, because he accepts all of them. But in part only, for he would never accept the fanaticism of religions. Unfortunately, however it is the fanatics who take charge of religions, emphasizing what in them brooks no compromise and underplaying the common element in them. As Voltaire says 'Which is more dangerous, fanaticism or atheism. Fanaticism is certainly a thousand times more deadly, for atheism inspires no bloody passions, whereas fanaticism does; atheism is not opposed to crime, but fanaticism causes crimes to be committed.'[37] Due to failure to understand this much blood has been shed and innumerable atrocities done in the name of religion, on the Hindus by the followers of Islam, on Jews by tyrants like Hitler and the Romans who crucified Christ, by Christian rulers of India who tormented the weavers so much that they chopped off their thumbs rather than be forced to work for a pittance and on Christians, as Mill wrote:

> 'Socrates was put to death, but the Socratic philosophy rose like the sun in heaven, and spread illumination over the whole intellectual firmament. Christians were cast to the lions, but the Christian church grew up a stately and spreading tree, overtopping the older and less vigorous growths, and stifling them by its shade. Our merely social intolerance kills no one, roots out no opinions, but induces men to disguise them or to abstain from any active effort for their diffusion. With us, heretical opinions do not perceptibly gain, or even lose ground, in each decade or generation; they never blaze out far and wide, but contine to smoulder in the narrow circles of thinking and studious persons among whom they originate, without ever lighting up the general affairs of mankind with either a true or deceptive light.'[38]

As Hosea Bollou says 'A religion that requires persecution to sustain it is of the devil's propagation'. An Edict of Ashoka the ancient Indian ruler reads; '........ the sects of other people all deserve reverence for one reason or another..... He who does reverence to his own sect, while disparaging the sect of others wholly from attachment to his own, with intent to enhance the glory of his own sect, in reality by such conduct inflicts the severest injury on his own sect.[39]

The Vedas say that what people call by different names is One - *ekam sad vipra bahudha vadanti*. Idries Shah tells us about a novice who wanted to know if 'there was a basic urge toward mystical experience, shared by all humanity, and the teacher told him there was. He expressed it in the term *anguruzuminabstafil* and proceeded to explain that once a Persian, a Turk, an Arab and a Greek having just a coin were quarrelling because they wanted (what they thought) different things for it. A man came who knew all the four languages - Persian, Turki, Arabic and Greek. He heard them and took the money and brought four bunches of grapes giving them one each. That settled the dispute, for they had all wanted grapes, but knowing only their own language were using words all meaning 'grapes'; respectively *angur, uzum, inab* and *stafil*. This implies the fundamental view of religions is the same. But when the author goes on to say ' In the religious sphere the Koran maintains the unity of religions.....' [40] he is surely contradicting what the aforesaid anecdote asserts and making the very same mistake against which Ashoka's Edict cautioned, for on the contrary as Bacon, whom we have quoted, rightly observed in his Essay on Unity in Religion, 'But we may not take up the third Sword, which is Mohomet's Sword....' Some of the Moslem monarchs were so bigoted that they could not stand a Hindu even saying that his faith was just as good as Islam! Sultan Sikandar killed a brahmin of the name of Laudhan for daring to think that 'Islam was true, as was his own religion.' The Moslems did not spare even Sufis who were followers of the Holy Quran. A Sufi who was a distinguished mystic who came to the Western world in 1910 and lectured and taught there till his death in 1926, has recorded:

> 'In whatever period of civilization, therefore, the tendency has shown itself to judge the one who is advanced, there has always come a collapse of the whole civilization. Sarmad, a great Sufi saint who lived in Gwalior, was asked by the emperor Aurangzebe to attend the mosque, for it was against the rules of the time that anyone kept away from the regular prayers, which took place in the mosque of the state. Sarmad, being a man of ecstasy, living every moment of his day and night in union with God, being God-consciousness himself, perhaps forgot or refused. A certain time of prayer or a certain place for prayer to him was nothing; every place to him was a place of prayer. As he refused to attend prayers he was beheaded for breaking the rules which were made for everyone. The consequence was that the whole Mogul empire declined and its downfall can be dated from that time'.

Though it might be somewhat farfetched to attribute the fall of the Mogul empire to this incident, it does show the fanatic nature of Islam (Significantly Idries Shah omits any mention of this great Sufi writer quoted above).

hazrat Inayat Khan calls Hinduism a 'perfect religion'. He records:

> 'The Hindus have always known this philosophy of (nemesis befalling an evil deed such as that of Aurangzebe aforesaid), for the reason that they had a perfect religion, a religion in which one aspect of God was characterized as human; and their various Devas are nothing but various characteristics of human nature, each of them adored and worshipped. In this way not only God but the whole human nature

> in all its aspects. was adored and worshipped. It is that which makes the Hindu religion perfect. When people say "This place is sacred and that other place is not sacred; that particular thing is holy, and all other things not holy" in this way they divide life into many pieces, the life which is one, the life which cannot be divided'.[42]

Hinduism is most tolerant of religions. It does no parade its superiority as Islam does. The Holy Quran declares the Moslems to be the best community and raised up to guide and govern humanity as viceregents of God on earth and Islam to be the chosen religion destined to triumph over all other religions.[43] We have already quoted before from the Holy Quran to show that as regards Hindus (Kafirs) the view of the 'Book' was that they should all be slain unless they accepted Islam.

The Holy Quran was against the Christians too. Chapter 18 (Al-Kahf: the Cave) gives a warning to the Christians, 'And warn those who say: God has taken a son. They have no knowledge of it nor had their fathers; a grievous word it is that comes out of their mouths; they speak nothing but a lie'.[44] It is stated in Āl 'Imrān (3) 61 that the Christians disputed this refutation of Jesus Christ being the Son of God. 'When the Prophet failed to satisfy them, however, he challenged them to settle the dispute by the old Arab method sanctioned by the Quran of reciprocal curses (*mubāhalah*). The Christians disapproved of it and withdrew, as the New Testament forbids cursing. Then the Prophet dictated his terms, asked them to embrace Islam, and upon their refusal, to accept his suzerainty and pay *jizyah*. They were made subjects of the Prophet and had *jizyah* imposed on them by force.'[45] According to the Christian religion idol worship is condemned and God, strangely enough is spoken of as being jealous! 'I am the LORD thy God, which have brought thee out of the land of

Egypt, out of the house of bondage. Thou shalt have no other gods before me. Thou shalt not make unto thee any graven image, or any likeness of any thing that is in heaven above, or that is in the earth beneath, or that is in the water under the earth: thou shalt not bow down thyself to them, nor serve them: for I the LORD thy God am a jealous God, visiting the iniquity of the fathers upon the children unto the third and fourth generation of them that hate me; and showing mercy unto thousands of them that love me, and keep my commandments.'[46] Thus we find three things being considered mandatory, first that the God of the Christians condemns idol worship even as Allah of the Moslems, second that the Christians conceive God to be jealous (which is hardly a godly virtue) and third that mercy is confined to those who keep the commandments (which though of universal moral value have the special Christian touch of strictly keeping the sabbath). The specific commandment is '..... in it, i.e., the sabbath, thou shalt not do any work, thou, nor thy son, nor thy daughter, thy manservant, not thy maidservant, nor thy cattle, not thy stranger that is within thy gates, for in six days the LORD made heaven and earth, the sea, and all that in them is, and rested on the seventh day; wherefore the LORD blessed the sabbath day and hallowed it'.[47] By a quirk of imitation of the erstwhile British conquerors, we in a sense have in a small measure adopted the sabbath too in making Sundays a non-working day, as one of the many habits and behaviour of the Raj. As regards the Christian mercy mentioned by the Lord in the 'Book of Exodus', it does not seem to have the universality spoken of by the Bard:

> 'The quality of mercy is not strain'd
> It droppeth as the gentle rain form heaven
> Upon the place beneath: it is twice bless'd;
> It blesseth him that gives and him that takes......
> It is an attribute to God himself,
> And earthly power doth then show likest God's
> When mercy seasons justice'.[48]

But obviously Christian mercy was not like the rain falling on all alike. It encompassed only the Christians who kept the commandments. Quite unlike is the Hindu religion which maybe in stray departures, is the most tolerant in the world. Contrary to the general belief, Hinduism is not merely idol worship. it believes both in dualism as well as monism. The concept of *Brahman*, the Absolute, is of the Formless and Qualitiless. Lord Krishna says in the *Gita* that they also doubtlessly attain God who worship the Imperishable, Unmanifest, Inexpressible Omnipresent, Unfathomable, Immutable, Immovable and Constant[49]- The concept closely resembling Allah or Khuda of Islam. The *Gita* even says that those who worship with firm faith other gods must also be considered as worshipping God.[50] This is the catholicity of Hindu religion. In fact after having given the entire discourse of the *Gita* in its 18 chapters to his disciple, Krishna finally say 'now ponder over it well and do as you desire' - *vimṛashyai tad asesena yathe 'cchasi tathā kuru.*[51]

We will revert to the influence of Hinduism and of the *bhakti* movement. Coming back to Fariduddin Attar, his life is most interesting and discloses the mystic nature of Sufism. It is related that a Sufi once came to his eyes with tears in his eyes. Fariduddin, being engaged in his business resented the intrusion and asked him to go his way. The Sufi said it would not at all be difficult for him to do that, for he had no possessions except his cloak, but this would be difficult for Fariduddin for how and where would he in that case carry with him his costly drugs. The implication, of course, was that one who has wealth and possessions remains attached to the world. How then could he reach God? The incident had a great impact on Fariduddin. He sold his shop and took the Sufi teaching under Sheikh Ruknuddin. what really was the Sufi attitude to wealth, it is difficult to say, for it is bound with contradictions. Mulla Nasrudin's anecdote about his throwing money into a pool for the frogs which we have related aforesaid, seems to point out that wealth should not be shunned. Idries Shah says, 'the Sufi attitude toward money is a special one, far removed form the shallower, philosophical or theological assumption that money is the root of evil, or that faith is in some way opposed to money'.[52] We will not dispute with the author whether this philosophical attitude is shallow or not for everyone is entitled to his views. But Fariduddin's sudden decision to abandon his pharmacy would point out to the fact that to him money did not have any such significance as Idries Shah mentions as 'the Sufi attitude' to it. Kabir, who is considered to have the Sufi strain in him, says about wealth: *kabīra so dhana sancie jo āge ko hoi, sīsa caṛhāe poṭalī le jā ta no dekhā koi* [1 Gather the wealth of good deeds which will stand you in good stead, and plead for you in the other world. I have never seen, says Kabīr, anyone carry on his head his bundle of riches when he is dead!].[53]

Although Fariduddin had a great love for and understanding of all art and beauty he never underestimated the importance of the body. He considered body and soul as an integrated whole, as the poet, Browning say:

Let us not always say
'Spite of this flesh today
I strove, made head, gained ground upon the whole!'
As the bird winds and sings
let us cry 'All good things
Are ours, nor soul helps flesh more now,
than flesh helps soul!'[54]

After some time Fariduddin left the Sufi group being giving the teaching of Sufism and went to Mecca and other places. During this period he wrote his biographies of early Sufis in prose entitles *Memoirs of the Friends*. The Sufi chemist was now aged, and Jalaluddin who was still young and was destined to become a distinguished Sufi, met him and was greatly drawn towards him.

Attar's death was very tragic and even though a hundred and ten year's old now, he retained his ready wit and the typical Sufi manner right till the end. When the Mongol nomads invaded Persia in 1220 they caught hold of him and were about to kill him when one of them restraining the slayer's hand said 'Don't kill this old man, I'll give you a thousand pieces of silver in return of his life'. Fariduddin said to his captor to wait, saying he would get more for him from someone else. Another man who was heartless and unfeeling contemptuously offered a little straw 'Sell me him' Attar said 'that's all I'm worth'. His captor was furious and immediately slew him. We find a parallel in the death of the Hindi Brajbhasha poet Ghananand, who though not a Sufi, had the Sufic element of aestheticism in him, for in one of his poems he wrote; 'He only may know my verse who is a great lover and speaks a language filled to the brim with love'. Of Ghananand's death a commentator, Shri Viyogī Harī, gave the following account:

> 'In 1739 when the soldiers of Nadir Shah's army reached Mathura, someone told them that the emperor's chief scribe who lived in Vrindavana, had a lot of wealth with him. The soldiers went and surrounding him, began to shout "zar! zar! zar!", meaning "bring us all your wealth" (*zar* means "wealth" in Persian). Ghananand, not having any wealth at all, threw three handfuls of dust on the invaders, and reversing the letter of the word uttered by them, exclaimed "raj! raj! raj!" (*raj* meaning "dust"), as much as to say "I do not have anything with me except the dust of this holy city" (Mathura is associated with Krishna). The enraged soldiers hacked off his hands'.[55]

One of the most distinguished of Sufis was Jalaluddin Rumī. He founded the order of the Whirling Dervishes of whom we have mentioned before also. Many prominent Sufis belong to this order as for example Ali el-Hujwiri. He settled in India and was buried after his death in Lahore becoming a place of pilgrimage for all classes, kings and commoners. Hujwiri's teacher was Abu el-Qasim Gurgani of the Naqshbandi order, and his work the *Revelation* is the first one written in Persian about Sufism and the Sufi Orders. It deals with the lives of prominent Sufis, the different periods in which they lived, the doctines they propagated and subjects like prayer, charity, faith and mysticism. While at Lahore he wrote a number of books of which *Kashf al Mahjub* is the most well-known, and is a kind of textbook for those in India who study Tassawuf. It is also studied in Islamic countries.

The Naqshabandi order was introduced in India by Khwaja Baqi Billa Berang and was developed by his disciple, Sheikh Ahmad Faruqui Sirhindi who lived in the sixteenth-seventeenth century. It repudiated the Vedantic teaching of monism. Being uncompromising, the Naqshabandis were censorious of Akbar's liberalism and of his efforts to achieve a synthesis of religions in his Din-i Ilahi, which was strange as it had a Sufi touch in the belief that the soul was ultimately absorbed in God, and in the House of Worship the emperor opened at Fathpur Sikri he invited Sufis too to put up their point of view. The Sufis often appeal to reason rather than dogma. The Jesuits condemned Akbar for acknowledging 'reason to be the basis of religion' and English historians failed to appreciate the emperor's quest for truth, as eminent a writer as Vincent Smith calling it 'a monument a Akbar's folly', 'outcome of ridiculous vanity' and 'a monstrous growth of unrestrained autocracy'.[56] In fact Akbar was a mystic and when he was only fifteen he suddenly went away some distance from his camp and meditated for several hours. Badauni says that the emperor passed whole nights remember God and sat 'many a morning alone in prayer and meditation on a large flat stone in a lonely spot'. As the English poet Lord Tennyson says about him.

'I can but lift the torch
Of Reason in the dusky cave of Life,
And gaze on this great miracle, the World,
Adoring That who made, and makes, and is,
And is not, what I gaze on – all else, Form,
Ritual, varying with the tribes of men'.[57]

Akbar delighted in Sufism and had Hafiz and Rumī read to him. Once while he was out hunting on the bank of the Jhelum in January 1575, ten day's preparation had been made and birds and beasts within fifty miles had been encircled for this purpose. All of a sudden Akbar broke the hunt and set all the animal free, declaring that 'not a feather of a finch was to be touched'. He distributed alms to fakirs and laid out a garden and a monument to commemorate the spot where the realization had come to him. This is much like the Mulla Nasruddin story we have related before, about the Mulla being compelled by a king to accompany him on a bear hunt. In view of this it is amazing that the Sufis of the Naqshabandi Order should be so incensed against Akbar. Anyway Akbar was the sole exception to bigotry and soon after they found their champion, Aurangzebe, who was applauded by them even though he got a Sufi executed! The bastion of the Naqshabandis was Sirhind. Ahmad Sirhindi of this order styled himself as Qayum (meaning 'God'). The qayum he said is God's viceregent on earth and he governs the universe. The sun, the moon and indeed everything is under his control. No one's prayer can reach God unless it is routed through him. Sirhindi said that God had appointed him and his three successors as Qayums. He claimed to have been made by God with the material left after creating Mohammed, the Prophet, and that he was Majaddid Alif Sani, the renovator of Islam and the controller of the universe for the second millenium! Aurangzebe became the disciple of Masum the second Qayum and he spurred on the fanatic emperor in his persecution of the Hindus. Thus the Qayums of the Naqshabandi order were bigoted and arrogant. In this context it is difficult to accept the greatness of the Naqshbandi Order Sufis unless Hujwiri and his teacher Abu el-Qasim Gurani are taken to be opposed to the Sirhindis. The Sufi doctrine is really so esoteric that at times it touches the fantastic and conveys little meaning to the general, even intellectual run of people, like the pieces of glass in a kaleidoscope which have not created any pattern. This can of course, be passed by with the observation that Sufism is not for the common man. But a doctrine so against reason as that for example about the 'patch' of the Dervish orders is certainly fantastic. Considering Hujwiri's sayings on the patched robes one reaches this conclusion. Quoting professor Nicholson's translation:

> 'To take pains in sewing patched robes is considered allowable by the Sufis because They have gained a high reputation among the people; and since many imitate them and wear patched robes, and are guilty of improper acts, and *since the Sufis dislike the society of others than themselves*–for these reasons they have invented a garb which none but themselves can sew, and have made it a mark of mutual acquittance and a badge. So much so that when a certain dervish came to one of the Shykhs wearing a garment on which the patch had been sewn with wide stitches, the Shaykh banished him from his presence'![58]

The creed of exclusivism, however, is not the belief of Sufism, for despite their esoteric rituals they have a universal view of humanity. It is Islam which claims to be exclusive and which, because of this, differentiates between people of the

Book and those not of it, thus creating a barrier between its followers and the rest of humanity. A distinguished Sufi says:

> 'But it [the religious bond] has caused diverse sects, which have opposed and despised one another for thousands of years, and have caused endless splits and divisions among men. The germ of separation exists even in such a wide scope for brotherhood, and however widespread the brotherhood may be, it cannot be a perfect one as long a it separates man from man.
>
> 'The Sufi, realizing this, frees himself from national, racial and religious boundaries, uniting himself in the human brotherhood, which is devoid of differences and distinctions of class, caste, creed and race, nation, or religion, and unites mankind in the universal brotherhood'.[59]

The 'patch' symbolism denotes different things–*raqua*' meaning 'nonsensical'; *raqaa*', the wine-drinker; *artaqa*' signifying 'heedlessness'; *rāpa*' signifying the divine nature of Sufism; *rupa*' at meaning 'chessboard' the black and white tiles of the floors in rooms where Sufis meet; *muraqqa*' meaning 'patched garment'; 'walking fast' and repairing a well, the 'well' being the well of knowledge. Sufism is both universal and individual. It is universal in the sense that it is not confined to any one country. Branches of these orders are spread over India, Africa, Indonesia and other countries. There remain no monastries, for it is a way of thinking not an association of people. The main orders have been given representative names, the 'Howling Dervishes' for the Rifa'is, the 'Shaven' for Qalandaris, the 'Musicians' for the Chistis, 'Dancers' for Mevlevis and the 'Silent' for the Naqshbandis. The Orders follow the rituals and methods devised by their founders. Rumī advocated dances to inculcate the Sufi doctrine. As we have said before, these would perhaps be analogous to the *sankīrtana* initiated by Chaitanya. We have narrated before the technique of the *latifa* which is very similar to the *chakras* of Tantra, because the areas involved are very much the same - the self under the navel, the heart, the spirit opposite to where the heart is, the portion between the heart and the spirit, which would be the spinal column through which the Tantric *kundalini* rises, and thereafter the forehead and the brain. The closeness between the two concepts, the Sufi *latifa* and the Tantric *chakras* is too obvious to be missed or denied. Another technique of the Dervish orders is *tajalli* or irradiation. This if genuine, results in a permanent increase in the capacity to know intuitively what is to happen. It is much like the *siddhī* of Hinduism. the author has personal experience of a man who had this insight. He was known as the 'Jhāri wale baba', presumably because it was said in his youth he would keep hid in bushes (Hindi *jhāri*) remaining nude. The man was neither a sage nor a miracle-worker, but at times he could *know* what was to happen in the future. Once he very accurately foretold both the date and the way my daughter's marriage would come about and did the same for a near friend of mine. Even more amazing was his foretelling of my transfer from one government office to another. When I scoffed at it as I had only a few month's to retire, he said emphatically 'what I have told you *must* come about. If I did not have this intuitive power, what importance would you attach to me?' And surprisingly it happened just as he had said. This man had the power of *tajalli*, even though it is not likely that he was a Sufi of the Dervish Order. This I relate as my own experience, but such gifts of *siddhī* or *tajalli* are divinely given to others too, as for example the wizard in numbers, Shakuntala Devi, who can give an instant solution to any geometrical or arithmetical problem, however complicated, much quicker than a computer can! Another practice of the Dervishes is the *quiff* in which the Sufi commands his pupil to halt and stand perfectly still. After sometime he lets him relax.

This practice is carried out by the teachers of the Naqshbandi order and they believe thereby they can transmit *baraka* (grace) to the student of the Naqshabandi school.

The Sufi teacher is believed to be perfected in four stages or 'Journeys'– the condition of *fana* or annhilation in which the Sufi achieves objective reality; the stage of *baqa*, i.e., the teacher to whom all come; the stage of universal instruction in which the teacher can teach all things to all men; the fourth and final stage in which even after physical death the spirit of the teacher yet keeps on guiding his disciples.

The dervish aims at self-realization, 'He who knows his essential self' says he, 'knows God'. The similarity between this concept and that of the *Bhagavadgita* is very striking. After having given the entire teaching, the lord says to his disciple, Arjuna, 'has your delusion born of ignorance been dispelled?' - *kaccid ajñāna - saṁmohaḥ praṇaṣṭas te* and Arjuna's reply to the Lord is 'My delusion is destroyed and by your grace I have known my inner self' - *naṣṭo mohah smṛtir labdhā tvatprāsādān mayā*[60]. No wonder Aldous Huxley calls the *Bhagavadgita* 'the most systematic scriptural statement of the Perennial Philosophy'. He further adds 'Nevertheless, one has the impression, while reading certain Sufi texts, that their authors did in fact conceive of all *haqq*, the real, as being the divine Ground or Unity of Allah, underlying the active and personal aspects of the Godhead.... The Sufi, Mansur, was executed for giving the words "union and "deification" the literal meaning which they bear in Hindu tradition... Krishna, who is here the mouthpiece of Hinduism in all its manifestations, finds it perfectly natural that different men should have different methods and apparently different objects of worship.... A similar attitude of charitable inclusiveness, somewhat surprising in a Moslem, is beautifully expressed in the parable of Moses and the shepherd told by Jalaluddin Rumī in the second book of the *Masnavi*.'[62]

In acquiring this self-knowledge there are certain hindrances called 'veils'. These are ten in number as follows:

1. Desires mostly unreasonable. 'This is good for me, I must have it'. The corrective to this is the practice of austerity.

2. Separation, i.e., being self-centred. This is removed thinking of the ultimate reality.

3. Hypocrisy, i.e., self-pride which is removed by doing what the Lord wants, being kind and humble and not running after wealth.

4. The desire for praise and love. This is removed by taking an objective view of things.

5. Illusions. These are removed by thinking about the glory of God.

6. Avarice and miserliness resulting in envy. This is removed by *yakīna* (being sure about things).

7. Greed. This is the irrational desire to have more and more wealth. It is like fire in which one keeps heaping more and more fuel. Austerity in living and charity are the corrective to this.

8. Impatience. This is the effort to obtain instantly the desire which takes hold of the mind, and the remedy is patience.

9. Inconstancy. This is removed by making the mind calm by practices aimed to achieve calmness.

10. Laziness or sloth. In Hinduism this is known as *tāmasa* for Hindus believe according to the *Sānkhya* system that every being has three qualities (*guṇas*) the pure (*sattva*) the one causing passion or too much activity (*rājasa*) and the *tāmasa guna* leading to inactivity or sloth. The kind of person one is, is determined by which of these three qualities predominate in him. The fault of laziness can be removed by

being alert, and for this the Sufi dervish teacher prescribes appropriate exercises.

With this digression, we now revert to the renowned Sufi, Jalaluddin Rumī. He was born in Bactria in a good family and lived and taught in Iconium in the Asia Minor. He belonged to the thirteenth century. It is said he spurned the thone of the Ottoman empire which was offered to him. He wrote his works in the Persian language and they have won acclaim, so much so, that they are often called the Koran of the Pehlevi language. he took a wide view of the Holy Quran, saying that it could be interpreted in seven different. ways. Dr Johnson says about him, 'he makes plain to the pilgrim the secrets of the way of unity, and unveils the mysteries of the path of eternal truth'. There are three outstanding works of his, the *Mathnawi-i-Manawi*, popularly known as the *Mansavī*, *Fihi Ma Fihi* which has become the basic book on Sufism for scholars, and thirdly, *The Diwan of Shams* of Tabriz. Rumī's family descended from Abu Bakr Mohammed's companion. His father was related to king Khwarizm Shah, and Rumī was born in 1207. The king of Balkh, where Rumī was born, persecuted the Sufis. He got one Sufi saint cast in the river. When the Mongols invaded Balkh the great Sufi, Najmuddin, was slain by them, The soldiers of Jenghiz Khan revaged Turkestan and the Sufi saint fled to escape being killed. Rumī 's father went away to Nishapur along with his son. There they met Attar, another distinguished Sufi who spoke highly of Jalaluddin saying that he would turn out to be the light of the world to guide mankind. Attar too, fell soon after a victim to Mongol wrath. Rumīs father fled to a place near Konia and the king there treated him well and appointed him as a professor. There they met another great Sufi master, Ibn El-Arabi of Spain. Rumī started his work and teaching when he was forty and began to write poetry. But he considered verse to be only a medium through which love is expressed and according to him real love was inexpressible in words. As Kabīr says:

akatha kahānī prema kī, kach kahi na jāī|
gūṁge kerī sarakarā, baithe musakāī||

['Love's tale cannot be told. It's as though a dumb man were eating sweets and smiling on enjoying their relish' (but because of being dumb unable to tell of it)].

Or as the Nāradā Bhakti-Sūtras say:

mūka asvadana-vat 'The nature of love is indescribable as the taste of a dumb person' [sūtra 51]

The poet William Blake says:

'Never seek to tell thy love
Love that never told can be
For the gentle wind does move
Silently invisibly.'

It is in love that a man finds the fulfillment of his desires. Rumī Says in his *Mansnavī*:

'Love gives sweetness to bitter things
It turns copper to gold
Because of it sickness is health
Stings are as honey
Lions harmless as mice
Wrath is turned to mercy
Through love the dying are revived
And kings become slaves.'

Jami, the renowned Persian poet, says in *Yusuf Zuleikha*: 'A seeker went to a Pir to learn. The Pir said if you haven't yet moved on love's path, go and become a lover first and then come to me'. But love's path is not easy. A Persian verse says

'Love is not meant to be practised by those delicate. Before one embarks on its path he must have a heart strong as a lion's and be able to bear all kinds of calamities.' It is like the heat of a furnace. If one suddenly gets too close to it, he may be burnt. Maybe for him, to begin with, the light of a lamp's enough. In the same way the poet, Rasakhan says 'Love's wayward path is slender as the tendril of a lotus, yet hard as a sword's blade. It is straight and then again sinuous,'[63] and again, 'Everyone keeps saying "Love ha! love". But they don't know how dolorous it can be ; as a noose round the neck leaving the victim gasping for breath'[64] Rumī emphasizes that one cannot be enlightened by his own efforts. A guide or a teacher is essential. For example one may be seeking gold, but if he does not know what gold is, he'll not be able to recognize it as such even when he gets it. Reason, says Rumī, has its place. Unless it is combined with faith, it is valueless. For example, one selects his doctor after discrimination. But once he has chosen him he must have complete faith in him and take the treatment he prescribes. The materialist moves only one plane, while the mystic has a wider view and moves on many different planes. That's why he is not understood by the materialist, and knowing this, mystic does not preach to all and sundry. 'Those who fail to grasp a thing' says Rumī 'believe it to be useless. If one strikes flint with steel it will produce a spark, but will it do so if you strike the steel on the ground?' Wisdom and ignorance complement each other, as night and day or sun and shade. If there was no light, darkness would be without significance. The Sufi masters bring enlightenment but one should beware of false teachers. Only when their teaching brings continued enlightenment, it should be accepted as truth.

Rumī wrote about God and the soul. In *Fihi Ma Fihi* he says that a man passes through three stages. In the first he worships anything even earth and stone, in the second he worships God, and finally he says neither 'I worship God' nor 'I do not worship God'. According to the Sufis only God can save us the pain of suffering provided we surrender ourselves to him and consider him to be the agent of all that happens. In the *Masnavī Rumī* says

> I am a cup if he makes me a cup
> Or a dagger if he makes me that;
> If he makes me a fountain I sprout water,
>
> If he makes me fire I give heat.
>
> If he makes me a friend, I give friendship.
> I am as a pen for him to write;
> Who am I to question him?

Another great Sufi, Sachal of Sind has a similar idea:

> 'The world is a picture of the Lord
> He is everywhere, the ravisher of hearts
> A nightingale, a flower, a garden and spring's verdure.
>
> 'He is the dervish with a coarse garment, the wearer of silk,
> He is speech and he is silence,
> A Sunni, a Shia and the sage of enlightenment
> A lover, beloved, blandishment, coquetry.
> he shows one way to one, a different way to another
> He deceives all, making of the same cloth innumerable patterns.'

In the *Gita* the Lord says: 'There is nothing at all apart from Me, O Arjuna, all the world is held together by Me as gems on a string. I am the taste in the waters, the light in the moon and sun, I am *Aum* in the Vedas, and manhood in men. I am the pure fragrance in the earth, the brightness in fire, the life of all creatures and the virtue of austerity in ascetics. I am the Timeless Seed from which all creatures spring. I am the understanding of the wise and the glory of great men. I am the strength of the strong shorn of lust and craving. I am that desire which seeks righteousness. And whatever qualities there are, the pure, the active and the dull, know them to be from Me alone; but though arising from Me, I am beyond them'[65]

A Sufi may be unconventional in his attitude, but this is because he is able to visualize what others can't see. Jalaluddin illustrates this by a fable. A man who was drunk saw the king go past him riding a very good horse. He said something nasty about the horse. Next day the king sent for him to punish him for it. The man said 'It was not me who said it. It was a man who was drunk. An now he is no longer there, for he has gone'. The man's reply pleased the king who rewarded him for it. In this way the man, who was a Sufi, succeeded in explaining that often people act unconscious of what they do and the responsibility of the act is not theirs. Like Omar Khayyam whose verses Edward FitzGerald has immortalized in his superb translation, Rumī also uses the symbology of the wine and the grape to emphasize the nature of the soul:

> 'Before there was the garden, vine or grape
> There was the Soul drunk with wine'.

The Soul, Rumī believes, is imprisoned in the body and so we are not able to realize its true nature:

> 'Every night Thou freest our spirits from the body
> its snare, making them pure as rased tablets.
> Every night spirits are released from this cage,
> And set free, neither lording nor lorded over.
> At night prisoners are unaware of their prison;
> At night kings are unaware of their majesty.
> Then there is no thought or care for loss or gain;
> No regard to such a one or such a one'.[66]

We find this concept in Hindu philosophy also. Shankarāchāraya says, 'The *sūkshma sharīra* is free from all union and unaffected by limiting factors. It performs all actions as the instrument of the *atman*, as chisel and other tools do for a carpenter. For this reason the *atman* is free from all union'.[67] So too, in the *Brihadāraṇyaka Upanishad* the sage. Yājñavalkya taught Maitreyī thus about the soul:

> 'All relations like husband, wife and sons, all castes like the brahmins and Kshatriyas, all wealth, all the worlds, and all the gods; in truth all things and persons existing, are dear to one not in themselves but because they please his own soul....... The worlds, men, gods, creatures and all that exists are indeed the soul. As the notes of various musical instruments..... cannot be isolated from the sound they produce, so too there is nothing apart from the soul.
>
> 'Both in arising and dissolution, this one reality is the fountainhead of all things, as the ocean is where all waters merge, touch in which all tactile sensations rest, the nose that smells all odours, the tongue that savours all tastes, the ears that hear all sounds, the mind that makes all deliberations, the intellect that is the source of all knowledge, the hands that perform all actions, the organs of generation that is the source of all (sexual) enjoyment, the excretory organs that are the instruments of all excretions, the feet that are the means of all walking, and voice which is the chanter of all the Vedas.
>
> 'As a lump of salt when dissolved in water cannot be taken out again but wherever one tastes the water it is salty. So indeed, my dear, is this great reality – endless, infinite and pure knowledge. Each soul

> arises from it with its own separate element and when these elements are destroyed, it goes back to it. When it departs thus, the soul has no individual consciousness'.[68]

'Prayer', says Rumī 'has form, sound and a physical reality'. This is so because when one prays he utters words of prayer and so the thought transforms itself through these words to activity. Work is a must for the Sufi. Rumī says it must not be given up for all that the Sufi seeks is obtained through it. That is why all Sufis are employed in some vocation, as for example Kabīr, the weaver. Constructive self-endeavour is the aim, as wool is woven into a carpet, earth becomes a mansion and cotton cloth. Rumī encourages comprehensive action, as in the making of a tent, some sewing, some weaving, some making ropes. In fact most tasks are done by people working in unison. This concept, too. is very much like that which lord Krishna speaks of in the *Gita*: 'Not even for a moment can anyone abstain from work. He will be driven to it helplessly by the qualities of Nature. Do your prescribed duty, for action is better than inaction. You cannot even exist if you do not work........ I have no duty to perform in all the three worlds O Arjuna, nor anything lacking which I need to obtain, yet I am engaged in work. For if I ever abstained from tirelessly working, people will in all ways follow My example. Were I to abandon work, these worlds would perish and I would be the cause of the people's fall from morals and of their destruction'.[69] And in the eighteenth chapter of the *Gita* about renunciation, and relinquishment of works. The Lord said 'Works of sacrifice, charity and penance ought not to be abandoned. They should be performed, for they purify men of wisdom. But works should be done after giving up attachment and the desire for reward'.[70]

People may appear evil to some and good to others, says the Sufi, even as 'the fish and the hook are present together.' As in Hindu philosophy, Sufism advocates detachment, as Rumī says, 'The person whose belly is full, looks at a loaf of bread with indifference, while the hungry man wishes to grab it'. The Sufi sees meaning in what may be meaningless to the ordinary man. 'Discard the shell' says Rumī and take the pearl. You will not find a pearl in every shell.' What is just a stone to an ordinary man, he says, is a gem to the Sufi. It is only the worthy man who can become spiritual. To such a one spirituality comes of itself as a tame bird. It will not frequent an unworthy place as a peacock woudn't. Only when the Sufi learner is on the spiritual path, he can communicate with others. The Buddha was for the middle path. If the strings of a lute are too tight it will not give the right note. Nor will it if they are loose. So too is Rumī's view. There should be a balance between extremes, or one's effort will go waste. Both attraction to anything or repulsion to it is to be shunned. In much the same manner Lord Krishna says 'The person who neither rejoices nor hates, grieves, nor desires, who has renounced both good and evil, is indeed My dear devotee'.[71] He considers those persons to have transcended the qualities (*guṇas*, goodness, activity and dullness) 'Who neither dislike illumination, activity and delusion when they arise, not long for them when they cease to be'.[72]

Rumī speaks of the inner senses which guide the outward ones and which are to the outer ones as 'gold is to copper'. Thus it is the spiritual in man that is of primary importance. But how is this spirituality to be achieved? Largely it consists in moving God-ward. Rumī says one comes to this world of dimension, but he is from non-dimension. And further says Rumī:

'God's chains bind man completely
Yet rust has gathered in his heart
So that he heeds not the divine:
He follows vice, blind to its evil,
Goes on life's journey sinful and God-less,
Layers of dust clouding the mirror of his mind
Made rusty as rusted iron,
And like a jewel whose brightness has gone'.[73]

Hazrat Inayat Khan says that one who lives the inner life lives in God, God is in him and he is in God, as Lord Krishna says in the *Gita* – 'I am in them [who worship Me with devotion] and they are in Me'.[74] According Hazarat Inayat Khan five things are needful for attaining this inner life: mastery over the mind, finding the spiritual guide or guru, the Murshīd, and having found him repose in him the utmost confidence. The Murshīd is a saintly person, and Rumī says

'One minute in a saint's company
Is better than a hundred years of prayers and piety'.

The Murshīds speak very little, but they always advise that one must place others above himself and bring round one whom he takes to be his enemy, to friendship. 'If one rebukes you' says Sāha Latif, do not speak in return'. The Murshīds also never argue but teach by stories and illustrations. They have great love for the seeker (the *tālib*) and welcome anyone who is eager to learn of whatever class community or religion he may be.

The third thing necessary in going through inner life is the receiving of knowledge assimilating it and reasoning it out oneself. The fourth stage is meditation (*Ryazat*). Meditation brings perfect pēace. As the *Gita* says – 'Without self–control (*sādhanā*) there can be no wisdom, and without wisdom there can be no meditation; without meditation the mind can find no peace and how can one who lacks peace be ever happy?'[75] The fifth necessity for leading the inner life is avoiding to hurt the feelings of others, keeping one's balance under all circumstances, love, forgiveness and detachment amid crowds (*vairāgya*), that is to say living in the world, yet not being of it, as a lotus rearing its head over the waters of a dirty pond. As the Sufi puts it:

> 'O Lord I am a beggar. yet what I ask of you is more than what a thousand kings may want. Everyone asks you for something he longs for. I have come to ask you to give me yourself alone,' (i.e., I do not wish for anything other in the world).

Sufism sometimes expresses itself in mystic language which mey seem baffling to the ordinary reader, as for example the following verse in Rumī's *Dīwan of Shams of Tabriz*:

> 'Be in the brotherhood,
>
> Go on the ruined road where these are whose houses have been pulled down,
>
> Drink the cup of feeling so that you are not ashamed,
>
> Close your eyes and see with your inner eye,
>
> Open the arms of your soul if you seek an embrace,
>
> Break the earthen images and see their faces
>
> Why take a great amount of dowry for a weak hag,
>
> Or get recruited in the army for three loaves......?
>
> Leave difficult talk, to know the real answer,
>
> Be silent to be able to speak well,
>
> Ignore life and world to see the World's life'.

The verse appears to be meaningless, but what Rumī is essaying to stress through it is that Sufis ('the brotherhood') ought to see the actual Reality hid witin the outward one. This is possible by communion, works and concentrated thought. The inward truth has to be known. It lies behind the false patterns one sees. The seeker (*tālib*) must actively learn from the guru (*Murshīd*) - 'open his arms to embrace'- and not stand by awaiting to be taught. The old hag is worldly experience which really conceals the truth. Thought must be of things universal. It cannot be shackled by any fixed patterns. Men have the capacity to form a world-vision but they limit themselves to small compartments. Speech which has substance in it follows silence. Thus the poem is allegorical. The Sufi teaching can often be misunderstood by those who fail to go deep enough. For example the observation of Rumī about silence preceding meaningful speech. In a letter to the editor of a paper a correspondent wrote about Atal Bihari Vajpayee the prime minister of India 'I hope his thoughts are clear not needing pauses'.[77] This was a comment on Vajpayee who is an expert orator. Now this letter displays ignorance of the Sufi concept of such silence. Far from its being a liability, according to Rumī it is a necessity.

Rumī propagated his teaching through music and dancing and specific exercises aimed to create harmony. Women have been given short shrift both in the East as well as in the West. With all the pretensions to give them a good deal by reprentations in all branches of services and professions they are generally in the East confined to their homes to carry out household chores, and in Moslem countries they are pushed into thick cloth veils to cover themselves from head to foot with peep-holes to look through. Among Hindus countless women are burnt and killed in all kinds of torturous ways. The great poet, Milton, put woman subordinate to man 'He for God only, she for god in him,'[78] and even the religious poet of the

Ramayana Goswami Tusidasa equates woman with a low-caste and a beast, fit only for being beaten! The Holy Quran says. '........ and as to those [women] on whose part you fear desertion, admonish them, and leave them alone in the sleeping places, and beat them; then if they obey you, do not seek a way against them; for God is High, Great'.[79] Thus has male chauvinism delegated women an inferior position and role. No wonder 'foreign observers' are taken aback by Rumī's very cogent and justified observation that woman is not a mere plaything, but a ray of deity'. The view is corroborated by Ramakrishna, guru of Vivekananda, who though referring to 'woman and gold' in the sense of 'lust and wealth', looked on all women, even prostitutes with the same sanctity as Kali, the Divine Mother. 'the sage would even see the Divine Mother in prostitutes whom he came across on the way, and bow to them reverently.'[81] It was this same spirit that impelled Rumī to consider woman a ray of the deity. In his *Dīwan of Shams of Tabriz*, Rumī examines all religions and concludes that the truth does not lie in any such outside creed but inside the man himself. We have already quoted before the poem in which he says that he sought God in church, temple, Kaabaa Kaf, Kandahar and other places, but he was not anywhere in these. God, he discovered was within his own heart. He was in no other place Idries Shah says that this conclusion 'has caused a certain amount of confusion to the liberalists'.[82] The liberalists are those who are believed to be broadminded, and if this view of Rumī confuses them, it negates their very liberalism and in fact depicts their hideboundedness.

Rumī died in 1273, leaving his son Bahaudin to carry on the headship of the Mevlevi order. He was mourned by all alike and his funeral was attended by people of all classes and creeds. His teaching about God being inside one's heart had been known to Hindu seers round about 800 years before the birth of Christ: 'The body is like a city and the lotus-like heart within it like the royal place in this city. Within the heart there is a small space. What exists in that space is *Brahman*, (the Absolute). That indeed is to be sought after, desired and understood. If a disciple were to ask "What can one possibly find in that small space worthy of desiring and understanding?" the teacher says "This tiny space in the heart contains all that there is in the vast space of the universe, heaven and earth, Fire and air, sun, moon, stars, lightning and all that belongs to the man at the present time and what does not."[81] Rumī's greatness lies in rediscovering this truth and his emphasis on love being supreme.

Ibn El-Arabi ('the Greatest Master) was a descendant of Hatim Ei- Tai, one of the most charitable persons living at that time and whom FitzGerald spoke of in his *Rubaiyat*. He was born in 1164 in Spain when it was under Arab rule. His father was a friend of the Sufi, Abdul-Qadir Jilani Sultan of the Friends (1077-1166) and he predicted that Ibn El-Arabi would be of outstanding merit. El-Arabi was given the best education available and learnt law and Islamic theology at Lisbon, the Quran at Seville and jurispudence at Cordoba under Sheikh El-Sharrat. He befriended Sufis and from an early age began to compose verses. He lived in Seville for about thirty years and his poetical works won high acclaim there. They have been said by professor R.A. Nicholson to be love songs but sometimes having an underlying mystical sense and hidden meaning. His prominent works are *Interpreter of Desires* and *Bezels of Wisdom*. Since El-Arabi's thought contains the Hellenic philosophy to a large extent, even though it is streaked with other ways of thought too like the Vedanta of Hinduism, Christianity, Islamic theology, ascetism and mysticism, it would be profitable to briefly dwell upon the Greek thought of Plotinus which greatly influenced that of El-Arabi. Plotinus's doctrine is contained in the 54 treatises of the

Enneads. The transcendent First Principle is called the One or God. It is beyond mind and being, beyond thought language, knowledge or description. This, of course, is much like the Hindu concept of *Brahman* (the Absolute). The primary activity is contemplation which produces the lower as fire generates heat, a flower yields perfume, the sun its light but in doing so fire, sun and flower do not undergo any change. The link between the higher and the lower is the Soul. There is the Higher soul (the World soul) and the lower soul or Nature. It is the Soul which contains the body and not the body the soul.

Man's spiritual state depends on his attitude. If he allows the Soul to devote itself selfishly to the body, the Soul becomes entrapped in it and the man's fall is steep, even to the level of brutishness. The mere fact of being in the human body does not imply imprisonment to the Soul. That comes only if the Soul surrenders to the body. One can see how very similar is this to the teaching of the *Gita*: 'Let not a man degrade his Soul, but himself uplift it; for the elevated Soul will be his helper, and if debased it will turn against him. The Soul is a faithful friend when attuned to the spiritual, but it is an adversary when the lower instincts prevail'.[84] Man can pass, says Plotinus, from the narrowness of earthly life to the universality of the transcendent Soul, and then pass beyond the Soul to take his rightful place in the world of the Divine Mind. Thence he can even pass even higher, though rarely, to that ecstatic union with the One in which Mind attains to the highest by leaving itself behind. This view is also similar to that of the *Gita*: 'Maybe one among thousands strives for emancipation, and of those who achieve it, some rare person knows Me as I am'.[85] Evil and suffering, are, according to Plotinus, the inevitable consequences of life. Suffering is a necessary consequence of embodiment. The wise man is beyond the reach of suffering not because his body cannot suffer, but because he is utterly detached in spirit. The most important part of his self abides above in the spiritual world, and does not come down into the conflict and turmoil of bodily life. Lord Krishna says in the *Gita* 'There is nothing in this world as pure as wisdom' - *na hi jñānena sadrisham pavitram iha vidyate* (*Gita*. 4: 38), and the ignorant man lacking in faith, and of doubting mind is destroyed. Much the same is the view of Plotinus, who holds out no hope for the non-philosophical man.

This digression on the philosophy of Plotinus has been given because a great deal of El-Arabi's teaching comes very close to it. He studied for some time under a Spanish woman named Fatima, daughter of Waliyya. He often experienced psychic states and it is said he wrote some of his works while in a state of trance. He believed, like Plotinus, in a Reality behind the outward appearances of the mundane world. In his work *Bezels of Wisdom* he says that materialism can never take a man God-word. There are angelic powers hid in man and the Sufi should, he said, bring them out. Another view of his was that one must not be a diehard religionist. Instead of speaking of Mohammed of Mecca and Medina, he spoke of 'the eternal Mohammed'. Writers have read in this a meaning that El-Arabi signified Christ and all the prophets, but it was not this that was the significance of what he meant. It was rather that this 'eternal Mohammed' was the First Principle or the One, the Absolute which, as Plotinus said, underlies everything. A Sufi said that God is given names which are different. 'When he is seen as Mohammed he is Mohammed and when seen in another form he is called by the name in that form'.[86] El-Arabi's liberal view that there was an esoteric relation between outer religion and its personal enlightenment incensed Moslem theologists against him. A hardened bigoted Moslem called him a liar, a heretic and a hypocrite. However the more sensible ones who appreciated El-Arabi's spiritual attitude, like Kamaludin Zamlaqani and Sheikh Muhiyuddin Ibn, were all praises for him. Some of his observations are doubtless puzzling for example his saying even in dreams the thought process needs to be controlled as it will result n awareness of 'the intermediate dimension' and thus prove very valuable. Everyone, he said, should try to attain this ability.

Rumī, as we have said, considered woman to be a ray of the deity. In like manner El-Arabi says 'The sight of God in woman is the most perfect', in other words woman is the very image of God.[87] When El-Arabi was thirty-seven he went to Ceuta. The distinguished Sufi Ibn Sabain was giving lessons there in his school. It is said he had a dream in which he divined that El-Arabi had arrived there. Sufism has the belief that dreams and reveries are able to reveal and foretell events. In reveries the mind comes into contact with the Supreme Reality and this reveals the happenings of the conscious world.

El-Arabi's work *Interpreter of Desires* was particularly obnoxious to orthodox Moslems and even to foreign commentators like D.B. MacDonald who considered it to be a confused mix-up. The verses of this book, however, are sublime, full of strange imagery and double meanings. It was this work mainly which led to the accusation of heresy against him. In 1202 he went on a pilgrimage to Mecca visiting North Africa on the way. The Persians who had settled there welcomed him, but a fanatic made a murderous attempt to do away with him. Luckily he was saved. The Persian chief had a lovely daughter, devout, learned and religious. Presumably he was greatly influenced by her, though there is nothing to show that he fell in love with her or she with him. However his love poems were dedicated to her. El-Arabi conceived human beauty to be divine reality, which in not at all strange, for even the renowned English poet, John Keats, inspired by the picture of a lovely woman and her lover painted on a Grecian Urn, wrote:

> 'When old age shall this generation waste,
> Thou shalt remain, in midst of of the woe
> Than ours, a friend to man, to whom thou say'st,
> "Beauty is truth, truth beauty" - that is all
> Ye know on earth, and all ye need to know'.[88]

And Bion Smyrnaeus says 'Beauty's a woman's glory, strength a man's.[89]

El-Arabi was portraying the beauty of woman in this same way as a deep reality, a creed of the love of which he speaks in his verses, one of which, translated by professor Nicholoson is as follows:

> My heart is capable of every form:
> A cloister for the monk, a fane for idols
> A pasture for gazelles, the votary's Kaabaa
> The tables of the Torah, the Quran.
> Love is the creed I hold: wherever turn
> His camels, Love is still my creed and faith.[90]

The orthodox were shocked by El-Arabi's utterances on the beauty of women and the universalized concept of love. On his visit to Aleppo which was the centre of Moslem orthodoxy he found the divines scoffing at his erotic verses. He wrote a commentary there on the *Interpreter of Desires* to explain that the inner meaning of these verses was in consonance with their views and so succeeded in satisfying them.

For Sufis like El-Arabi and Jili matter emanated from God. El-Arabi says 'Glory to God who created things being himself their essence.[91] Their philosophy is known a the doctrine of *Wahdatul Wajud* according to which God is the Universal Consciousness and the Reality of Realities (*Haqiqat ul Haqaiq*), the universal body (*al-Jism-al-Kulli*) and prime matter (*hayula*). We have mentioned that El-Arabi distinguised between the higher Self and the lower. The human body's higher principle is the *Jism-al kulli* (the universal body). The Universal Soul is the *al-nafs al-kulliyah*, and the human spirit is universalreason (*al-aql al kulliyah*).[92] In effect this view resembles very much the Hindu one that God projects himself in the word as creation and yet transcends it. This view finds place in the *Gita* and the *Upanishads*. The *Shvetāshvatara Upanishad* says: 'Spreading out net after net of this vast creation, he (*Brahman*) with draws them again; the Lord Supreme creates all life from the gods to the humblest creatures, holding sway under them all..... As a spider weaves a web around itself *Brahman* sends forth from Nature the threads of existence, may he absorb us in himself as the spider does the threads from his own navel'.[93] In the *Gita* Lord Krishna says; 'My form unseen pervades the entire universe. All beings are in Me but I am beyond them. But in truth these creatures are not contained in Me. Do you see my wondrous power? I sustain the universe and yet am away from it. It is My Spirit which give these beings life. As the mighty air moving everywhere stays contained in space, so to all creatures abide in Me'.[94]

In this way El-Arabi also believed that there was no existence save God's. Those who think there is any other existence other than his are mistaken. God is both ruler as well as ruled, the Creator as well as the creation. When a person loses his egoism or 'I-ness' and realizes his inner self he realizes this oneness between God and himself. The *Gita* in like manner says 'That yogi has realized the soul when seeing, hearing, smelling, touching, eating, walking, sleeping or breathing, he knows it is not he who does all these things.

Whether he speaks, relinquishes or grasps, opens his eyes or closes them: he understands it is only the interplay of the senses with their objects'.[95]

But, says El-Arabi, thereby one does not become God, nor does God become him. *Haqq* remains *haqq*, *khalq* remains *khalq*. As Burckhardt says: 'The state of supreme union has been described by El-Arabi, as a natural interpenetration of Divinity and man. God as it were takes on human nature; Divine nature (*al-lahut*) becomes the content of human nature (*an nasut*), the latter being considered the recipient of the former, and from another angle man is absorbed and as it were enveloped by Divine Reality. God is mysteriously present in man and man is obliterated by God. These are the two aspects of one and the same state which are neither merged together nor yet added one to the other'.[96]

Haqq and *Khalq* are the transcendent and immanent aspects of the one. Thus God and the universe are co-eternal. Creation (*takwin*) is merely the manifestation of that which is already existing and this (the pre-existing) becomes external existence. (*zahur*). God's nature cannot be known by the human mind for it is Oneness (*ahdiya*). Only God himself can know his real nature. Here also we see the similarity between El-Arabi's doctine and that of the *Gita* in which Arjuna says to the lord: 'You alone, O Supreme Being, can know what you are'[97] Jili calls this state of Oneness *Huwiya*, i.e., 'He-ness'. El-Arabi says 'If you regard him through him, then he regards himself through himself, which is the state of unity, but if you regard him through yourself, then the unity vanishes and there are many'.[98]

The similarity between El-Arabi's thought, particularly relating to God, and Hindu philosophy is obvious. Although he comes very close to a personal God, i.e., God assuming human form. Idries Shah admits that El-Arabi comes close to this concept: 'This is not a reincarnation theory, however much it may resemble one'.[99] On the surface it is not, but reading betwees the lines it is. That is mainly why it annoyed devout. Moslems and they dubbed him as 'chief among heretics' 'a pretender' and so forth. But the only fault with him was that he was not a fanatic.

Saints do not narrow down perspectives. They only emphasize that human being should be good and virtuous and do deeds which help mankind. In fact this is what all religions emphasize. In the Holy Bible the is the parable of the good Samaritan:

> 'And behold a certain lawyer stood up and tempted him (Jesus) saying, Master what shall I do to inherit eternal life? He said unto him, what is written in the law? how readest thou? And he answering said, Thou shalt love the lord Thy God with all thy heart, and with all thy soul, and with all thy strength, and with all thy mind; and thy neighbour as thyself. And he said unto him thou has answered right: this do and thou shalt live. But he, willing to justify himself, said unto Jesus, And who is my neighbour?
>
> 'And Jesus answering said, A certain man went down from Jerusalem to Jericho, and fell among thieves, which stripped him of his raiment, and wounded him, leaving him half dead. And by chance there came down a certain priest that way: and when he saw him he passed by on the other side. And likewise a Levite, when he was at the place, came and looked on him, and passed by on the other side. But a certain Samaritan, as he journeyed, came where he was: and when he saw him, he had compassion on him, and went to him, and bound up his wounds, pouring in oil and wine, and set him on his beast, and brought him to an inn, and took care of him. And on the morrow when he departed, he took out two pence, and gave

them to his host, and said unto him, Take care of him; and what so ever thou spendest more, when I come again, I will repay thee. Which now of these three, thinkest thou, was neighbour unto him that fell among the thieves? And he said, He that shewed mercy on him. Then said Jesus unto him, Go, and do thou likewise'.[100]

The Holy Quran also believes in the doctrine of karma; that is to say the evil deeds will be punished but good ones rewarded: 'He who has done an atom's weight of good shall see it. And he who has done an atom's weight of evil shall see it.'[101] Further, 'And We will set up a just balance on the day of resurrection, so no should shall be dealt with unjustly in the least; and though there be the weight of a grain of muṣtard seed, We will bring it, and sufficient are we to take account'.[102] The difference so far as Islam is concerned, however, is that for Believers, i.e., Moslems there is exclusive standard of judgment; 'And He it is who accepts repentence from his servants and pardons the evil deeds, and he knows what you do. And he answers those who believe and do good deeds and gives them more out of His grace; and (as for) the unbelievers, they shall have a severe chastisement'.[103] Thus while the Holy Quran promises God's forgiveness and grace to the followers of Islam, these are not extended to the followers of other religions. Hinduism, however, makes no such distinctions. We have already given instances of its catholicity. Lord Krishna says in the *Gita* 'Both the ignorant and the wise work, O Arjuna; but while the ignorant man is attached to works, the wise man works for the world's welfare'.[104] The Lord promises same-sightedness, 'All beings are the same to Me' and only devotion to God is necessary for forgiveness and grace.[105]

The Sufis, likewise, believed in active social service. A teacher advised his followers to 'live in society and bear the blows and buffets of the people'[106] Sheikh Nizam-ud-dīn Aulia pointed out two aspects of devotion to God – obligatory (*lāzamī*) and *mutā 'addi* (communicable). In the first benefit accrues to the devotee only, while in the other kind, the *muta 'addi* in which a man helps his fellow beings the reward is 'endless and limitless'.[107] The Chishtī saints (of whom we will speak about late too) advised their disciples to keep only what was absolutely necessary.[108]

Pacificism and non-violence were also enjoined by Sufis. Sheikh Nizam-ud-dīn Aulia said, 'If a man places thorns in your way and you do the same, it will be thorns everywhere'.[109] This was directly contrary to the militant Islamic concept of Jihad which was based on out and out violence and the slaughter of non-Moslems, Hindus in particular. Patience, endurance, elimination of anger, introspection and giving up thoughts of revenge for any wrong done, were qualities advocated by the Sufis. Many of the saints were vegetarians and were against slaughter of animals. Kabir says, 'You slaughter animals wilfully and say "It is sanctioned by my faith". But, says kabīr, when you are called to account for your deeds what answer will you give? Will this be believed reason enough for your cruelty?' – *kabīra jia ju marahi joru kari kahate hahi ju halālu, daphataru daī jaba kāḍhi hai hoigā kauna havālu.*[110] The Sufis were instrumental in bringing about a social and cultural revolution. Barnī remarked that as a result of their teachings 'vices among men have been reduced'.

The Sufis believe that evil may be transformed into good as a dirty pond, if it gets connected to a perennially flowing stream will after a short while become clean. So too when one breaks the barriers of his individuality and becomes part of universal life the forces restricting him and keeping him away from the stream of humanity cease to operate. Dalpat, a renowned Sufi who spent most of his life in Hyderabad wrote:

You alone, O God, are in all
Why then do you remain hid?
You make men perform good and evil
What need is there for hell or heaven?
Why should there be union and separation
When you and I, Lord are ever one?

And, as we have said before, the Sufi believes that the way to God is through love. Shah Abdul Latīf says:

Everything that comes from the Beloved is sweet
Provided your heart can savour that sweetness.

But love is a kind of gift from God. Jesus said to Nicodemus, a ruler of the Jews, 'The wind bloweth where it listeth, and thou hearest the sound thereof, but cannot tell whence it cometh, and wither it goeth'.[111] So too love does not come for the asking. It comes of itself and goes oı itself. A man asked Sādik, a prominent Sufi, to fill him with God's love. Sādik called a potter and asked him, 'Do you select the kind of clay you use for your pots, or does the clay make the offer itself?' The potter said, 'How can the clay do that? Of course it is me who chooses the clay for my pots'. Sādik told the seeker, 'God's love is just like that God is the judge of the type of person on whom to confer it'-

He utters God's name whom He causes to utter,
He chants God's praises whom He chooses to chant.

The Sufi view is that learning is not only useless in seeking seeking God's love, in other words for devotion (*bhakti*); it is a positive hindrance. Rohi, known as Bedil, a renowned Sufi, says 'The man who gets entangled in learning cannot reach the heights of love'. Another prominent Sufi teacher would advise the intellectuals of the city who wished to be taught Sufism to first return and forget all they had learnt.

We find this idea in the *Upanishads*. The *Īhsa Upanishad* says: 'Those who depend on rituals enter into blinding darkness; but into greater darkness those who seek support in empty learning'.[112] At times the Sufi teaching comes very close to Shankara's Vedanta, that the world is illusion and for the knower of Brahman it does not exist. There is a saying among Sufis that 'the world does not consist in family and possessions, but that it consists in the forgetting of God; that your having a family and possessions does not make you worldly, that you become only when you forget him [God]. Having all these, if you constantly remember him, the world does not exist for you. The world comes into being as soon as you begin to be unconscious of him, and exists only as long as you remain so'.[113]

We have spoken about the almost universal belief in karma. Like Hindus, Sikhs and Moslems, and other faiths to a high place is given to the guru or Pīr. Or as the Sufis term him, the *Murshīd*. It is said that there were two friends, one of whom sought the spiritual guidance of sadhus while the other kept busy with sensual pleasures. The two were on their way for some work. The pleasure-seeker happened to find by his good luck a bag full of gold, while the other man stepped on a thorny growth and bled where a thorn had pricked him. On return the man who had found the gold began to scoff at his spiritual friend saying 'That's what one gets by spirituality.' The other man went to his guru the sadhu, and wanted to know why it was so. The sadhu said 'That pleasure-seeker was to find a huge treasure, but because of his actions this ended up in just that bag of gold. You were fated to go to the gallows, but because of your spiritual bent of mind you got off with just the prick of a thorn'. Thus this Sufi anecdote depicts the belief in karma.

Sind is the centre of Sufi influence, and there were gatherings of Sufi saints there from the earliest times, as for example in the Jhok village Rohri, Tando Saneended and Kumber. The bards there sang the *kāfī* which is about the pangs of separation. Many songs are sung there about Maruī who is story is as follows. She was a girl living in Malir village. Umar, prince of Amarkot saw her and bewitched by her beauty eloped with her to Amarkot and asked her to marry him. 'You will live here in grandeur' he said, 'like a princess'. But she refused his proposal, telling him that she was already engaged to a man who was her lover, in her village. She spurned the splendour of the royal palace and preferred her humble home and tattered clothes. Ultimately it turned out that the charming beauty was really Umar's foster sister. He took her back and got her united with her village lover. The song about Maruī is very dear to Sindhis and fills them with wistful yearnings for home-coming. Shah Latīf interprets it spiritually as the Soul's longing for God who is its abode.

The attitude of Sufis to music and song is one of the many aspects in which it departs from the Islamic way of thinking. The Mogul emperor, Akbar, was an exception to Islamic fanaticism and, himself fond of music, invited singers like Tanasena in his durbar, and delighting in Sufism, had Hafiz and Rumī read out to him. But he earned thereby the wrath of Moslem chroniclers and historians. The puritan Aurangzebe was much closer to the Islamic tradition in having an abhorrence for music. It is said that some music lovers were taking out a mock funeral procession (*janāzā*) of music to impress Aurangzebe and somehow persuade him to change his attitude. When the emperor heard the commotion outside his place, he asked what it was about. 'Sire, they are taking out the *janāzā* of music' he was told. 'Then' said Aurangzebe, 'ask them to bury it so deep that it never comes out again'! The Sufis call the hearing of music *sāma* and believe it helps in the concentration of the mind, and causes ecstasy (*wājid*). A writer says, 'The ordinary people hear *sāma* as a natural instinct, the novice for *shauq* and *khauf*, the Aulias for the bounties of God, the *arifs* (gnostics) for the knowledge of God, and the perfect for revelations. The hearers of *sāma* shed tears, some in fear of God and others in joy. The perfect who have reached their destination cannot be thrilled by *sāma*'.[114] The Sufi prizes music even as the Duke, Orsino:

> 'If music be the food of love, play on,
> Give me excess of it; that surfeiting,
> The appetite may sicken and to die.—
> That strain again; – it had a dying fall;
> O, it came over my ear like the sweet south,
> That breathes upon a bank of violets
> Stealing, and giving odour'.[115]

According to El-Ghazali of Persia music can lead to emotional effect but not on all men alike. The Sufi teacher is the judge of this and it is he who must decide whether the seeker can benefit from it. If such benefit cannot be obtained, one should abstain from music and dancing. In fact instead of being beneficial, these can be, in that case positively harmful. A *tālib* approached Sheikh Gujrani about this. The Sheikh asked him to fast for a week and the have tasty dishes prepared. If he still preferred music to such food, by all means take part in it! It is perhaps because of this that Shakespeare speaks of music being the 'food of love'. True love is difficult to acquire and unless one has it he cannot enter into the soul of music. It is the lover who serenades to the beloved.

El-Ghazali got an appointment as a professor at the famed Nizamiyya Academy of Baghdad at the early age of thirty-three. He became an authority on Islam. However he soon realized that authoritative religion could never disclose reality, and being a conscientious man resigned from his post.

A misconception about Sufism is that it is allied to any religion. Idries Shah says The Sufis appear in historical times mainly within the pale of Islam....... Scholasticism and mysticism are opposed to one another. But the Sufis gave rise to, among others, a school of each. Were these Moslem schools? No, they were Christian, associated with the Augustinians and St. John of the Cross as professor Palacios and others have established'.[116] In fact the Sufis were neither followers of Islam in its strict sense, nor were they Christians. The Sufi movement was one of ascetism. Before the coming of Islam in the mid-seventh century there were two rival empires to the north of Arabia, Persian and Byzantine whose religions were Zoroastrianism and Christianity respectively. The Byzantine rulers persecuted the Christians and the Persian ones did the same to non-Zoroastrains including Christians of Iraq and Mesopotamia. To escape such persecution the heretics and Gnostics went away to the deserts.[117]

The Arab Moslems overran all countries connected with Sufism including Iraq, Syria, Egypt and others. To Moslems, whether a person was Christian or Hindu or of any other faith except Islam, he was a Kafir and had no right to live in the world which was meant for Moslems alone. So it was Islam or the sword. Many, therefore, embraced Islam to escape death. Even then the Moslems made a difference between converted Moslems and the other ones, and the Abbasi Caliphs crushed the latter. This made them turn to ascetism, for as ascetics denying worldly pleasures, they could bear their tortures with more endurance. Thus Abu nasr Sarraj the earliest writer on Sufism says in his book *Kitabul Luma fit-Ta-swauf*, 'as a system it was not evolved by the Sufis but has been long prevalent among ascetics in the pre-Islamic period'.[118] Although these early Sufis had faith in Mohammed and the Holy Quran, they were not bigoted. There are fundamental differences between them and the followers of Islam, the men of the Book. The Sufis believed in duality of matter and spirit and the unity of God and man while the followers of Islam were for dualism of God and man. Islam believes in 'Iblis' an isolated evil spirit. In Sufism worldliness is connected with evil. In Islam the world is for enjoyment and thereby attaining heaven. The Sufi is for renouncing the world. In Islam not following the Quran leads to hell and to escape hell one has to try for heaven. The Sufi's aim to find salvation in this very life, and he stands for meditation. One of the earliest Sufis, Al-Hasan al-basri said, 'A grain of genuine piety is better than a thousand-fold weight of fasting and prayer; renunciation in fear of hell or in hope of paradise is no renunciation. True renunciation is for the realization of God and this comes by purifying one's heart'.[119] It is said the Prophet asked the Sufi, Rabia in a dream if she hated Satan, and she replied 'I am so absorbed and full of the love of God that there is no room for love or hatred for anyone else'. One of her favourite prayers was 'O God, if I worship Thee in fear of hell, burn me in hell, and if I worship Thee for Thine own sake, withhold not thine everlasting beauty.'[120]

As regards Sufism and Christianity, there are also fundamental differences between them and the Sufi's view is much more broadminded than that of Christianity which conceives God to be 'jealous God' condemning those who hate him and showing mercy to those who love him and keep his commandments (Exodus 20:5-6). The Sufi is free from such restrictions and gives everyone the liberty to have his own opinion. Hazarat Inayat Khan, the renowned Sufi says:

> 'The God of the Sufi is the God of every creed and the God of all. Names make no difference to him. Allah, God, Gott, Dieu, Khuda, Brahmā or Bhagavān, all these names and more are the names of his God; and yet to him God is beyond the limitation of name. He sees his God in the sun, in the idol which diverse sects worship; and he recognizes him to be beyond all

> form: God in all, and all in God, He being the Seen and the Unseen, the only Being. God to the Sufis is not only a religious belief, but also the highest ideal the human mind can conceive'.[121]

In the Holy Bible the Lord says in his commandments 'Thou shalt have no other gods before me'. Image worship, the making of 'any graven image' is strictly forbidden.[122] There are some beliefs essential for Christians which, even though not denied by the Sufis, are not obligatory on them, as for example the Immaculate Conception about Mary who gave birth to Jesus parthenogenetically, and the Bodily Assumption (that at death she was physically transferred to heaven). Then there is the dogma accepted by most Christians that though God is one, he exists in three Persons, the Father, the Son, and the Holy Ghost.

Thus Sufism is neither Islamic, nor Christian, nor Hinduism nor any other religion. It has its own individual way of thinking, though some of its concepts may seem analogous to those of other religions. Being Moslems and accepting the Holy Quran and the Prophet, the Sufis gave it a liberal interpretation shorn of all dogma and bigotry. Akbar, the Mogul emperor, was a stickler for the Holy Quran, despite the view of some writers that in his later years he ceased to be a Moslem. In his 'Infallibility Decree' in which he took on himself to decide any matter in which *mujtahids* differed he specified that such a decision would not be in opposition to the injunctions of the Quran, but nonetheless he found differences arising not only on questions of detail, but of fundamentals too: 'One pronounced a thing lawful, another would pronounce the very same thing unlawful. They called one another fools and heretics. In order to support their arguments they quoted form ancient authorities and proved that there existed as great a difference of opinion among them as among their modern representatives'.[123]

As Sufism is not any religious system one has to consider what it really is. Professor R.A. Nicholson (*The Mystics of Islam*) considers it as 'undefinable'. But that would be a negative way of thinking, for we surely can't conceive all the rich and subtle observations of hundreds of Sufi saints and masters as not pointing to any truth at all. It is clear that the Sufi believes more in experience than in knowledge. Its central doctrine is decidedly love. Love is a very tricky word and it is understood in so many wrong ways by different people that one may conclude it is never understood at all. For one thing different people interpret it according their own personal experiences of it. To one lecherous and carnal it means only sex. As for example a prominent writer and columnist wrote about the revered saint Mirābaī that she was an adulteress! Obviously this man's experience was restricted to the sexual act. He never knew that love was something quite apart from it. When the bond between lover and beloved is that between man and God, love becomes divine. Yet since the human mind is unable to grasp the nature of divine love even if he can feel it, he has to employ erotic symbology, as the great Sufis Rumī El-Arabi and others did, or as Krishna devotees like Surdasa, Mira, Rasakhan and many others did in writing about the love of Rādhā and the milkmaids of Braj for Krishna. The difference between carnal love and divine love is that one is momentary while the other is everlasting, as Lord Krishna says in the *Gita — amritasya 'vyavasya sukhasyai* ('nectar-like everlasting bliss')[124] But carnal love, as Shakespeare says, cloys the appetite it feeds.[125] Another difference is that while carnal love satiates the body by reliveing its passion, divine love uplifts the soul. Nevertheless as the symbolism is the same in both cases, Sufism has a resemblance to Vaishnavism. The prominent Vaishnava Sufis were Farid Sani, Shah Hussain, Sultan were Farid Sani, Shah Hussain, Sultan Bahu, Bullhe Shah, Ghulam Jilani Rohtaki and the Qadiris. Farid imagines himself to be a wife whose Husband is the Lord. She sleeps with him daily and the day she does not, her body pines for Him. She does everything possible to please Him, even putting off her attractive dress and covering herself with the cloak of an ascetic.[126] Bullhe Shah was greatly influenced by Hindu ideas, adoring the Prophet as Vaishnavas adored Krishna, wifely devotion like that of Farid Sani, the concentration on the *anahat* sound, breath control, monism and transmigration of souls. Thus his belief was in the Vaishnava kind of devotion and also in tantra. He speaks in the same term as the Krishna-devotees: 'Krishna plays on his flute and when I hear its tune, I forget everything... when I heard his flute's notes I wept with the woe of parting. I was a *gopi* rushing madly towards Krishna, where else should I go? God sports with him (himself imagining to be a *gopi*) and when he does not even glance at him, he is disappointed.[127] Ghulam Jilani Rohtaki's book *Jog Sāgara* is full of Hindu beliefs and he calls on his followers to follow Hindu scriptures and practices, 'Those who have trodden the path of yoga have known the Truth; If you adopt the eight steps of the yoga system, your mind will be purified'.[128] He says 'Sing the glory of Hari with every breath'. He is for the 'soham jāpa' ('What God is so is my soul').[129] He also advocates chanting God's name, giving charity, the acquisition of knowledge, bathing, worship, remembering Hari and following the teachings of the Vedas and Shastras.[130] Thus while love is very much the creed of the Sufis, it is spiritual love, which is permanent, blissful and takes one to God, despite its being sometimes expressed in erotic verses as in El-Arabi's *Interpreter of Desires* Is Sufism a religion? In the sense in which religion is the creed of a particular community or sect, it is not. The Sufi tolerates all religions. He does not belong to any particular religion, yet accomodates all. He dose not subscribe to the didactism of religions, for he believes that 'truth is that which cannot be fully spoken and that is not necessarily the truth that can be spoken'.[131] Sufism is neither a school of thought, though it is a medium through which one acquires wisdom, nor is it any philosophy. Though one may trace its source to mysticism, it is that only in the sense that it seeks soul-knowledge. Good and evil are comparitive terms. What seems good to one may be evil to another and it hard to say where evil ends and good beings, for in a moment one may turn into the other as the poet, Tennyson says:

> Oh yet we trust that somehow good
> Will be final goal of ill,
> To pangs of nature, sins of will,
> Defects of doubt, and taints of blood;
>
> Behold, we know not anything;
> I can but trust that good shall fall
> At last–afar off–at last to all
> And every winter change to sping.[132]

The sage, Ramakrishna, records 'Says God "I am the snake that biteth and the charmer that healeth; I am the judge that condemneth and the executioner that whippeth."[133]

Man has a tendency to take the credit for what is good himself and blame God for all his evil acts. Ramakrishna illustrates this through one of his parables:

> 'A brahmin was laying out a graden and looked after it day and night. One day a cow strayed and ate a sapling of a much cared for tree. He thrashed it so much that it died, and to justify himself he said that it was his hand that did it and since heaven's god, Indra, was a hand's presiding deity, it was he who was responsible. Indra, in his heaven, heard this and taking an old brahmin's form came down and extolled the beautifully laid out garden. The owner said proudly that he himself had done it. Indra (the

disguised god as man) folded his hand and said "If it's you who take the credit for all this, isn't it hard lines for poor Indra to be held responsible for killing the cow?'[134]

Hazrat Inayat Khan considers that God is aware of our sufferings, but he himself is above all earthly joys and sorrows. God is surely merciful and forgiving and this power of his can be exercised in a moment, provided the plea for forgiveness is sincere. And this comes only with complete faith in God (*aṇanya bhakti*, i.e., 'singleminded devotion'). A deathbed repentance is no good if the entire life of the human being has been passed in doing evil and dwelling on sensual pleasures: 'For this reason the teachers of humanity have taught man faith is the first lesson in religion. Those are forgiven the sins of their whole life, who have always believed that any moment death might come and have safegaurded themselves against doing anything that does not meet with the pleasure of their Lord, and whenever, owing to human imperfection, they have failed in doing right, they have most earnestly asked forgiveness'.[135]

The *Bhagavadgita* also emphasizes that the devotees of God are absolved of sins 'Those persons worship me who, by their virtuous deeds have destroyed their sins'.[136] But the Lord also says in the *Gita* that though a person attains that to which his thought turns at the hour of death, such a thought is fashioned by the kind of life he has lived.[137] This is very much like the thinking of the Sufi, Hazrat Inayat Khan whom we have quoted aforesaid. A saying of Shri Ramakrishna also illustrates this point:

> 'The entangled creatures attached to worldiness, talk only of worldly things in the hour of death. What will it avail such men if they outwardly repeat the name of God, take a bath in the Ganges, or visit sacred

> places? If they cherish within themselves attachment to the world, it must show up at the hour of death. While dying they rave nonsense. Perhaps they cry out in a delirium "Turmeric powder! Seasoning! Bay-leaf!" The singing parrot, when at ease repeats the holy names of Rādhā and Krishna, but when it is seized by a cat at utters its own natural sound: it squawks "kaa! kaa!"[138]

Just as love for the Sufi means divine love so too learning means wisdom. We have dwelt on this before also. It is said that the great saint of Punjab, Bullhe Shah was sent to school along with boys of his own age. While the other boys mastered the entire alphabet, he was stuck up with Alif. The teacher tried his best to make him learn the other letters but to no purpose. So he sent him home saying that there was some deficiency in his mind. His father got him private tutors but it was no use. Seeing his father's despondency, Bullhe Shah ran away from home so that he may not prove a burden, and began to live in the forest.

There he saw Alif manifested in everything–trees, hills, rocks birds and beasts, and within himself too. After a few years he went back to his teacher who by now had forgotten him and bowed to him humbly saying, 'I have learnt the lesson you were so good enough as to teach me. Will you teach me anything more?' The teacher recollected him then, but laughed at him, for he recalled that the boy was not able to proceed beyond Alif. Bullhe Shah asked his permission to write what he had learnt and his teacher said 'All right if you are so insistent, write it on the wall!' Bullhe wrote the letter 'Alif' on it and lo! it, of itself, divided into two. The teacher was amazed and said 'What you have learnt in that one letter I have failed to learn in these many years. In have failed to learn in these many years. In truth *you* are my teacher'. Bullhe Shah then sang a song:

Leave your learning aside
Fill not your room with tomes
You burden the mind with learning,
Cease; for it has no use.
In purshing the false, lose not the true
One Alif is all you need to know.

It is the One which is revealed in many forms in this world. And Alif represents that one, and it is derived from a dot, i.e. zero (In Arabic zero is written as a dot). It is this nothingness that is the origin of everything, as Omar Khayyām says:

'A hair perhaps divides the false and true;
Yes, and a single Alif were the clue,
Could you but find it–to the treasure house,
And, peradventure to the Master too.
My soul said, "I desire the mystic knowledge:
Teach me if it be in thy power."
I said, "Alif". She answered, "Say no more;
If one is at home, a single letter is enough".'[139]

Again, we find the same thought in the Upanishads In the Chāndogya Upanishad. Shvetaketu was being taught by his father about the Being from which all shapes and forms were produced, even though no one could see it:

> 'Fetch a fruit of the banyan tree, son' his father said. When the lad had brought it, he told him to split it open. 'What do you see inside?' he asked. 'These tiny seeds, sir', Shvetaketu said. 'Break one of them son. What do you see inside the seed?' 'Nothing at all, father' said Shvetaketu. 'From this same subtle essence, which you do not see, this huge tree arose.

> Believe me, dear lad. This subtle essence is the soul of all beings. It is the true. And that is what you are Svetaketu'.[140]

Sri Ramkrishna said, 'Too much study of the scriptures does more harm than good. The important thing is to know the essence of the scriptures. After that what is the need of books? One should learn the essence and then dive deep in order to realize God'.[141] And again, 'The vulture soars high up in the air, but all the while he is looking down into the charnel-pits in search of putrid carcasses. So the book-read pundits speak glibly and volubly about Divine knowledge, but it is all mere talk, for all the while their minds are thinking about how to get money, respect, honour, power etc., the vain guerdon of their learning".[142]

Reverting to El-Ghazzali, after resigning from his post of professor the Nizamiyya Academy at Baghdad, he spent twelve years in wandering and meditation. This is the period prescribed for dervishes to realize truth.

We have aforesaid mentioned some characteristics of the Dervish Orders like the significance of the patched up garments they wear. Almost all Sufis belong to one or the other of these orders, as for example the Rafa'i, Qalandari, Chishti, Mevlevi and Naqshbandi. Many of these Orders though accepting Islam admit traditions of other religions too. So they are less reigid and exclusive. Most Moslem interpreters of Sufism try to downplay its broadmindedness, but some like the celebrated Hazrat Inayat Khan have no trace of such bigotry. One of the most prominent Sufi saint was Ali el-Hujwiri, who wrote a number of books while at Lahore, the most well-known being *Kashf el-Mahjub* (the Revelation of the Veiled'). This became one of the most significant of books for the students of Tassawuf in India as well as in other Islamic countries. Hujwiri studied under Abu el-Qasim Gurgani of the Naqshbandi Order which as we have mentioned was uncompromisingly communal. Obviously Hujwiri's thought was fashioned on the same lines. No wonder a writer has said, 'Ali el-Hujwiri's tomb may still be seen in Lahore [now in Pakistan] near the Bhati gate... Most of the Moslem invaders and wandering dervishes on entering the land, made a point of paying their homage at his shrine'.[143] Who were these Moslem invaders who showed such reverence to Hujwiri's tomb? Surely they could not have had even an iota of the Sufi spirit, which Robert Graves defines as follows: 'To be "in the world, but not of it", free from ambition, greed, intellectual pride, blind obedience to custom, or awe of persons higher in rank–that is the Sufi ideal'.[144] This sounds much nearer to the creed of the *Gita* than to any other philosophy. The *Gita* says that one should live in the world as the lotus in the waters of a pond, with its petals above the surface of its dirty waters. So too Sri Ramakrishna says, 'Live in the world like a waterfowl. The water clings to the bird, but the bird shakes it off. Live in the world like a mudfish. The fish lives in the mud, but its skin is always bright and shiny'.[145] Hazrat Inayat Khan says 'The Sufi... frees himself from national racial and religious boundaries, uniting himself in the human brotherhood, which is devoid of the differences and distinctions of class, caste, creed, race, nation or religion, and unites mankind in the universal brotherhood'.[146] Obviously the Moslem invaders who are said to have invariably made it a point of paying homage at Hujwiri's tomb would be the persecutors of mankind not their saviours, and so unSufistic as would, if Hujwiri was a true Sufi, make him turn in his grave; for it is not the invaders who are the ones admired but the philosophers who believe in 'the human brotherhood–the Diogeneses not the Alexanders.[147] For the invaders were Tīmūr-i-lang whose motive was, as the Holy Quran enjoined 'slay the idolaters wherever you find them, and take them captives and besiege them and lie in wait for them in every ambush... for God is Forgiving, Merciful'.[148] In pursuance of this, the invader,

Tīmūr, says in his Memoirs 'The sword of Islam was washed in the blood of the [Hindu] infidels...'[149] Tīmūr's other motives were greed for wealth and lust for power. The other invader was Nadir Shah of whose pillage a chronicle recorded: 'But how to relate the ruin and desolation that overwhelmed this beautiful country! Wazirabad, Imanabad and Gujarat, towns which, for population, might almost be called cities, were levelled with the earth. Nothing was respected, no sort of violence remained unpractised; property of all kinds became the spoil of plunder, and women the pray of the ravisher'[150]

Thus it is evident that Hujwiri may be the Moslem ideal but not of Sufis. The Sufis believed in oneness of lover and Beloved as in the saying of Jalaluddin Rumī about the man knocking at the door of the Beloved which we have quoted before. 'Wherever you are whatever be your state' says Rumi 'always be a lover'. But Hujwiri's view is quite different 'The created (*makluq*)' he says 'cannot become one with the Creator (*Khaliq*) and the event (*hadis*) with the Eternal'.[151] The early Sufis, like Hujwiri, were of the Ijadist Order which initially lasted till the invasion of Tīmūr in 1398. It was revived during the rule of the Moslem bigoted emperor Aurangzebe and the period after when Nadir Shah pillaged and sacked Northern India. These Ijadists were not of the general Sufi belief and they were more or less Moslem fanatics. They insisted that seekers of God must accept Islam and the Prophet, and if they do not, they must be converted by force. Muinuddin Chishti, founder of the Chishti order in India said 'If a Kafir utters *la ilaha ill Allah* for a hundred years he will remain a Kafir and if he says *Mohammed Rasul Allah* even once he will cease being a Kafir'![152] Farid Ganj-i-Shakar locked up a Hindu in his room for three days and set him free only after he agreed to embrace Islam.[153] It was the same attitude of bigotry with others of this Order.

Secondly the saints of the Ijadist Order considered knowledge of the Shariat to be vital. Hujwiri said that the highest stage was possible only by knowledge of the Holy Quran and its traditions.[154] According to Nizamuddin Aulia there could be no salvation for a man who did not follow the Shariat.[155]

The Ijadist Sufis were somewhat confused about the nature of God. Some of them believed him to be personal, with attributes. Others that he is the Absolute and unknowable. Thus they approximated to the Hindu concept of God as the Personal Ishvara and also the Impersonal *Brahman*. They did not believe God to be immanent, that is to say pervading creation and yet they recognized him to be present in the universe in his knowledge and through the manifestation of his attributes. This too is very much like what the Lord says in the tenth chapter of the *Gita*. When Arjuna asked the Lord about his divine manifestations through which, pervading the universe, he abided, he related all of them and finally told him 'I uphold the universe by just a frament of Myself'.[156]

While Mansur said 'I am the Creative Truth', Hamid-ud-din Nagori held that one who considers God and man as two, i.e., sees duality, is always in conflict with himself. Thus these Idajist Sufis kept veering between didactism and liberalism. In fact they were apprehensive that if they spoke fearlessly about what they really thought, they would be branded as traitors to Islam.

The soul, they thought did not exist before creation, it was only in the idea of God. After creation the soul was in essence different from God. However again we find these Sufis to veer to the Hindu idea of the Vedanta of Shankaracharya. The universe, they said, has no real existence. It exists only in God's will The soul falls under the influence of ignorance and thinks the world to exist separately. So too, the *Ātmabodha* (self-knowledge) of Shankara says: As the dream world is real so long as one is dreaming, but is proved unreal on waking, even so the world of attachment, aversion and so forth, has reality no longer for the knower (*Brahman*)'. Love according to the Ijadist Sufis meant not the lover-Beloved relationship but obedience to God who doesn't tolerate any violation of his commandments. This idea too is analogous to the Hindu one contained in the *Upanishads* except that there the commandments do not mean any injunctions of the scriputres but the cosmic Absolute formless Brahman:

> 'It's his fear [*Brahman's* fear] that makes the fire burn and the sun gives heat; it's his fear that makes the gods of Heaven and wind perform their functions along with Death's god, who is the fifth'.[157]

Why and how does creation come about? The Ijadist order believes God loved his *jamāl* (beauty) and *jalāl* (majesty) and out of these created man so that he may love and obey him. Nizamuddin Aulia considers love of God (*mohabbat-i-zat*) to be a divine gift.[158] The Hindu view is that the world is a *līlā* (sport) of God. The Ijadists also believed in the vision of God, but this is not possible by means of the intellect. God can be seen only with the inner eye, not with the human eye. This again is very much like the *Gita's* in which the Lord on Arjuna's supplication showed him his cosmic form. But that was not possible with his human eyes. The Lord said 'But your eyes by themselves cannot see me thus; I will give you divine sight so that you may see my wonderful form'.[159] Sri Ramakrishna also believed that such vision was possible, but only when there was an earnest and overpowering desire to see God:

> 'A disciple asked his teacher "Sir, please tell me how I can see God". "Come with me" said the guru "and I shall show you". He took the disciple to a lake and both of them got into the water. Suddenly the teacher pressed the disciple's head under the water. After a few moments he released him and the disciple raised

> his head and stood up. The guru asked him, "How did you feel?" The disciple said "Oh! I thought I should die; I was panting for breath". The teacher said "When you feel like that for God then you will know you haven't long to wait for his vision".'[160]

El-Ghazzali, however, approximates to the above idea of Sri Ramakrishna, discounting the belief that God-vision can be obtained by the eyes. He says that it is not related to the eyes or any other organ. It is a complete knowledge which God can create in man without the mediation of any of the senses.[161] Nizamuddin Aulia thinks that God vision will be had by everyone on the Day of Judgment. But since all religions do not envisage such a day, this could not be universally possible.

Regarding God's grace and good and evil, the Ijadist Order follows the usual Moslem belief that God's adversary is Satan, and in the world Satan keeps foiling God's designs. That is why God's grace takes a back seat, so long as Satan is not vanquished. In fact in a ritual performed at Mecca during the Haj pilgrimage known as 'stoning the devil? pilgrims throw stones at three pillars symbolizing Satan.[162]

In their views about renunciation the Ijadists are closer to Hinduism and Jainism inasmuch as most of them are in favour of shunning worldliness. Baba Farid considers such a renouncer the wisest of persons. He says that desires are endless and even if one's desires are satisfied he keeps on wanting more and more.[163] He was also one of those few who practised what he preached, living a life of poverty *faqr* and often undergoing fasting and at the end of a fast taking only one capful of syrup and even out of that giving half or even two-third of it to his companions.[164] Nasirud-din Chiragh Dehlvi also believed that desires have no end and one follows another without ceasing. He also said that one should keep away altogether from the world because if one got involved even a little he gets more and more involved and finally ends up by being absorbed in it irretrievably.[165] About this Ramakrishna Paramahansa has a parable which illustrates the point Dehlvi makes, very well:

> 'There was a sannyasi whose only possession was two pairs of loin-cloth. One day a mouse nibbled at one piece. So the holy man kept a cat to protect his loin-cloth from the mouse. Then he had to keep a cow to supply milk for the cat. Later he had to engage a servant to look after the cow. Gradually the number of his cows multiplied. He acquired pastures and farm land. He had to engage a number of servants. Thus he became in course of time a sort of landlord. And last of all he had to take a wife to look after his big household. One day one of his friends, another monk, happened to visit his home and was surprised to see his altered circumstances. When asked the reason, the holy man said "It was all for the sake of a piece of loin-cloth!" '[166]

The attitude of these Sufis of the Ijadist Orders was not at all consistent so far as renunciation and the acquisition of weath were concerned. Some, like Sadrud-din Arif spurned wealth and considered it the root of all evil. But his own father, Zakaria, had a trunk full of gold *tankas*![167] Many were lured by wealth and had a number of wives. Still they called themselves renouncers! Some were content with whatever God gave them, and met the expenses of their families from *fatuh* (voluntary charity), others took up jobs and enjoyed royal patronage. Muinuddin Chishti had contacts with Mohammed Ghauri and Kaki had as his disciple, Sultan Iltutmash. The Ijadist poets were equally inconsistent and their vision was narrow. Farad Faqir was a bigoted Moslem condemning Hindus and their main avatars Rama and Krishna and urging everyone to embrace Islam. Yet he is for the lover-Beloved Vaishava attitude and wrote he sought God as in the love of Zuleikha and Yusuf! So too Ghulam Rasul says 'I am the woman who likes to see thy Beautiful Face', but later on declares the path of Mohammed to be the only true one! We will now pass on to El-Ghazzali of the Dervish Order about whom something has already been said before.

After El-Ghazzali left his job, he wandered about and spent his time in meditation. This was largely to get rid of the ego (*ahankāra*) as Shankaracharya calls it; the I-sense. He says about it in *Vivekachuramani* (The Crest-jewel of Wisdom):

> 'Abandon at once the idea of "I" in the *ahankāra* which is the cause of change, which experiences the consequence of karma and which is the destroyer of rest in one's own real self. One believes erroneously that this "I" is the soul... Therefore having destroyed this *ahankāra* be happy in the enjoyment of spiritual bliss'.[168]

However Shankaracharya realized that the destruction of this I-sense is no easy task: 'The great *ahankara* even though seemingly uprooted, will if excited only for a moment by the mind come to life again and cause a hundred distractions just as clouds are scattered by the stormy breeze'.[169] During his search for enlightenment El-Ghazzali happened to a go to a mosque where he heard the preacher end his sermon with the words 'So too says our leader Ghazzali'. Ghazali was aghast and said that he would go away somewhere where there was no talk about him. He went away to Syria and stayed there two years seeking sotitude trying to overcome sense of self and fighting against passions and purifying his soul so that he could turn his heart towards meditation of God. He had some esctatic experiences, but did not consider that thereby his goal had been achieved, for as the *Gita* says, unless one can conquer the lower self by the higher, nothing is achieved. In one of his books '*The Alchemy of Happiness*' (his other ones being '*The Destruction of the Philosophers' and the*

'Niche for Lights') he refers to one of the stories of Bayazid to illustrate this point. A man came to Bayazid and said 'I have been fasting and praying for thirty years to come closer to God but I've failed to do so'. Bayazid said even if he did so for a hundred years it would be of no use because he had not been able to eradicate his sense of selfishness. 'Then what sould I do to succeed?' the man asked. Bayazid asked him to put off all his clothes, wear a loin-cloth and go to the bazaar with a bag full of walnuts offer one walnut to every boy who agreed to slap him and then go to the court where the qazi was deciding cases! 'But that's impossible', the man said. 'Give me some other way'. 'This is the only way' Bayazid said. 'I've already told you the reason why it's impossible for you to be close to God'. Ghazzali believed that the crux of all religions lay in Sufism, but it was only meant for the chosen few who could imbibe the Sufi spirit-in Milton's words 'fit audience though few'. In his work *Mizan el Amal* El-Gazzali said that apart from what the teacher explains to his students there is the inner experience which can be known only to a handful of people. The same point is elaborated in the *Mishkat el Anwar* ('Niche for Lights'). Everything has an outward and an inward significance. While the outward is knowable generally, the inward is a matter of experience, not of understanding. Taking for instance love, to which all Sufis give prominence. It is not to be understood or talked about, irrespective of whether it is physical or spiritual. The sweet nothings of loves in lovemaking are meaningless as a Sanskrit love poet writes, 'Sounds she uttered then, without meaning, yet not meaningless'.[170] Abu Nasar Mohammed of Farabi (870-950) a philopher and a Sufi, believed love to be beyond material objects and not to be grasped by knowledge or to be understood by the intellect. Through love everything in the universe as well as every human, is perfected.[171] Things like spiritual love are even more difficult to express for they are known to the heart or else not known at all. That was why

Ghazzali termed them as esoteric and inexpressible in words. First of all is the philosophical part of his work, then the metaphysical as in the '*Achemy of Happiness*' and the *Niche for Lights*, the third the hidden meaning, finally transmitted by word of mouth to those few who have been able to fully absorb his doctrine. Learning, by itself, cannot convey the Sufi ideal. It cannot grasp the inner experiences of saints or Sufis. Just as a child can't follow the thinking of an adult, divine knowledge evades the man of learning. These were the principles Ghazzali incorporated in his '*Revival of Religious Sciences*' but orthodox Moslems to whom the Commandments of Mohammed were sacrosanct, were incensed by these observations and publicy burnt his book in Spain. Ghazzali insisted on a correct approach to wisdom. In the '*Alchemy of Happiness*' he says 'There are many degress of knowledge. The mere physical man is like the ant crawling on paper who observes black lettering and attributes its production to the pen and to nothing more'.[172]

As we have mentioned, Ghazzali spent twelve years in solitary meditation trying to get over the I-sense and realizing the true self. According to the Dervish Order self-realization is necessary and in fact knowing one's real self is like knowing God. As Shakespeare says: 'This above all: to thine own self be true'.[173] Without knowledge of the self one cannot realize the truth of any religion. This is a belief of the Sufis and particularly those of the Dervish Orders, for which Moslems condemn them calling it paganism. The factors which the Dervishes consider as retarding this self-knowledge are ten in number, namely unreasoned desire which is got rid of by austere living; the feeling of separateness which is countered by sincerity and the realization of the brotherhood of man; the vanity and hypocrisy of people, which is corrected by humility and plain living; self-love as in Malvolio, 'O, you are sick of self-love Malvolio, and taste with a distempered appetite'.[174] This can be overcome by an objective view of oneself. The fifth impediment is illusions, countered by thinking of the Lord's glory; sixth avarice giving rise to envy, removed by the feeling of certainty (*yakina*); seventh greed countered by austerity and piety; eighth, irresponsibility removed by patience; the ninth overtiredness, overcome by prescribed exercises and finally negligence or sloth which is removed by being alert.

The Dervish order prescribes stages in the lives of persons much like the *asharamas* of Hinduism (*brahmachaya*, *grihastha*, *vanaprastha* and sannyasa the student, householder, forest-dweller and hermit). The Sufi stages are, however, three. The first stage of the dervish is serving others (*khidmat*); the second, the young people moving about in social assemblies and gathering knowledge; the stage of retirement the third and final one (resembling the *vanaprastha*-sannyasa *asharmas*) which is for the aged and senior citizens (the people of retirement – *Ahl-i-khilwat*). These people spend their time in solitude (but do not retire to the forests like the *vanaprashtas*) and carry on exercises suitable to their age.

Since the ordinary man is unable to understand the Sufi experience at times, Ghazzali says that allowance must be made for him for he is not able to grasp them as a blind man can't comprehend what's around him. Yet it would be unwise to deny something just because it can't be seen by a particular person. Dervishes do not favour ecstatic states and anyone exhibiting it. Sheikh Junayd once pulled up a man who fell into a frenzy at a Sufi meeting. Ghazzali points out that what seems to be the same, may have different functons. For example one is aware that the sun and the moon are large in size, but one may see them reflected in a small pool of water. A knife is handy in slicing fruits and vegetabels, yet the same knife may be used in stabbing and killing a person. In the '*Revival of Religious Sciences*' Ghazzali speaks about the self in its different aspects. It can be the means of sensual pleasures in its lower aspect which commands the undeveloped man, hence known as the Commanding Self. When the self calms the mind, removes confusion and harnesses emotions to the man's betterment, it is the Peaceful Self. When this same self brings to the notice of the man where he has gone wrong, it becomes the Accusatory Self. Men wrongly conceive uniformity in what is not constant. This recalls both the *Gita's* principle of the higher Self a man's helper when it is uppermost and his enemy when the lower self overpowers it[175] and also the Buddhist idea that there is constant change in that which appears to be changeless, as the river seems one but at every point the flowing water does not remain the same, or the flame of a candle burns steadily but the flame at any one instant is not same as the one before. In the same way, says Ghazzali in the '*Revival*', a human being keeps changing and what pleases him at one stage of his life no longer does so in another. Children like to play and do not know what marriage is. The aged man turns from sex to contemplation and when he is near death his thoughts turn to the other world. As Shakespeare say about man's seven ages:

> 'All the world's a stage
> And all the men and women merely players:
> They have thier exits and their entraces;
> And one man in his time plays many parts...'[176]

In his works Ghazzali presents many aspects of his teaching outwardly, though the inner meaning stays the same. In the *Minhaj el-Abidin* he speaks figuratively of consciousness going through seven modifications which he calls 'valleys' – of knowledge, turning back, obstacles, tribulations, lighting, abysses and praise. The bliss of a man depends on his thinking. If it is confined to the purely sensual it is merely outward happiness. When it seeks moral virtues it is of the inner kind and he has real knowledge. The right seeker contemplates a perfect Being and so has the greatest degree of happiness.

El-Ghazzali was doubtless one of the foremost Sufis of the Dervish Order, but his teaching has been often misrepresented as leaning toward orthodox Islam and Christianity. One great failing of religions has been to consider them or their adherents as superior to others. There can be no God's chosen people nor can any religion impress by condering itself superior. A Moslem commentator and translator of the Holy Quran says, 'the Book (the Quran) is so called because it is a collection of the best religious teachings and because it is a book that is or should be read and as a matter of fact it is the most widely read book in the whole world'![177] The Quran itself says, 'The (true) religion with God is Islam'. In the footnote the translator says 'the man who accepts that religion enters peace'![178] The persistent and often horrible incident of persecution of Hindus under the Moslem rule from Mahmud Ghazni to Aurangzebe, the rape of their women and the streams of blood which flowed in the name of Islam, hardly denotes that Islam offers even a distant semblance of peace as claimed for it. Ghazzali was not really the 'virtual father of the Moslem church' as professor Hitti is said to have observed.[179] Ghazzali's contribution really was that he realized Islam's shortcoming in so far as its unyielding bigotism was concerned and that was why he left his professorship to be in isolation and think it over for twelve long years. What he was searching for was the inner Self, in other words the Soul, the divine knowledge beyond oridinary understanding. It was these progressive ideas that enraged orthodox Moslems who did not appreciate what to them was mere calptrap, and led to the burning of his book '*Revival of Religious Sciences*' publicly. Ghazzali's service to the 'Moslem church', as professor Hitti puts it, was to remove that stigma from religion which Lucretius speaks of, 'How many crimes have been committed in the name of religion!'

Mention has already been made of the Naqshabandi Order of which the earliest saint was Khwaja Baqi Berang (d.A.D. 1603). Sheikh Ahmad Faruqi Sirhindi (1563-1625) gave it prominence. We have mentioned the uncompromising attitude of those of the Naqshabandi Order and nothing more needs to be said about them. Another school of Sufism which flourished mainly in Punjab was that of the Qadiri Order. Its original founder was Qadir Jilani (A.D. 1087-1166) and it came to Punjab with Sayyid Ghaus Wala Pir. Sultan Sikandar Lodi was his devotee. This order spread very rapidly and comprised more than twenty sub-sects. Dara Shikoh, who was an admirer of Hindu philosophy and had the *Upanishads, Bhagavadgita* and the *Yoga Vashishtha* translated into Persian, got initiation from Mullah Shah Badakhan. Dara was a broadminded and cultured Moslems. But his liberalism antagonized orthdox bigoted followers of Islam. Dara and his son Sipihr Shukoh, just a boy, were paraded through the streets of Delhi with ignominy, seated on the back of a small female elephant covered with dirt. Though Dara pleaded to be spared, Aurangzebe was not the man to show that mercy of which Seneca says 'It is impossible to imagine anything which better becomes a ruler than mercy'.[181] Dara was condemned to be executed for 'infidelity and deviation from Islamic orthodoxy'. The end was painful. The slaves sent to carry out the sentence rushed at the boy Sipihr who clung fast to his father and dragged him away. Then they fell on Dara. 'All this time Sipihr Shukoh's agonized shrieks were reaching his father's ears. A minute after the room grew still; the daggers of the slaves finished the work; the struggle ended in a pool of blood'.[182] This indeed is just one brick of the foundation on which, the 'Moslem church' as professor Hitti puts it, was founded, for it must not be forgotten that Dara was in spirit, a Sufi.

Among the Qadiri sect some practices of the Malamatias were also brought in, such as music and dancing. The Qadiris were often confused and full of contradictions in their views. One of them, Bahu, was a stickler for Islam, so much so that he tried to forcefully convert Hindus, yet he said that the Shariat is ignorant of that which is love's path. He considered worldliness to be a great impediment in living and likens worldly life to a corpse and worldly people to dogs and vultures eating it. Yet he lived a princely life marrying four wives, the number sanctioned for Moslems. On the one hand he was communal, on the other he considered the Self to be above communalism. He says that God is nearer to man 'even than thy own blood vein. The blind cannot see him'.[183] Besides Bahu believed in meditation, breath control (*prānāyāma*) and favoured the path of the yogis. Those who have realized reality, he says, keep quiet. Instead of going on the Mecca pilgrimage, he says he realized God in his heart. He also stressed, like other Sufis, that love's way is the best and love is like a lamp which lights up the path of the seeker.

Another Order was that of the Chishtis, whose founder was Khwaja Muin-ud-din Chishti. He was born in Sanjar, a town in Sietan and came to India at the end of the twelth century. He settled in Delhi but later shifted to Ajmer. His follower was Khwaja Bakhtiar Kaki and Kaki's disciple was Khwaja Fariduddin Masud Ganj-i-Shakar who founded the Chishti Order in the Punjab. Ganj-i-Shakar first lived in a town of Hissar district and then moved to a town of the name of Pakpatan where a tribe of backward Hindus lived. Nizami wrote it was because of Ganj-i-Shakar that the Chishti Order spread all over India and in many prominent places.[184] Farid's disciple was Sheikh Jamaluddin who was a distinguished scholar. He wrote a *dīwan* in Persian and a work in Arabic, the *Mulhamat*. Other disciples of Farid were Sheikh Ali Sabir who was responsible for the Sabiri Silsilah Order in the Saharanpur district of the United Provinces (now Uttar Pradesh), and Nizamuddin Aulia under whose guidance the Chishti Order reached its zenith. However Nizamuddins's thought depicts the same contradictions as Bahu's. He says that the person who does not conform to the Shariat is to be condemned. On the other hand he says that love of God's essence (*mohabbat-i-zat*) is a divine gift and the lover and Beloved must become one, an idea that is much akin to Vaishnavism.

Some writers have attributed fantastic miracles to Muin-ud-din Chishti, the founder of the Chisti order. It is said that Prithviraja did not like his entry in Ajmer and deputed some magicians and soldiers to prevent his entry, but Muin-ud-din threw some pebbles at them and they became blind! Further one glance of his caused three hundred yogis and pundits to lose their power of speech! Another screwy incident narrated is the a yogi named Jaypal brought with him thousands of his followers and interrupted the flow of water to the Anasagara lake. One of Chisti's followers took out a small amount of water in a vessel at which all the streams and wells dried up. Then Jaypal let loose lions and tigers to devour Chishti and his men, but he made a circle on the ground and as soon as they entered it they were all killed. Ultimately Jaypal acknowledged Muin-ud-din's superiority and became his disciple, presumably converted to Islam, as he took the name Abdulla, and he is believed to be ever present at Chishti's *dargaha* in Ajmer. Thus the old wives' tales go on and on, and the likely explanation for them is the author narrating these is his own deprecation of the 'professional Hindu ascetics' who he is convinced were 'wedded to a deteriorated tradition', and who 'tend to burst into print, to provide material for documentary photographers, to recruit disciples from abroad, to try to spread their teaching as widely as possible'.[185] Another misconception is the author's view of Hindu *shlokas* (*Shlokas*) which he considers as containing 'a great deal of popular wisdom', and that Hindus 'actually adopted the Arabic word for a dedicated Sufi–*Fakir*–and applied it to themselves'.[186] The Hindu ascetics lived long before the advent of printing and as for photography it is comical to think it existed in those times when neither the Islamic not the Christian civilizations had taken birth. These were the sages of the *Upanishads* which go back to the 7th-8th centuries before Christ, and of the Upanishads Schopenhauer observed 'In the whole world .... there is no study .. . so beneficial and so elevating as that of the *Upanishads*. They are products of the highest wisdom. They are sooner or later bound to become the faith of the people', and Deussen considered that they formulate 'philosophical conceptions unequalled in India or perhaps any–where else in the world'.

Some writers have the mistaken concept of a Hindu ascetic as one who does the rope-trick or subjugates his body to all kinds tortures, but an ascetic is simply a person of 'severe self-discipline' or one who 'leads a severely simple life without ordinary pleasures' (Advanced Learner's Dictionary of Current English, Oxford University Press). Thus anyone, a Moslem, Christian, Hindu or a follower of Jainism, a Sufi in fact of any religion, if he leads a life of detachment, is an ascetic. The ancient *Upanishads* were taught orally by sages to worthy disciples who were eager to learn. We are told that when the great emperor, Alexander, wished to see the Indian sage, Dandamis and sent him a message that he should come to him on pain of being beheaded, the sage merely smiled and gave a reply so befitting that Alexander yielded, his curiosity getting the better of him, and he himself went to the sage. The story is told in Megasthenes' *Memoirs*:

> 'When therefore the messenger (of Alexander) came to Dandamis, he addressed them thus: "The emperor Alexander, the son of the great Jupiter, who is lord of the human race, has ordered that you should hasten to him, for if you come, he will give you many gifts, but if you refuse he will behead you as a punishment for

you contempt". When these words came to the ears of Dandamis he rose not from his leaves whereon he lay, but reclining and smiling he replied in this way: "The greatest God", he said "can do injury to no one, but restores again the light of life to those who have departed. Accordingly he alone is my lord who forbids murder and excites no wars. But Alexander is no God, for he himself will have to die. How then, can he be lord of all, who has not yet crossed the river Tyberoboas, nor has he made the whole world his abode, nor has crossed the zone of Gades, nor has beheld the sun in the centre of the world? Therefore many nations do not yet know his name. If, however, the country he possesses cannot contain him, let him cross our river and he will find a soil which is able to support men. All those things Alexander promises would be useless to me if he gave them: I have leaves for a house, live on herbs at hand and water to drink: other things collected with labour, and which perish and yield nothing but sorrow to those seeking them or possessing them, – these I despise. I therefore now rest secure, and with closed eyes I care for nothing. If I wish to keep gold I destroy my sleep; earth supplies me with everything, as a mother does to her child. Whenever I wish to go, I proceed, and wherever I do not wish to be, no necessity of care can force me to go. And if he wish to cut off my head, he cannot take my soul; he will only take the fallen head, but the departing soul will leave the head like a portion of some garment, and will restore it whence it received it namely to the earth. But when I shall have become a spirit I shall ascend to God, who has enclosed it within this flesh. When he did this he wished to try us, how, after leaving him, we would live in this world. And afterward, when we shall have returned

> to him, he will demand from us an account of this life. Standing by him I shall see my injury, and shall contemplate his judgment on those who injured me: for the sighs and groans of the injured become the punishments of the oppressors.
>
> 'Let Alexander threaten with this them that desire riches or fear death, both of which I despise. For brahmins neither love gold not dread death. Go, therefore, and tell Alexander this: "Dandamis seeks nothing of yours, but if you think you need something of his, disdain not to go to him"'.[187]

The view that Hindu religion is pessimistic and unduly ascetic has for long been a chimerical idea of Western thinkers. Dr Albert Schweitzer for example, refers to 'life-negating ascetics' imposing their gloom on their followers. However, this is not so. Both Hinduism and Buddhism stress suffering only because it is there and is inevitable and undeniable. For that matter Gray's Elegy could be bracketed with the view of these ascetics and termed life-negating:

> 'The boast of heraldry, the pomp of power,
> And all that beauty all that wealth ever gave,
> Awaits alike the inevitable hour,
> The paths of glory lead but to the grave'.[188]

Yet it was these lines that moved General Wolfe when he was on the way to take Quebec; and which he read then and said that he would have rather written this Elegy than take Quebec! The Hindu ascetics did not gloat over sorrow or eulogize it. In fact they evolved ways to remove to and stressed that everlasting bliss was to be desired and coveted not transitory joys. The *Isha Upanishad* says, 'Always performing works here one should wish to live a hundred years',[189] and the *Rig Veda* has this verse:

'Here now remain, nor ever part
Enjoy the whole expanse of life,
With sons and grandsons joyous sport
Be glad in heart within your house'.[190]

Thus the disparaging comments on Hindu ascetics are without any justification and largely due to ignorance of Hinduism. So are the comments about *shlokas* and the word '*Fakir*'. In Hindi the word (*Fakir*) does not have the same significance as in Arabic, and specifically implies a beggar or mendicant. The Chambers Etymological English Dictionary defines it as 'a (esp. Mohammedan) religious mendicant in India (Ar. *faqir*, a poor man, *fakr*, *faqr*, poverty)'. Thus it was not Hindus who adopted this Arabic word, but it has entered English dictionaries just as many other words of Arabic or Sanskrit origin like 'cadi' (*kazi*), 'Kafir', 'karma', 'dharma' and so forth. Besides a Sufi is hardly a Fakir. As we have said the Sufi is not a mendicant and his 'religion' is not confined to Islam alone. Idries Shah himself has said 'the Sufi attitude toward money is a special one, far removed from the shallower, philosophical or theological assumptinon that money is the root of all evil, or that faith is in some way opposed to money'.[191] As we have mentioned many Sufis, like Sheikh Farid, Bahauddin Zakriya, and others married many wives and had a lot of wealth. How then can the Sufis and Fakirs be bunched together? As regards *shlokas* too the view expressed is completely mistaken. It is said to be supported by 'Abbe Dubois' great work Hindu Manners, Customers and Ceremonies (Oxford, 1906 pp; 474 et seq)'.[192] With deference to this 'great work', the interpretation of this Sanskrit word is completely mistaken. The *shlokas* are certainly in no sense 'Like the fables of Aesop or the tales of Saadi' for merely good advice upon which one could rear one's children, or for their inner meaning'.[193] They mean simply couplets or stanzas of mainly Sanskrit works. The *shlokas* were generally meant to impart divine knowledge and philosophical thoughts and weren't by any stretch of the imagination fables or advice. Anyone who considers them to be so has obviously never made any study of them in the original or any of the authoritative translations of them by authors who have acquaintance with the original Sanskrit.

A Minor order which existed in India in the fifteenth to early seventeenth century was that of the Shattaris. Its founder was Abdulla a descendant of Shahabuddin Suhrawardi. Humayun, the Mogul emperor, was initiated in this order and was Shah Mohammed Ghaus' disciple. Others associated with the Shattaris were Wajid-ud-din Gujrati (1599) and Sant Shah O Pir (1632). Anayat Shah, Bullhe Shah and Raza Shah were of the Shattari order as well as of the Qadiri. Some Sufis were of a minor order known as Be-Shara, as they did not follow the religious practices of *Shara*. A few of them considered themselves to be a branch of the Suhrawardi order. Their main sects were the Qalandiri, Madari and Malamati.

Some of the saints in these order were Lal Shahbazi, Rasul Shahi Musasuhagi, and Sharaf-ud-din Bu Ali of Panipat (a Qalandri). The Malamatis could hardly be termed saints as they were in the habit of taking intoxicants like wine, opium, hemp etc. They neither performed the *namaz* regularly, nor observed the Ramadan fast.

Hindu creeds and religious thought influenced a number of Sufis to a very great extent. Vedanta, Vaishnavism, the school of Natha Yogis and the *Bahkti* Movement, all had their impact in some way. The Sufis were also influenced by Buddhism, particularly its emphasis on meditation, ascetism, monasticism, celibacy revering saints and in the belief in *Fana*. Gorakhnath the founder of Nathism had a number of Moslem disciples, such as Apanath and Rattan Haji. The Mogul emperors Akbar, Jahangir and Shah Jahan were indulgent to the yogis. Breath-control (*prāṇāyma*) was advocated by Pātanjali in his *Yogasutras*: 'After posture is attained there follows *prāṇāyāma* which means retention of the breath after it has been inhaled or exhaled .... By practising *prāṇāyāma* the evil karma of the yogi is destroyed. Impurity is eliminated the light of knowledge shines. And further, the mind becomes fit for concentration.'[194] The Sufis considered breath-control and other such practices to produce the state of ecstasy (*hal*). The Sufi *zikra* also showed the influence of yoga. According to a writer on Sufism, the Sufis said that in the repetition of *la ilaha ill-Allah* they concentrate on *la ilaha* while exhaling and on *Ill-Allah* while inhaling. [195] We have mentioned in the earlier part of this book the *latalif* (subtle ones) of the Sufis. These are analogous to the six *chakras* of yoga (the *mulādhāra, svādishthāna, manipura, anāhata, vishuddha and ājnā*). The Sufi *chakras are nafs, qulb, ruh, sirr khafi* and *akhfa* respectively below the navel, on the left side of the chest, on the right side of it, between the *qalb* and the *ruh*, the forehead and in the brain. The Sufis and the yogis were very closely connected, but for one thing–the Sufis emphasized love which had no place in yoga which had as its objective absolute freedom 'when the *guṇas* (qualities), being devoid of the object of the Purusha, become latent; when consciousness in established in its own nature...... With the attainment of this absolute freedom the final goal of the yogi is achieved'.[196] For the Sufi however without love there is no achievement. As Rumī said 'Wherever you are, whatever is your state, always try to be a lover'.

The *bhakti* movement also had a great impact on Sufism. The Sufis of the Qadiri order studied the *Upanishads* and other books of Indian philosophy. As we have narrated before Ibn El-Arabi wrote love poetry in his '*Interpreter of Desires*', which was sublime and in the Vaishnave *bhakti* style and that was why fanatic Moslems called him a liar and a heretic and when he went to Mecca he narrowly escaped being assassinated. Arabi's doctrine of *wahdatul wajud* had much in common with the Vedanta. This doctrine was also advocated by Hafiz Barkhurder, Bullhe Shah and Ali Haider. Farid Sani and Shah Hussain endorsed the *bhakti* cult. Another idea which the Sufis adopted was that God redeems the sins of the *bhakta* (devotee). As the Lord says in the *Gita - pratijānīhi na me bhaktaḥ praṇashyati*: 'know for certain my devotee can never perish'.[197] So too the Sufis believed that God is the redeemer of the devotee. Shah Hussain and Bullhe Shah say that only the grace of God can wash away one's sins.

Another belief of the Sufis was the wife-husband relationship in the Vaishnava *mādhurya bhāva*. They sometimes considered themselves as lovers and God as the Beloved. When Nizam-ud-din Aulia died, Khusro, his disciple. spoke thus; *gorī soye chaina se mukha para bikhare kesa| cala khusaro ghara āpane, raina bhai cahuṃ desha||* 'The fair one is sleeping with her tresses spread on her face. Come home now Khusro for the day is spent and darkness envelopes the world'.[198] Farid Sani considers God as *kanta* (husband). Yet another development of the Sufis inclining to Hindu thought was that Moslem and Hindu came together. Kabir was greatly instrumental in bringing this about. He said: *kārī piyarī duhahū gāī, tākara dūdha dehu bilagagāī* - 'One cow is black, another yellowish, but is not the milk of both the same?[199] And again:

> 'Those who believed that in this Kali-age
> The *kalimā* would bring one near to the divine
> Could themselves not know God though they essayed
> Self-centred, they did only works that bind.
> The Vedas and the Quran also speak
> Or works that led to repeated births and deaths:
> Do you think the Hindu's sacred thread

Or the circumcision of the Turk
Can by themselves know race or religion?
It's only the man who can diligently search
Inside himself who can have God-vision.

The same Soul dwells in beings everywhere
How can it ever be affected by caste
Or by the accursed body formed of water and air?
For the Soul is immortal, and the body does not last'.[200]

It may be added, however, that the Sufis were embarking on an impossible task in attempting Hindu-Moslem unity even though their effort was laudable, for Islam has always remained, and will ever be, impervious to any effort to dilute its bigotry, for that is eternally embodied in its scriptures.

A doctrine which finds place in Sufism is the concept of maya. In Islam we have Iblis or Satan who is God's opponent. The Holy Quran says 'And when We said to the angels, Make obeisance to Adam, they did obeisance, but Iblis (did not): he refused and was proud, and he was one of the unbelievers'.[201] The man difference between the concept of Satan and that of maya is that while Satan remains ever God's defier, maya is the slave or *shakti* (energy) of God. The *Shvetashvatara Upanishad* (4:10) says 'know then that nature is maya and the great lord *mayavin* (the make of maya). In the *Ramacharitamanasa* the lord is called *mayapti* or the master of maya (*Uttarakanda*, 62 B) and its prime mover (*maya praraka- Aranyakanda*, 15). So really God has no opponent according to the Vedanta, but his delusive power is maya through which truth is concealed (*āvarana*) and misrepresented (*vikshepa*). For example, every man knows that death comes to all. He sees people dying, his friends and relations, yet the thought of death never enters his mind. Thus this truth (of the inevitability of death) remains hidden from him by maya's power of *āvarana*. Then again one knows that when death comes something–call it the *atman* or *ruh* or spirit - leaves the body, so that the person who was erstwhile speaking, moving, seeing etc., cannot any longer do so, even though his entire body is intact (as the *Brihadaranyaka Upanishad*, Chapter 4 says) 'This lifeless body is then of no account, as a snake's abandoned slough lying on an anthill. And the soul that has left it shines with the light of the supreme *Brahman*'. Yet people think, when they think about themselves, that they are the body. They say 'this is *my* head, these are *my* eyes, limbs, hands, feet and so on'. Thus in so doing maya's power *vikshepa* (misrepresentation) works in making the person mistake the body as reality instead of the soul. Bearing this difference in mind between the Moslem Iblis or Satan and the Hindu concept of maya, it may be said that the Sufi saints muckraked maya as the power of delusion. Bahadur, the Punjabi Sufi poet, pictures maya as a woman magician who plays on the lute and makes everybody dance to her tune. Shah Husain considers the world as God's sport (*līlā*). This, too, is the view of Hindu philosophy: 'This world' says Sri Ramakrishna 'is the *līlā* of God. It is like a game. In this game there are joy and sorrow, virtue and vice, knowledge and ignorance, good and evil. The game cannot continue if sin and suffering are altogether eliminated from creation'.[202]

Kabīr also mentions maya which he says makes people sin and has 'spread her net in the world as a cheat keeping shop in the marketplace'. It tastes, he says 'sweet as jaggery and so it makes everyone its prey', and is a demoness 'who tears everyone to pieces with her teeth'. Maya captivates 'even the wisest of men. They cannot escape, for it sends bewitching arrow-like glances after them by which they are helplessly enslaved'.[203]

Although the Sufis did not believe in the Hindu theory of avatars, Some of them express, like the Punjabi Sufi poets, Ghulam Husain and Barkhurdar their affinity of Lord Krishna.[204] Nissar wrote his *Yusuf Zalaikhan* in the Vaishnava manner, and it has many references to Hindu philosophy. According to him as a consequence of reading it sins are redeemed and virtues attained. The barren woman gets children, the poor wealth, the fools wisdom, the miserable happiness. the learned joy in knowledge, prisoners freedom, those diseased heath, those separated union and the lovers, love's fulfillment.[205]

Another influence on Sufism in general, and particularly in Punjab, was that of Vaishnavism, *bhakti* and *Vedanta*. So great was this influence that many Moslems got reconverted to the Hindu faith. This alarmed the orthodox Moslems who raised the cry of Islam in danger and they rallied round their leader, Ahmad Sirhindi who in retaliation enunciated his own doctrine of *wahdatushshahud*. A section of Moslems were won over, like Farad Faqir and Ghulam Rasul who became Ijadist Sufis. Some, like Bullhe Shah and Ghulam Jilani Rohtak did not leave the Vaishnave path. Yet another section denounced the Vedantic and pantheistic creeds and were for neo-Platonism as expressed by Ibn El-Arabi's doctrine of *wahadat-uwwajud*, but they continued their doctrine of Vaishnava love and the Beloved lover relationship. Among these Sufis were Hafis Barkhurdar, Karim Buksha, Ali Haider, Ahmad Yar and others.

In order to comprehend what the creed of the neo-Platonic Sufis was, one has to go back to the Hellenic philosophy of Plato. The word neo-Platonism literally means ' a mixture of Platonic ideas with Oriental Mysticism'. Plato reversed the earlier Greek beliefs by holding that the soul is far more real than the body. It is, he said, truly divine, a being immortal in its own right and not the gift of any higher divinity. It has existed, therefore, always and will continue to exist after it has attained final release from the body after the chain of births and rebirths.[206]. For this reason the care of the soul is the most important thing. Cicero, the philosopher, says:

'If I am in error in believing that the soul of man is immortal, I err willingly; nor have I any desire, while life lasts, to eradicate the error in which I take delight. But if, after death (as some small philosophers think), I shall feel nothing, I have no fear that those departed philosophers will ridicule my error'.[207]

And again;

> 'The divine soul is drawn from its lofty home, and, so to say, plunged into the earth, an abode which is by its nature the antithesis of divinity and eternity'.[208]

Plato also emphasized that there is reward in the next world for good works and punishment for those evil, thus reiterating the Hindu karma theory. It these elements of neo-Platonism that these Sufis adopted. According to them God revealed himself in the world of forms, he being its essence.

To sum up, the Sufi orders were basically of three kinds. One stuck to orthodoxy like the Idajists and were opposed to any compromise with faiths other than Islam. The second showed affinity to Vaishnavism and many of the other Hindu beliefs. In between were those who were neither strictly orthodox nor inclined to the Vedanta, but still not averse to love as expressed by Vaishnavism, like El-Gazzali and others.

REFERENCES

1. For example Professor, M.A. Shushtery. *The Sufi Mystery* p., 58 says 'The classical Sufis of Islam, the great Vedantists India and the Mystics of Europe lived between the 8th and the 15th centuries'.

2. The Sufi Mystery, ed. N.P. Archer. Philosophy, Training, Orders and Ethics, p., 59 R.A. Nicholson. *The Idea of Personality in Sufism* p., 8 op. cit.
3. *Four Sufi Classics*. London : Octagone Press, On Love, pp., 211-12 [Adapted].
4. *The Sufi Mystery*, ed. N.P. Archer. London; Octagon Press, 1980, p., 61 (The author is indebted to *The Sufi Mystery* for the material about these early saints).
5. Related in *Four Sufi Classics*. Octagon Press, pp., 191-92.
6. *The Sufis*. Idries Shah. Doubleday 1964. Robert Graves. Introduction, p., vii.
7. *Four Sufi Classics*. London : Octagon Press, 1980 'On Humour'. p., 213.
8. Trans; Muhammad Ali : Lahore : Anjuman-I-Ishaat-I-Islam. 1928. 9 : 29.
9. *Bhagavadgita*. 12 : 3.
10. Aeschylus. *Agamemnon. Chorus*. 171 and 250
11. *Katha Upanishad*. 1. 29.
12. Samuel Taylor Coleridge. *The Ancient Mariner*.
13. *The Sufi Message of Hazrat Inayat Khan*, vol., 1. London : Barrie and Rockliff, 1960. p., 56.
14. Roger Bacon. *Opus Majus*, trans.; R.B. Burke, 1928.
15. The Holy Bible. New Testament. *St John*, 18 : 37 - 38.
16. *The Sufi Message of Hazrat Inayat Khan*. London : Barrie and Rockliff, vol. 1, 1960, p., 240.
17. *The Word of God and the Word of Man* Trans.; Dougtas Horton, 1958.
18. E. Swedenborg. *Arcana Coelesta*.
19. *Gita* 2. 16.
20. Murti, T.R.V. *The Central Philosohpy of Buddhism*.
21. Robert Burns. *Tam o' Shanter*.
22. *shreyah cha preyah cha manushyam etah tau samparitya vivinakti dhīrah/sheryo hi dhīro abhipreyaso vrinīte preyo mando yogashemād vrinīte. Katha Upanishad* 2.2.

23. *Abt Vogler* IX.
24. *Seven Meditations*. Isherwood. *Vedanta for the Western World*.
25. Evelyn Underhill. London: Methuen, 1911, p., 81.
26. *St. Matthew*. xix 16.24
27. *Katha Upanishad*. 2 : 3 and 6.
28. The Holy Bible. St. Luke. 16 : 13.
29. *Bhagavadgita*, 14 : 24.
30. Kabīr *Padas from the Guru Grantha Sahīb*. Bahadur, K.P. *A New Look at Kabīr*. New Delhi : Ess Ess Publication, p., 212.
31. *Metamorphoses* I., 131. *Amor sceleratus habendi*.
32. The anecdotes about Zen are mentioned in D.T. Suzuki. *Zen and japanese Culture* London : Routledge and Kegan Paul, 1959.
33. The Holy Quran. Trans.; Muhammad Ali. Lahore : Ahmadiyya Anjuman-I-Ishaat-I-Islam, 1928, 9 : 4 : 29 (pp., 194 - 5) and 9 : I : 5 (p., 191). Italics author's.
34. Idries Shah. *The Sufis*. New York : Doubleday Dell Publishing Group Inc. 1964, p., 403.
35. *Gita*. 9 : 31 and 9 : 29.
36. ibid. 18 : 65.
37. Voltarie. Philosophical Dictionary, 1964.
38. John Stuart Mill. *On Liberty*. London : John W. Parker and Son, West Strand M. DGCC. Lix, pp., 65- 66.
39. Adlous Huxley. *The Perennial Philosophy*. London : Chatto and Windus, 1946, p., 206 op. cit.
40. *The Sufis*. Idries Shah. Anchor Books pp., 23 - 24.
41. *The Sufi Message of Hazrat Inayat Khan*. London : Barrie and Rockliff 1960, vol. 1, p., 83.
42. ibid.
43. Harsh Narian. *Zizyah and the spread of Islam*. New Delhi : Voice of India, 1990, p.1 (quoting A'l 'Imrān [3] 110., An - Nūr [24] 55; an-Naml [27] 62, Āl 'Imrān [3] 19. 85, At-Tawbah [9] 33 and various other sources.).

44. Trans.; Muhammad Ali. Lahore : Ahmadiyya Anjuman-I-Ishaat-I-Islam, 1928, p., 293. The translator's note says 'Antichrist (*Dajjāl*) is nothing but Christianity in its present form'.
45. Harsh Narain. *Jizyah and the spread of Islam*. New Delhi : Voice of India, 1990, 1990 pp., 13-14.
46. The Holy Bible *Exodus* : 20. 2 - 6.
47. ibid. 20 : 10 - 11.
48. Shakespeare. *The Merchant of Venice*. Act IV scence I.
49. *Bhagavadgita* 12 : 3 - 4.
50. *Gita* 9 : 23.
51. ibid. 18 : 63.
52. Idries Shah. *The Sufis*, p., 105.
53. *The Sākhīs*. Maya. Tran.; author's.
54. Robert Browing. *Rabbi Ben Ezra*.
55. Rama Chandra Shukla. *Hindi Sahitya kā Itihasa*, p., 320.
56. Vincent Smith. *Akbar, the Great Mughal*, 1962.
57. Alfred, Lord Tennyson. *Akbar's Dream*.
58. Quoted in Idries Shah. *The Sufis*, p., 325. Italics author's.
59. *The Sufi Message of Hazrat Inayat Khan*. vol. 1. London : Barrie and Rockliff, 1960, pp., 18 - 19.
60. *Bhagavadgita*. 18 : 72 - 73.
61. *The Bhagavad - Gita*. Trans.; Prabhavanand and Isherwood. Mentor Books Introduction.
62. ibid.
63. *Premavātikā* 6.
64. ibid. 23.
65. Bhagavadgita. 7 : 7 - 12.
66. *The Sufi Message of Hazrat Inayat Khan*. London: Barrie and Rockliff, vol. 1, 1960, p., 196. op. cit.
67. *Vivekachuṛāmaṇī*, 102.
68. Brihadarāṇyaka Upanishad. 4 : 1 - 13.

69. *Bhagavadgita*. 3 : 5, 8, 22- 24.
70. ibid. 18 : 5 - 6.
71. *Bhagavadgita*, 12 : 17.
72. ibid. 14 : 22.
73. Jalaluddin Rumī
74. *Bhagvadgita*. 9 : 29.
75. ibid, 2 : 66
76. Ansari of Herat.
77. A.K. Chadhry. *Are you Listening Mr Vajpaee. The Pioneer* 17 April 1998.
78. *Paradise Lost* Book iv line 295.
79. The Holy Quran. Trans.; Muhamad Ali, Lahore : Anjuman-I-Ishaat-I-Islam, 1928., p., 86 Part V, ch., 4 Sn., 6 verse 34.
80. Idries Shah. *The Sufis*. Anchor Books, 1924, p., 152.
81. Prem Lata. *Sri Ramakrishna Paramahamsa*. New Delhi : Sumit Publications, p., 102.
82. Idries Shah. The *Sufis*. Anchor Books, 1964, p., 152.
83. *Chandogyaupanishad*. 8 : 1 - 6.
84. *uddhared ātmanā 'tmānaṃ*
   nā 'tmānam avāsadayet|
   ātmaiva hy ātmano bandhura
   ātmaiva ripura ātmanaḥ||
   bandhura ātmā 'tmanas tasys
   yenā 'tmaivā 'tmanā jitaḥ|
   anātmanas tu śatrutve
   vartetā 'tmaiva śatruvat|| *Gita* 6 : 5 - 6.
85. *manushyaṇāṃsahasreshu*
   kashcid yayati siddhaye|
   yatatām api siddhānāṃ
   kashcin māṃvetti tattvataḥ|| *Gita*. 7 : 3.
86. Jili. *The Perfect Man. The Sufis*. Idries Shah op cit pp., 160 - 61.

87. El-Arabi *The Bezels of Wisdom*. Idries Shah. *The Sufis*. opcit.
88. John Keats. *Ode on a Grecian Urn*.
89. *Fragment* 14. “Μορφά, θηλνγψέρηστδ' ‘*aλk’a*”
90. Quoted in Idries Shah. *The Sufis* New York : Anchor Books, 1964, p., 165.
91. A.E. Affifi. *The Mystical Philosophy of Muhyiud Din lbnal Arabi*, p., 54.
92. S. Radhakriashan. *History of Philosophy Eastern and Western* vol. 1, p., 500.
93. *Shvetashvatara Upanishad*. 5 : 3, 6 : 10.
94. *Bhagavadgita*. 9 : 4 - 6.
95. ibid. 5 : 8 - 9.
96. Titus Burckhardt. *An Introduction to the Sufi Doctrine*. Trans.; Mohammed Ashraf, p., 93.
97. *Bhagavadgita*. 10 : 15.
98. S. Radhakrishnan. *History of Philosohpy Eastern and Western*, vol. 1, p., 499.
99. Idries Shah *The Sufis*. Anchor Books 1964, p., 161.
100. *St Luke*. 10 : 25 - 37. The Holy Bible. New Testament.
101. 99 : 7 - 8. Trans.; Muhammad Ali. Lahore : Ahamadiyya Anjaman-I-Ishaat-Islam, 1928.
102. ibid. 24 : 47.
103. ibid. 42 : 25 - 26.
104. *Bhagavadgita*. 3 : 25.
105. ibid, 9 : 29, 30 - 31.
106. *Siyar-ul-Aulia*. p., 237.
107. ibid. p., 411.
108. *Fawa' id-ul Fuād*. p., 130.
109. ibid. pp., 86 - 87.
110. *Sskhis from the Guru Grantha Sahib*. Ess Ess Publications New Delhi, 1997 p., 280.
111. *St. John* 3 : 8. The Holy Bible. New Testament.

112. *Isha upanishad*, 9.
113. *The Cultural Heritage of India*. Calcutta: Sri Ramakrishna Centenary. Belur Math. III, p., 384.
114. Umr bin Shahbauddin Subrawardi (urdu trans.;) *Awariful Muarif.* (Trans; Rashid *Ahmad Arshad*, pp., 250, 246.)
115. Shakespeare. *Twelfth Night*. Act 1, scene 1 1. 1 - 7.
116. Idries Shah. *The Sufis*. New York : Acnhor Books, 1964, pp., 55 - 56.
117. Bertrand Russel. *History of Western Philosophy*, p., 345.
118. Shushtery, A.M.A. *Outlines of Islamic Culture*, p., 367.
119. Tiwari, R.P. *Sufimat-Sādhanā our Sāhitya*, p., 215.
120. Arberry, A.J. *Sufism*, London, 1950.
121. *The Sufi Message of Hazrat Inayat Khan*. London : Barrie and Rockcliff, vol. 1 1960, p., 13.
122. *Exodus* 20 : 3 - 4.
123. Sharma, S.R., *The Religious Policy of the Mughal Emperors*. Bombay, 1962, p., 16.
124. *Bhagavadgita* 14 : 237.
125. About women in general, 'other women cloy the appetites they feed'. *Antony and Cleopatra*.
126. *Guru Grantha Sahib* Trans.; Dr Dardi, G.S.W. 30 and 103.
127. Dr. Shah, H.S. *Sufi Kāvya Sangraha*, p., 97.
128. ibid. p., 154.
129. ibid. p., 157.
130. ibid., 153 158.
131. *The Sufi Message of Hazrat Inayat Khan* London : Barrie and Rocklift, 1960, p., 56.
132. Alfred, Lord Tennyson. *In Memoriam* L III.
133. Max Müller *Ramakrishna-His Life and Sayings*.
134. ibid. (Summarized version).,
135. *The Sufi Message of Hazrat Inayat Khan*. London : Barrie and Rockliff, 1960, p., 60.
136. *Bhagavadgita*. 7 : 28.

137. ibid. 8 : 6.
138. *The Gospel of Sri Ramakrishna*. Trans.; Swami Nikhilananda. Madras : Sri Ramakrishna Math, 1964.
139. *The Sufi Message of Hazrat Inayat Khan* London : Barrie and Rockcliff, 1960, p., 41 op. cit.
140. *Chandogya Upanishad* 6 : 8 - 16. Trans., author's.
141. *The Gospel of Sri Ramkrishna*.
142. *Ramakrishna - his Life and Sayings*. Max Miiller.
143. Subhan, John A. *Sufism, its Saints and Shrines*. Lucknow, 1938., p., 130 (italics author's)
144. Idries Shah. *The Sufis*. Introduction, p., viii New York : Anchor
145. *The Gospel of Sri Ramakrishna*.
146. *The Sufi Message of Hazrat Inayat Khan*. London : Barrie and Rockcliff, vol. 1, p., 19.
147. Diogenes was a noted cynic philosopher (c. 413-323 B.C.) who lived in a tub. According to one version Alexander the Great so admired him that he said 'If I was not Alexander, I would to be Diogenes'. According to another version Alexander with great vanity asked Diogenes to have whatever he desired. Diogenes, who was enjoying the sun's warmth while in his tub, snubbed the emperor by saying. 'I wish you would move off a little away for you are blocking my sun'!
148. Trans.; Muhammad Ali. Lahore : Ahmadiyya Anjuman-I-Ishat-Islam, 9 : 1 : 5 (p., 191) - italies author's.
149. Elliot and Dowson. *The History of India as Told by its Own Historians*. Trübner, 1871, vol. 3, p., 427.
150. ibid. vol. 8, pp., 78 - 80 (recorded in *Tazkirā*).
151. *Bazm-i-Sufia*. Rehman, Sabahuddin Abdul, p., 24.
152. Masood, Wahid Ahmad. *Swaneh Khwaja Muinudi-din Chishti*, p., 290.
153. Nizami, K.A. *Life and Times of Farid-ud-din Ganj-i-Shakar* p., 107.
154. Sabahuddin, *A.R. Bazmi-i Sufia* p., 11.

155. ibid. p., 230.
156. *Bhagavadgita* 10 : 16 and 42.
157. *Katha Upanishad.* 6 : 3. Trans.; author's.
158. Nabi, M.N. *The Development of Muslim Thought in India*, p., 63.
159. *Bhagavadgita* 11 : 8.
160. *The Gospel of Sri Ramakrishna.*
161. Nabi, M.N. *The Development of Muslim Religious Thought in India*, p., 67.
162. The *Pioneer.* 11 April 1998 p., 1.
163. Nizami, K.A. *The Life and Times of Farid-ud-Din Ganj-l-Shakar*, p., 87.
164. Nabi, M.N. Development of Muslim Religious Thought in India, p., 46.
165. ibid. pp., 99 - 100.
166. *The Gospel of Sri Ramakrishna.*
167. Nizami, K.A. Some *Aspects of Religion and Politics of India in the Thirteenth Century*, p., 226.
168. *Vivekachuramani* 308 - 311.
169. ibid. 312.
170. Sanskrit Love Poetry. Trans.; W.S. Merwin and J. Moussaief Masson. New York : Columbia University Press, 1977.
171. Shushtery, A.M.A, *Outlines of Islamic Culture*, p., 311.
172. *The Allchemy of Happiness.* Idries Shah. *The Sufis* Anchor Books, New York. 1964, p., 177 op. cit.
173. *Hamlet.* Act 1, scene 3.
174. Shakespeare. *Twelfth Night* Act 1, scene 5.
175. *Bhagavadgita* 6 : 6.
176. *As You Like It.* Act 2, scene 7.
177. The Holy Quran tran.; Muhammad Ali. Lahore : Anjuman-I-Ishaat-I-Islam, 1926, Introduction p., ix.
178. ibid. 3 : 18, p., 56 anf fn.

179. Idries Shah. *The Sufis*. New York : Anchor Books, 1964, p., 167.
180. *De Rerum Natura* I. 95. Tantum religio potuit suadere malorum!
181. Seneca. *De Clementia*. I. 19.1.
182. Jadunath Sarkar. *History of Aurangzib*, 1912. Vol. 2, p., 219.
183. *Diwan-i-Bhau*. ed., Ghafoor Khan.
184. Nizami, K.A. *Some Aspects of Religion and Politics in India in the Thirteenth Century*, p., 190.
185. Idries Shah. *The Sufis*. New York : Anchor Books 1964, pp., 405 - 6.
186. ibid, p., 406 and p., 404.
187. Megasthenes *Ancient India*. J.W. Mc Crindle pp., 127 - 129.
188. Thomas Gray. Elegy Written in a Country Churchyard, ix.
189. *Isha Upanishad* 1 : 2 Trans.; Dr S. Radhakrishnan.
190. *Rig Veda* 10 : 85 : 42.
191. Idries Shah. *The Sufis* Anchor Books, 1964, p., 105.
192. ibid. pp., 406-7.
193. ibid. p., 406.
194. Patanjali *Yogasutras* 3 : 51 - 53. Tran.; author's.
195. Bishop John. A. Subhan. *Sufism, its Saints and Shrines*, p., 150.
196. Patanjali's *Yogasutras* 5 : 34. Trans., author's.
197. *Gita*. 9 : 31.
198. *Jayasī Granthāvalī* ed. R. Shukla, p., 307.
199. Kabir. *Ramainīs*. Trans.; author's Ess Ess Publications, New Delhi 1997.
200. ibid.
201. Trans.; Muhammad Ali. Lahore Ahmadiyya Anjuman-I-I shaat-I-Islam, 1928. 2 : 34. Also 7 : 11, 12 : 15 : 31 - 37,

3

Fundamental Beliefs

Even though a string has a hundered knots, it remains one string.

Jalalauddin Rumī

The Sufi is broadminded enough to allow the doctrines of other faiths too in certain aspects of theirs provided they conform to truth. Truth is perhaps difficult to define, as we have mentioned one of Mulla Nasrudin's anecdontes to depict, in which to a king who was determined that truth would prevail in his kingdom was surprised when the Mulla said that there is real truth and relative truth, and proceeded to show that it was really so. But even though truth may be difficult to define it is easy to understand. Besides it is no dogma, for then truth would be confined to a particular thinking of a special race or community. That is why no religion can be the sole repository of truth and any religion which forces itself on others than its own believers, by so doing is a self-confession of its own falseness. As Fredrick (II) the Great says `All religions must be tolerated...' Therefore the Sufi concept of God is that he is God of all creeds, call him by whatever name you like – Allah, Khuda Bhagavan or such other name. The God of the Sufis exists everywhere, in the sun, fire and even in the idols worshipped by various creeds. He resides in the soul and the souls of all persons is the same, so there cannot be anything like racial or communal animosity. As a Bengali poet Pagālā Kānāi puts it : One says Durga or Hari, the other Bismilla: but they drink the same water. One wears a rosary the other is circumcised: then, O brothers, why do you fight and ruin yourselves?[1] The Sufi believes that God sends a divine messenger of earth in human guise such as Mohammed, Jesus, Abraham, Moses, Shiva, Buddha Rama, Krishna and so forth. Hazrat Inayat Khan says: 'To the Sufi therefore there is only one Teacher, however differently He may be named at different periods of history, and He comes constantly to awaken humanity from the slumber of this life of illusion, and to guide man onwards towards divine perfection.[2] This idea may not be exactly the belief in avatar, but it comes very near it, as in the *Gita* the Lord saya: 'Whenever righteousness declines, and unrighteous increases, then indeed, O Arjuna, I incarnate myself. To protect the virtuous, to destroy the wicked and to establish righteouosness, I come into being from age to age'.[3] At another place the Lord says: 'Seeing Me assume a human form fools despise Me: they do not know that I am the Supreme Lord of all creatures'.[4] As we have said before some Sufis like Ghulam Hussain, Barkhurdar and Nissar remembered God through Krishna who is a Hindu avatar. The Sufi calls the Master *Murshīd*, and he believes that everyone old or young, rich or poor, learned or unlearned is taught by the *Murshīd*. The Sufis do not restrict themselves to any one scriptures. They believe that all scriptures are to be revered, whether it is the Quran, Bible, Zendavesta or the Buddhist ones, the Vinaya-pitaka, Samyutta-nikāya, Dīgha-nikaya, Dhammapada and so forth. The greatest scripture is Nature which, so to say, speaks through every leaf, flower rock and tree, as Wordworth the English poet says:

> 'I have learned
> To look on nature, not as in the hour
> Of thoughtless youth; but hearing often-times
> The still, sad music of humanity,
> Nor harsh nor grating, though of ample power
> To chasten and subdue. And I have felt
> A presence that disturbs me with the joy
> Of elevated thoughts; a sense sublime

Of something far more deeply interfused,
Whose dwelling is the light of setting suns,
And the round ocean and the living air
And the blue sky, and in the mind of man'.[5]

And again,

'The world is too much with us; late or soon
Getting and spending we lay waste our powers
Little we see in Nature that is ours;
We have given our hearts away, a sordid boon!
This sea that bares her bosom to the moon;
The winds that will be howling at all hours,
And are up-gathered now like sleeping flowers;
For this, for everything, we are out of tune;
It moves us not'.[6]

Thus Nature is the world's scriptures and tells as eloquently as them the glory of the Lord, if only one has the eyes to see or the ears to listen.

To the Sufi all religions and places of worship are the same, whether the mosque or temple or church. The Hindus conceive righteousness as dharma and Sa'adi says, 'Every soul is born for a certain purpose and the light of that purpose is kindled in his soul'.[7]

For the majority of men the family circle is all they know and care about. They restrict themselves to their sons and daughters and there blood relations. A few move out of this circle to their friends and acquaintances. A still smaller number can reach out to those who are neither family members or relations, or friends. It is these who look on mankind as one universal brotherhood, and eschew the limitations of race and religion for these often separate rather than unite. The Sufi transcends such racial, national and religious boundaries and distinctions of caste, creed race or religion. As Lord Krishna says in the *Gita – kalyaṇkrit kashcid durgatiṁ tāta gacchati* — 'He who strives for the good of all mankind can never come to grief'.[8]

As has been said before love is one of the foremost concepts of Sufism. But what does love really mean? According to the Sufis it is the source of all good and noble qualities – hope, patience, forgiveness, kindness, tolerance, beneficence, generosity. As Virgil says love is all-encompassing and extends to the whole creation:

> Yes, all that breathes the breath of life
> Is aflame with the unresisting fire of love,
> Man, beast and the creatures of the sees
> And birds that keep flying in the air.[9]

Euripides says:

> He who thinks not that Love is a mighty god
> Higher than all the deities of heaven
> Is all uncultured; or, unversed in beauty
> Knows not the god who ruleth over man.[10]

And the Bible says `He that loveth not knoweth not God; for God is love'.[11] We have spoken in detail about the prominence given to love by Sufi saints. Rumī says `Hail to thee, then, O love, sweet madness! Thou who healest all our infirmities! Who art the physician of our pride and self-conceit! Who art our Plato and our Galen!'[12] While certainly love is the guiding principle of inner life, its expression takes various forms. One man may love the beauty of his beloved, another the soul within, as in one of his poems W.B. Yeats says:

> `How many loved your moment of glad grace,
> And loved your beauty with love false or true;
> But one man loved the pilgrim soul in you,
> And loved the sorrows of your changing face'.

To the Sufi both kinds of love are acceptable. Ibn El-Arabi's `*Interpreter of Desires*' has been mentioned aforesaid as love poetry and he realized that human beauty was connected with divine reality and wrote `Love is the creed I hold' Shah Abdul Latif says,

All is sweet that comes from the Beloved
There is no bitterness if you taste it from inside.

Of the other beliefs of the Sufis mention has been made in the earlier chapters of this book. The Sufi worships beauty in all its aspects. He believes that the learner (*tālib*) must know his inner self, Hazrat Ali says that if one knows himself, he knows God and Amir that before union with God can be attained one must lose his very self, and lqbal observes `I wandered in the pursuit and the destination'.

The Sufis believe in thought and reflection but more in personal experience. Paiseem observes in *Tongue of the Dumb* `a Sufi says: 'The moth, if it could think' might well believe that the candle flame is desirable because it seems to represent perfection. The flame is the product of the wax, the wick and the spark which kindles it. Is the human moth seeking the flame or the spark itself? Observe the moth. His destiny, to be destroyed by the flame is visible to you, and hidden to him."[14] It is as though one may imprison a scorpion in a glass vessel and put his finger against it. The scorpion thinks it can sting, but the man who has thus confined him knows that it can't. However reflection is secondary, what is of more significance is experience. As Rumī says `Only he who tastes, knows'. The Sufi believes that disbelief or wrong belief can sometimes be removed by a sudden twist in narration, much as the psychiatrist cures mental aberration by giving a mild electric shock. In his `Song of the Reed' Rumī employs such a device. He relates the story of a prince who seeing a lovely girl fell in love with her and obtained her. Soon after, however, she fell seriously ill and none of the physicians could cure her. So he went to a mosque and prayed for her recovery. He saw in a vision that a physician would soon come and cure her. True enough one came and after questioning her, found that her illness was due to her being in love with a certain goldsmith. The prince sent for him and got her married to him. At this stage the hearers thought that the tale had ended and all was that ends well. But it had not. The mysterious physician prepared a concoction for the goldsmith to drink and when the goldsmith drank it, it became apparent that his love was not sincere and when this was revealed to the girl she started hating him. The goldsmith died and the girl married the prince, her faithful lover. The story is meant to show that when one lacking understanding, wishfully thinks that everything is going right, really everything might go wrong, for the happening and sequence of events is not in our hands.

The Sufi believes that material things cannot bring true happiness for that so obtained is transitory, while only that can bring happiness which makes it everlasting. And that can be got only by soul-knowledge, In the *Brihadarnyaka Upanishad* we are told of the householder, Yānavalkya who had two wives, Kā tyānī and Maitreyī. Kātyānī was worldly minded but Maitreyī was spiritually inclined. One day Yājnavalkya said that he wished to renounce the householder's life and go to the forest to live as an anchorite and so wanted to make a final settlement of his property before he left. Maitreyī asked him 'if the entire world with all the wealth in it became mine, would that give me immortality?' 'Ah no!' said Yājnavalkya, 'you would just live the life of a very rich woman. Immortality cannot be got by wealth'. Maitreyī said what use would that be to her if it did not give immortality? Teach me that which can give me immortality. Yājnavalkya then taught her about the soul. What he said has been narrated earlier in this book, so it is not repeated here. In brief the purport was that everlasting happiness, which is the real purpose of life, can be got only by knowing what the soul is. The Sufi belief in the same:

> 'We know that we want good food and nice clothes, comfort of living and every convenience for moving about; honour, possessions and all necessary means for

> the satisfaction of our vanity, all of which for the moment appear to us as our life's only demands; but neither they nor their joys remain with us constantly. We then come to think that what we had was but little and that perhaps more would satisfy us, and still more would suffice our need; but this is not so. Even if the whole universe were within our grasp it would be impossible fully to satisfy our life's demands. This shows that our true life has quite different demands from those with which we are familiar. It does not want the joy experienced by this individual self only; it desires joy from all around. It does ot wish for momentary peace, but for one that is everlasting'.[15]

The Sufi distinguishes between intellect and wisdom. Intellect is mere learning. It gives knowledge but does not bring permanent peace of mind, while wisdom is the light within. The man of wisdom sees all human beings as one, and the divine in the entire universe.

Everyone who seeks truth is a Sufi. But as we have illustrated by one of anecdotes of Mulla Nasrudin, different people have varying views about truth. The *Murshīd* or teacher does not teach anything new to the *murīd* (the pupil). He only reveals in the seeker the light within his own self to which the *murīd* had been blind. In almost all religions the guru, which the Sufis call the *Murshīd*, is the guide and not to have one, is like a traveller trying to find his way in the dark. Once the *Murshīd* is chosen one should have complete faith in him. There are three ways of trusting, one is to trust no one till he proves trustworthy. But if one adopts this way he will always be suspicious, and the chances are that he may end up by distrusting everyone. The second way is to put one's trust on some teacher and go on trusting him till he proves himself to be untrustworthy. The third way is of absolute trust, and if the seeker has the will to learn, he will doubtless find the correct teacher. And the attraction of the *murid* to the *Murshid* is intuitive. It is like iron drawn to a magnet. The secrecy of the Sufi teaching is because one may easily misunderstand the Sufi concept, and this can lead to confusion. The teaching is given only when the pupil is ripe for it. It has been said before the Bayazid rejected an aspirant who could not get over his selfishness. To the question whether Sufism is a belief, the answer is that it is. The believer is an optimist who looks on things hopefully, while the disbeliever is a pessimist who always looks on the dark side and keeps finding fault with everyone and with everything. As a writer puts it. `The optimist proclaims that we live in the best of all possible worlds; and the pessimist fears this true'.[16] However belief does not mean that one should let himself be hoodwinked and he ought always place reins on his credulity if he feels he is being misled. There are four stages of belief for a Sufi. The first is *iman-e muhmil*, This is when a person believes in something but the belief is not firm enough and if others try to shake him from it, he easily gives it up. It is like the tale of the goat and the dog. A man was carrying a goat in order to keep it as a pet. Three men saw him and planned to somehow get it for themselves. Some distance away one of them accosted him and said `Fie on you, you are carrying a dog' (a dog is considered unclean among Hindus). The man told him he was mistaken 'it's not a dog he said' it's a goat? As he went on each of the other two schemers told him the same thing. However when the third man repeated this he said to himself `Maybe it's really a dog, for now three men have said so'. He put the goat down and the conspirators had a field day slaughtering the goat and having a grand feast! The next stage of belief is *iman-e kamil*. This implies belief in the scripture and a saviour. This is firmer than the first but can be dimmed when reason overpowers emotion. When the light of reason shines, man enters the third stage, *haq al-iman*. Thereafter is the belief based on conviction, known as *`ain al-iman*. This is based on the man's actual knowledge like something one perceives with his own eyes. The example given is that if one is told there is water here, do not cross it, when the man sees with his own eyes that it is land not water, his belief becomes firm and he cannot be shaken from it.[17] This however may not be so in all cases. As for example a mirage seen in the desert. When in the *Mahabharata* Duryodhana was paying his visit to the wonderful palace of the Pandavas at Indraprasta he was tricked into ḅelieving that what seemed to his sight water was really land and what seemed land was water. The system of Nyā ya, which is one of the six systems of Indian philosophy mention four means of right knowledge (*pramānas*), perception, the knowledge arising form the contact of a sense with its object; inference, knowledge preceded by perception; comparison, the knowledge of a thing through its similarity with another thing which is well known; and verbal testimony, the assertion of a reliable person.

It has already made clear aforesaid that Sufism does not subscribe to any religion, though it does not also confute any. It has often been termed as mysticism. It is that if one considers it as soul-knowledge but it is not confined to any particular class of people. It is universal in its scope and though as the quest of the soul it could be called mysticism, it is also beyond it. Nor is Sufism strictly theosophy if we take theosophy to mean any sect or fixed beliefs or disbeliefs. The *Murshīd* only brings light to the *murīd* and then leaves him free to believe or not to believe. The Sufi conviction is that the man's soul is divine *hum man am* which leads to the ultimate conviction, *haq al-iman*, parallel to the Hindu one *jo ham so ham*. Sufism is also not restricted to any one country or region. It does not indoctinate and it is more than mere philosophy. It is an imparter of wisdom, and could be a school of thought only in this sense.

The inner life lived is to attain perfection. It means getting closer to God, and consists in living a full and complete life. The striving towards understanding the soul and the attainment of such knowledge, banishes the fear of death. The person then realizes that the body is only a kind of garment for the soul. As Lord Krishna says in the *Gita*, `As a person discards worn-out clothes and puts on fresh ones instead, the embodied soul abandons useless bodies and acquires others that are new'.[18] Raymond A Moody, Jr. who investigated cases of people who had been declared clinically dead but thereafter came to life again says of such persons who had actually come back after seeing God, whom they said to be a `Being of Light', as follows:

> "I am thoroughly convinced that there is life after death, without a shadow of doubt and I am not afraid to die. I am not. Some people I have known are so afraid, so scared. I always smile to myself when I hear people doubt there is an afterlife or say, `When you are dead you're gone'. I think to myself, `They really don't know' "... "I don't fear death. Those feelings vanished. I don't feel bad at funerals anymore. I kind of rejoice at them, because I know what the dead person has been through"... `According to these new views, development of the soul, especially in the spiritual faculties of love and knowledge, does not stop upon death. Rather, it continues on the other side, perhaps eternally, but certainly for a period of time and to a depth which can only be glimpsed while we are still in physical bodies, "through a glass, darkly" '.[19]

The inner life, therefore according to Sufi belief is the acquiring of knowledge of the soul, the realization that there is life beyond the present life. This realization is something beyond the perception of the outward senses, it is more in the nature of reliable testimony as revealed by saints and prophets. As the Lord says in the *Gita*:

Acquire that knowledge
By humble reverence and inquiry
And by service;
The wise men who have known truth
Will instruct you.[20]

Thus it is not for us to sit in judgment on what the *Murshīd* teaches, because the ordinary man's knowledge is limited. George Herbert says `Judge not the preacher, for he is thy Judge,[21] and `Judge not, and ye shall not be judged'.[22] As the spiritual soul advances it expands in its outlook and proceeds on the path of goodness drawn to the good wherever and in whomever it finds it. It starts caring for others rather than for itself alone and to sacrifice its own interest for the sake of that of others. Dr Moody says `He (the Being of Light, i.e., God) kept stressing the importance of love... He pointed out to me that I should try to do things for other people, to try my best'.[23]

Hazrat Inayat Khan enumerates five things necessary to attain inner life, that is to say the life of the spirit. Of these the first is control over the mind. In the *Gita*, Arjuna, the Pandava warrior doubted if the mind could be controlled:

`This yoga of which you speak, O Krishna,
Requires evenness of mind:
But I do not see how that is possible
When the mind is so unsteady.
`The mind, O Krishna,
Is restless, obstinate and stubborn;
It seems as difficult to curb
As the wind'.

And the Lord's answer was:

`The mind doubtless is fickle
And hard to control, O Arjuna,
But it can be brought under control
By sustained practice and dispassion?'

Patience and effort, therefore are needed to tame the mind. Wrong impressions have to be replaced by right ones. But this cannot be done by oneself alone. The seeker must have a guide, guru or, as the Sufis say, a *Murshīd*. After having found one, he must have full confidence in him. Enumerating the nine kinds of *bhakti* (devotion) Lord Rama told Sabari, his devotee `One should sit at the feet of the guru without pride and also hold saints in greater esteem even that him, i.e., as God himself' — *guru pada pankaj* and *moteṁ santa adhika kari lekhā*.[25] The third stage needed for spiritual attaiment is getting knowledge of the inner world, assimilating it and using the intellect to understand it. The fourth requirement is that of meditation. This is also a yoga practice and is closely allied to concentration. Various societies and their founders advocate its practice for example the transcendental meditation of Maharshi Yogi (TM), that of Acharya Rajneesh (Osho) and so forth, but they all originate from the yoga system of Pātanjali, which itself is only a restatement of yoga, the science of which goes back to several thousands of years, as Lord Krishna tells Arjuna in the *Gita*: `I taught Vivasvā n this imperishable yoga, he taught it to Manu and Manu to Ikshkvāku. Thus handed down from one to another, this yoga came to be known to the royal sages and thereafter this ancient wisdom was long forgotten. I tell it to you today as you are my friend and devotee.[26] Meditation brings both joy and peace. Hazrat Inayat Khan mentions that a man to whom he was once talking suddenly closed his eyes and went into meditation. When he opened his eyes and was asked `It is beautiful, is it not?' he said `it is never enough'.[27] As has already been said Lord Krishna too praises meditation: `The uncontrolled man has no wisdom, then how can he have a steady mind. One who cannot steady his mind by meditation can have no peace and how can one who lacks peace ever by happy?'[28] The next need for attaining the inner life is loving people and not hurting their feelings. As the poet Rasakhan says: *miliye sabase durabhāva binā* (`meet everyone, bearing no ill will towards him').[29] Finally one must have detachment amid the crowd, what is called *vairagya*. In the *Gita* also Lord Krishna said that one should `not have attachment to wordly things or be entangled with wife, son, home and the like, resort to solitary places'; and have aversion to crowds – *vivikta - desha - sevitvam aratir jan - samsadi*.[30] When this quality of *vairagya* assumes permanence the person having it becomes a saint. His only desire then is to look God-ward and love all human beings without desiring anything in return. His life in this stage is one of complete desirelessness, and this is the quality of the saints, sages and God's holy messengers.

The Sufi believes that there are five characteristics of the spiritual person. These are 1. The religious, who goes regularly to the place of worship, reads the scriptures and follows their injections; 2. The philosophical who has the capacity to endure and tolerate. Outwardly, he shows no signs which could distinguish him from ordinary persons. He may be a businessman or be carrying on other occupations. Only those who come into close contact with him realize his inner spiritualism; 3. The third kind is the one who works for the good of others. He considers everyone his own and reaches out to all alike. A baby knows only love. He responds to it irrespective of the person who gives it to him. It may be his mother, grandmother or even a nurse. But after some time `the shades of the prison house begin to close' as the poet says. He starts thinking in terms of *my* mother, *my* father *my* home and so forth. When he becomes an adult he is circumscribed by his family. The majority of persons no go beyond that. There are only a handful souls who can move beyond. These are the godly beings who do not consider mankind as compartments but as one brotherhood of whom the Gita says: that he sees the soul in all creatures.[31]

4. The fourth form of the spiritual person is the mystic. It is very difficult for the ordinary man to understand him, because mysticism is not any knowledge. It is inborn and temperamental. Taking an example there was Dādū a sixteenth century Indian

mystic. A passage form his *Bāni* discloses the extreme difficulty of understanding the trend of the mystic's utterances:

> The waking sleep and the sleepers sleep till
> God's mercy they discern;
>
> The waking wake and the sleepers wake
> when His blessed name they learn.
>
> They that see are blind, and the blind are blind
> until the truth is known;
>
> They that see behold, and the blind behold
> when they make God's love their own.
>
> They that speak are dumb, and the dumb are
> dumb till the secret comes abroad;
>
> The speakers speak and the dumb too speak
> when they lift their hearts to God.
>
> They that live are dead and the dead are dead
> till they behold His face;
>
> The living live and the dead too live in God
> their Dwelling Place'.[32]

5. The fifth form of the spiritual man; too, is hard to grasp by ordinary men. He is known as *madzub*, equivalent to *Avadhuta* in Indian terminology. He is a man of self-realization and very presence has an overpowering effect, even though outwardly there is nothing special about him. Examples of such persons are Ramana Maharshi, Sri Ramakrishna Paramhansa, Shankaracharya and such other saints of India. Often they are gifted with superhuman power, even though they are loath to perform miracles or display such powers. Many foreigners went to visit Ramana Maharshi. Of these one was a famous British author Somerset Maugham and another, a reputed journalist Paul Brunton. Maugham tried to ask question, but found himself

tongue-tied. The Maharshi said 'All is finished. Heart-talk is all that is required. All talk must end in silence only'. Paul Brunton came to India in seach of a genuine saint a *madzub* in Sufi terminology. He travelled all over the country and met many men who claimed to be sadhus but proved themselves to be mere imposters. Disappointed he booked his passage by sea, homewards. But in the night thereafter he had a vision (not a dream) in which he actually saw Ramana Maharshi, and a voice spoke to him 'The man you seek is this. If you go to Tiruvannamalai you will find him there'. Brunton cancelled his voyage and despite being tired and having to brave India's hot weather, took a train right down from there to the south. He wrote about this in his book *A Search in Secret India*, and about his meeting with the Maharshi he said:

> 'My initial bewilderment, my perplexity at being totally ignored, slowly fades away as this strange fascination begins to grip me more firmly. But is not till the second hour of the uncommon scene that I become aware of the silent, resistless change which is taking place within my mind. One by one the questions which I had prepared in the train with such meticulous accuracy, drop away. For it does not matter whether I solve the problems which have hitherto troubled me. I know only that a steady river of quietness seems to be flowing near me, that a great peace is penetrating the inner reaches of my being and that my thought-tortured brain is beginning to arrive at some rest.
>
> 'How small seem those questions which I have asked myself with such frequency! How petty grows the panorama of the lost years! I perceive with sudden clarity that the intellect creates its own problems and then makes itself miserable trying to solve them. This is indeed a novel concept to enter the mind of one who has hitherto placed such high value upon intellect.[33]

Another account of such experience is that of Vivekananda, disciple of Sri Ramakrishna. Vivekananda was a rationalist, the admirer of Western ideas of Herbert Spencer, Immanuel Kant and so forth, and he considered Ramakrishna a monomaniac and raving mad. His biographer narrates his experience thus: 'The sage put his right foot on his body. Instantly he had a mystic experience, which he would remember all his life. Everything in the room began to whirl round rapidly and vanished into nothingness – the walls, the floor, the roof and all the objects of the room – and there was a great void. The whole universe as also Vivekananda's I-ness seemed to vanish. There was nothing, nothing at all – no experience, nothing to be experience. To the bewildered lad it seemed he was facing death, and he cried out "What is this you are doing to me? I have parents at home!" At this Ramakrishna, stroking Vivekananda's chest, laughed aloud and said "All right, let it be. It is enough for now. Everything will come in due time." Instantly everything was as it was before, leaving Vivekananda amazed'.[34]

This, then, is the nature of the soul of the fifth form of inner life. These men have unimaginable power, but exercise it unobtrusively, not by performing any miracles. There are Sufi saints who have these powers, if one has belief in the accounts of them given. For example it is said that Sayed Abdul-Qadir hurled his sandals in the air and they disappeared and thereafter reappeared by the side of the heads of two leaders of a gang of Arabs who had looted the members of a caravan and were mysteriously found dead. It is said that there were Sufi magicians too. The Ikhwan El Safa ('Brethren of Sincerity') are considered such by some. But their mission was really the spread of knowledge — philosophy, religion, science and so forth. Rumi, Ghazzali, El-Maari and other Sufis were their admirers. However there is difference between the power of saints to influence people by their very presence of touch (as in Ramakrishna's we have related). Magic is a very crude and inferior form of impressing others and is based on trickery and sleight of hand. And miracles are not performed by saints but by messiahs. El-Ghazzali also speaks of such powers in *Alchemy of Happiness* - ruling over one's own body, affecting recovery in someone diseased, extra perception, moving bodies from one place to another, insight and immediate consiousness of knowledge. Such powers have been known for long to Indian mystics, but seldom used. *Siddhīs* are such miraculous powers. They are eight in number 1. *Anima*, the power of becoming infinitely small; 2. *Mahima* the power of becoming infinitely light; 3. *Ciarima*, the power of becoming infinitely heavy; 4. *Laghuma*, becoming both infinitely light and small; 5. *Prapti*, obtaining whatever one desires; 6. *Prakamya*, doing whatever one desires; 7. *Ishtva*, absolute supremacy and 8. *Vasita*, the power of subduing anyone. The *Yogasutras* of Pā tanjali mentions various occult powers which can be gained by the practice of yoga, such as knowledge of the sounds of all creatures, of past lives, the thoughts of the minds of others, the power of disappearing from sight, knowledge of death, becoming swift as the wind, the knowledge of all the regions of the universe (*lokas*), becoming light as cotton, walking on water or even on a ray of light, the power of entering into anything, even a stone, of not being burnt by fire, wetted by water or moved by air. He can become light as an atom or large so much so that he can touch the moon by his fingertips![35] Thus miraculous powers of which Ghazzali and other Sufis speaks were known in India thousands of years before the birth of Christ. But miracles were performed only originators of religion or by avatars.

Before creation nothing existed. This void or nothingness is known in Sufi terminology as *zat* or *Ahadiat* (the Absolute equivalent to the Hindu concept of *Brahman*). The Absolute could be conscious of nothing except Existence, or *Wahdat*. From this came the sense of ego (`I exist') called *wahdaniat* by the Sufis. This was pervaded by the spirit or *Nur* known in Sufi terms as

Arwah. Light (*ākāsha*) and darkness (*asmaan*) came and the spirit found bodies (*ajsam*). The light of the spirit spread to souls, six kinds of them, the first three *tanzi* being imperceptible and three, *tashbi* which can be distinguished. Then followed the elements ether (*nur*), air (*baad*), fire (*aetsh*), water (*aab*) and earth (*khaak*). The light of intelligence which in the Vedanta is known as *chaitanya* filled every being, as Shams-e Tabrez said `When the Sun of His countenance became manifest, the atoms of both worlds began to appear; as its light fell, every atom donned a name and form'.[36] This creation goes on till it culminats in destruction, known to Hindus as *pralaya*. The Sufi idea about this is akin to that of the Hindus. The Sufi division of souls into angelic and non-angelic is much like that of the divine (*sura*) and demoniac (*asura*), and the *Gita* also mentions this kind of division. Shri Krishna says: `Two types of beings have been created in this world, the godly and the demoniac'[37] Just as Shri Krishna mentions the good qualities of the godly souls and the evil ones of the *asuras*, the Sufis consider the *asura* kind as being away from the stream of goodness and having no spiritualism, while the angelic souls are kind, love others than themselves, are innocent and faultless and do not fear death. Further the communication between the soul and God is not in any of the languages spoken by men. It is soul-language, which is also mentioned by Dr Raymond Moody Jr. in his narrations of out-of-the-body experiences:

> `For here again, people claim that they did not hear any physical voice or sounds coming from the being, nor did they respond to the being through audible sounds. Rather it is reported that direct, unimpeded transfer of thought takes place, in such a clear way that there is no possibility whatsoever either of misunderstanding or of lying to the light.
>
> `Furthermore, this unimpeded exchange does not even take place in the native language of the person. Yet he understands perfectly and is instantaneously aware. He

> cannot even translate the thoughts and exchanges which took place while he was near death into the human language which he must speak now, after his resuscitation'.[38]

The Sufi conceives two angels called *khair* and *kahr*. The first is a kind who is sent by God to protect or save someone from impending trouble. *Khar* records the deeds of a person's actions. Here also we find the idea of *khar* in Hindu mythology in which the record of the person's acrts are entered in a register called Agrasandhānī, maintained by the recorder chitaragupta. According to Sufi belief the angels of heaven are Called *nur* and others *naar*. According to another view the angels are of power and beauty called respectively *jelal* and *jemal*. The rays of the divine Sun form souls or angels. The divine current is known as *tajalli*.

From the angelic heavens the soul comes to the earth as a jinn or *genius*. The words jinn and genius are from the Sanskrit *jñāna* or knowledge. The jinns are therefore beings of knowledge. Like the Hindu yogic concept of *prāṇa* and other life-breaths the Sufi believes souls to be breaths of God. There are different kinds of souls – artists, musicians, thinkers, philosophers, inventors and so forth.

The Sufi belief is that the soul becomes conscious of five spheres. The first one on coming to the world is *nasut*, the sphere of the physical plane. The next one is *malakut*, the sphere of thought and imagination. The third is the sphere of spirituality in which man is in touch with the infinite, if only for moments. The other two spheres also known as *malakut and jabarut*, are experienced respectively in dreams and dreamless sleep. Here again we find a parallel between Sufism and Vedanta. The latter also distinguishes between the waking, dream and deep sleep states, adding that a fourth which really underlies the other three is the *Turīya* or Eternal Witness.

`There are three states only the waking, dream and deep sleeop. *Turīya* is not a fourth one; it is what underlies these there. But people do not readily understand it. Therefore, it is said that this is the fourth state and the only reality. In fact it is not apart from anything for it forms the substratum of all happenings; it is the only truth, it is your very being. The three states appear as feeting phenomena on it and sink into it alone. Therefore they are unreal... *Turīya* is only another name for the Self'.[39]

Sufism does not stop at advocating meditation and concentration. It goes on to emphasize love of God. The soul is called *ruh* in Arabic it is the same as the *atman* of the Vedanta. Intrinsically the soul is pure *sāf* but it becomes captive in the body as the embodied soul. As Rumī says in the *Masnavi* `life on earth is the soul's captivity.' The soul does not die. Death comes to the body not to the soul. This idea of Sufism is akin to what Shri Krishna says in the *Gita.*

na jāyate mriyate vā kadācin
nā 'yaṁ bhūtavā bhavita na bhūyaḥ|
ajo nityaḥ shashvato yaṁ purāṇo
na hanyate hanyamāne sharīre||

`The soul is never born nor does it ever die, and having come to be it is never non-existent. It is unborn, permanent and primordial and does not die with the body's death'.[40]

Someone asked a Sufi what happened after death. The Sufi said `Ask this of someone who will die, a mortal being. I do not believe that the soul will ever die'.

Purgatory is as much a Sufi belief as that of Christians. The Sufi term for it is *naza* which implies a kind of interlude between the world of existence and *jannat* or paradise (the *swarga* of the Hindus). After the night's darkness light is seen. Which in Sufi terminology is known as *nahazat*.

The Vedantic belief is that thought precedes action. As is a man's thought-act process that create *sanskaras* (tendencies) and ultimately determine the kind of future life that the being is likely to get. Hazrat Inayat Khan relates a story to illustrate this.

> `A man who had heard of there being a tree of desire was once travelling; and he happened to find himself under the shade of a tree which he felt to be restful and cooling, so he sat there leaning against it. He said to himself "How beautiful is nature; how cooling is the shade of the tree; and the breeze is soft exhilarating; but I which I had a soft carpet to sit on, and some cushions to lean against". No sooner had he thought about it than he saw himself sitting in the midst of soft cushions. "How wonderful" he thought, "If only I had a glass of cooling drink"; and there came a fairy with a most delicious glass of cold drink. He enjoyed it, but said, "I would like a good dinner". No sooner had he thought of a dinner than a gold tray was brought to him with beautifully arranged dishes of all sorts. Now he thought, "If only I had a chariot that I might take a drive into the forest"; and a four-horse chariot was already there, the coachman greeting him with bent head. He thought, "Everything I desire comes without any effort. I wonder if it is true, or all a dream". No sooner had he thought a dinner than a joid tray was thought this than everything disappeared, and he found himself sitting on the same ground leaning against a tree".[41]

As Virgil says in Aeneid `They can because they think they can' (*possunt quia posse videntur*), and Emerson `Great men are those who see that spiritual is stronger than material force, that thoughts rule the world'.[42] Thus thoughts become materialized, provided one has faith.

The soul, when it reaches the angelic world experiences indescribable joy, as of wine, the kind of which is not found on earth. The Sufis call it the bowl of *Jāma-e Kauthir*. The soul experiences the music of heaven called *Saut-e Sarmad*. (the music of the heavenly spheres), and this frees it from all worldly worries. The souls of this angelic heaven hover round a light which is divine. Besides they set the tune for souls which are descending to the earth. This is known is Sufi terminology as *Azal*. The force that guides the soul in the spiritual world is known to Sufis as that of *Yageen*. And if this is lacking it hinders the soul's progress. The soul is covered by many veils of illusion (as the Vedantic *koshas*). When by death these are forcefully removed, it is called *fana* (annihilation), but they can also be removed by the soul's own will and effort, and in that case the spiritual awakening is known as *bakā*. Then the soul realizes its own nature and the truth that it itself is the source, the traveller and the goal. This is the truth that all religions try to teach.

Life is never purposeless. As Sa'adi says `Every soul is created, having a purpose behind it. And the light of such purpose lies in the soul itself'. Again behind such outer purpose there lies the inner one. For example everyone wishes to have a house or some kind of roof over his head. And so he seeks a home and a family just as a bird has its nest, and in that it has its young ones. But man is different from other creatures inasmuch as he seeks something more than a roof over his head, a home and a family. The beast just lives, but has no power to reason, think or question. The human being endowed with mind and intellect has all such facilities. He has the desire to live, to know, to have soul-power, to be happy and to have peace of mind. In fact the greatest of men have been philosophers and have not even felt the need of a roof above their heads to achieve peace and happiness, as Diogenes who was content to live in a tub and who humbled the great emperor, Alexander and so too Dandamis, the ancient Indian sage whose story as told by Megasthenes has been related before. The real life is the deathless one, and that is the existence of the immortal soul, not the mortal body. The desire to live is inborn in man and human birth is a prized gift. Given it (according to the Vedanta it is got after eighty-four lakh births in inferior wombs) it is not something to be wasted. But the question arises what really is the difference between wasting it and utilizing it to the best advantage? Life is doubtless precious and is meant to be lived to the full, as the poet Browning says:

> `Grow old along with me!
> The best is yet to be.
> The last of life for which the first was made
> Our times are in his hands
> Who saith "A whole I planned
> Youth shows but half; trust God: see all, nor be afraid'.[43]

Or as for example, Socrates : `Be of good hope in the face of death. Believe in this one truth for certain, that no evil can befall a good man either in life or death, and that his fate is not a matter of indifference to the gods... And now the time has come when we must depart : I to my death, you to go on living, but which of us is going to a better fate is unknown to all except God'.[44] The death is of the body not of the soul. Kabīr says: *kabīra baidu kahai hau hī bhalā dārū merai vasai| iha tau basatu gupāla kī, jaba bhāvai lei khasai* ||. The physician says "I'll cure you", but he does not know that the soul is God's, and when he calls for it, it will go'.[45] Thus clearly life and death are not in our hands in the sense that they are is uncertain and the period of existence is unpredictable. But till we have the gift of life how should we use it? Says Shankaracharya, the great apostle of *advaita* (nondual) Vedanta 'Therefore the wise man, having renounced his desire for sensual pleasures, strives for his salvation and seeking a true teacher accepts without reservation, his teaching[46] Shankaracharya also conceived the world of existence to be illusory as is the nature of dreams:

> The universe though it be the subject of daily experience, and though it be the object of our constant

intercourse is unreal like a dream inasmuch as its existence even in the moment next to its birth is not probable. For example: dreams are unreal during waking; nor is the waking condition possible in dreams. Both, however, are not to be found in deep absorption, as in dreamless sleep, which again is not experienced in either. Thus all the three conditions are unreal, being the illusive creation of maya with the three *gunas* (qualities): the real permanent and unique one is the spirit which stands aloof from these three *gunas* as the witness of all these conditions.'.[47]

Very few persons realize that while death is for the body, the soul never dies, as Shri Krishna says in the Gita. Kabīr says: *Kauna marai kahu pandita janā/so samajhāi kahau hama sanā/māṭi māṭi rahī samāi pavanai pavana liyā san·gli lāi/ kahai kabīra suni pandita gunī rūpa bhuvā saba dekhai dunī/*

['O wise men ponder carefully
Who is it that dies, and then tell me.
Dust unto dust this bidy is,
And with the wind the soul flies;
O pundits, all the world knows this
Says Kabīr, that only the body dies'.][48]

Rumī, the renowned Sufi saint, expresses the idea of the soul being imprisoned in the body in a verse of his which we have already quoted before.

In the *Masnavi* Rumī speaks of this desire of the soul of free itself. But it is not necessary that such freedom can come only when at death the soul leaves the body. It can come in life as well, and that is when the l-sense is eliminated. Shri Ramakrishna illustrates this by one of this parables:

`The feeling "I am the doer" is the outcome of ignorance. But the feeling that God does everything is due to knowledge. God alone is the Doer; all others are instruments in His hands.

`The misfortune that befalls a man on account of his egotism can be realized if you only think of the condition of the calf. The calf says, "Hamma! Hamma!" that is "I!I!" And just look at its misfortune! At times it is yoked to the plough and made to work in the field form sunup to sundown, rain or shine. Again it may be slaughtered by the butcher, In that case the flesh is eaten and the skin tanned into hide. From the hide shoes are made. People put on these shoes and walk on the rough gound. Still that is not the end of its misfortunes. Drums are made from its skin and mercilessly beaten with sticks. At last its entrails are made into strings of the bow used in carding cotton. When used by the carder the strings give the sound "Tuhu! Tuhu!"; "Thou! Thou!" – that is "It is Thou, O Lord! It is Thou!" It no longers says "Hama ! Hama !" "I!I!" Only then does the calf's troubles come to an end, and it is liberated. It does not return to the world of action.'[49]

So too Shri Krishna says in the Gita

`When he sees, hears, smells, touches
Eats, walks, sleeps, or breathes,
The yogi who has realized the soul,
Knows it's not he who does all these things.
`Whether he speaks relinquishes, or grasps,
Opens his eyes, or closes them:
He understands it is only the interplay
Of the senses which with their objects'.[50]

Next to the desire for living, comes the thirst for knowledge. The desire is for knowledge of the divine. This knowledge is quite different from mere learning. A human being is aware of the external world through his five senses. But knowledge of the divine is something beyond. The mind has only the power of intellect. It can focus an learning only. The *Īsha Upanishad* says:

> `Those who depend on rituals
> Enter into blinding darkness;
> But into greater darkness those
> Who seek support in empty learning.
>
> `Into blinding darkness fall
> Those who worship unmanifest Nature
> Into greater darkness those
> Who think there is this life and no other'[51]

The quest of knowledge of this spiritual kind is a long one. According to Dr Raymond A. Moody, it goes on life after life. He says `He (the Being of Light, i.e., God) seemed very interested in things concerning knoweledge, too. He kept on pointing out things that had to do with learning, and he did say that I was to continue learning. He said... that there will always be a quest for knowledge. He said that it is a continuous process, so I got the feeling that it goes on after death".[52] The sage Sri Ramana Maharshi says:

> `"Who AM I?" I am not this physical body; nor am I the five organs of sense perception; nor am I the five organs of external activity; nor am I the five vital forces, nor am I even the thinking mind... Nor is there any such thing as the physical world apart from and independent of thought... Just as the spider draws out the thread of the cobweb from within itself, even so out of itself the mind projects the world and absorbs it back into itself.

> 'The world is perceived as an apparent objective reality when the mind is externalized thereby forsaking its identity with the Self When the world is thus perceived, the true nature of the Self is not revealed: conversely. when the self is realized, the world ceases to appear as an objective reality'.[53]

The third thing necessary for accomplishing the inner purpose of life is the desire and achievement of power. But this power does not mean that of position, majesty, wealth or worldly ascendancy. All these succeed only in producing vanity. What is meant is the inner power which the Sufi terms as *Iman* (conviction) and the Sufi believes that such power is built by *Yaqeen* (belief). The Sufis believe that the source of all inner power is that of the Almighty. All other power is shortlived and limited. Such inner power is got by self-effacement or self-denial. To a person who has got this praise or blame is all one and wealth of no consequence says' indifference to praise or blame, vanity or arrogance and wealth and poverty is a godlike virtue.[54]

This self-effacement is attained by having faith in God and losing oneself in him. The way in which this is attained is known as *fanā* in Sufi terminology. 'I am nothing' says the Sufi. 'You are everything'. This attitude is known by Sufis as that of *bakā*. *Fanā* and *bakā* are not got by torturing oneself by stern austerities but by knowledge of the man's inner Self. Kabīr was against such practice:

> 'It vexes me to see men perform
> Various vain rites,
> So I keep chanting you name, Rāma
> Day and night.
> 'One pours on holy books
> One stares with a vacant look;
> One discards his clothes
> One wears out his body with yoga
> But Rāma is not in their thoughts.

`One pretends humility
One prides on charity
One flaunts a peacock's tail
One's in his cups always
One practises Tantra, one utters *mantras*
One puts his trust in herbs;
One has faith in breath-control
Or holy pilgrimage,
Yet they love not Rāma's name.
To darken their limbs, some expose
Them to the sun; but without Rāma
One cannot attain *moksha*.
Say Kabīr, the guru said the truth
Is the One Cosmic Absolute,
I followed in his steps
And by Rāma's grace, I escaped
The rounds of births and deaths.[55]

In the *Gita* too the Lord is not in favour of those who carry out stern austerities. Such persons, he says 'not only torture themselves but Me too whose Spirit is in them'.

The fourth constituent of the accomplishment of the inner purpose of living is man's constant search for happiness. For understanding the pursuit of happiness one has to realize first of all what happiness is. There is a difference between pleasure and happiness, although both elate a person. The most distinguishing feature between the two is the duration of delight. Pleasures are momentary and shortlived. As has been quoted before they have been described so by the poet as poppies which are deprived of the bloom the moment one tries to pluck them. Happiness of the contrary is lasting and that which is the happiness of the Spirit, that real inner happiness is everlasting. All pleasures end in satiety. As Cicero says `In everything we do, all our keenest pleasures end in satiety;.[56] For example, the pleasure of wealth lasts so long as the wealth lasts, of beauty of form so long as youth is there, and with age health and the efficacy of the limbs fades away. The pleasure of pomp and power last so long as one is in that position. Sexual pleasure is momentary even though it is extolled to the skies by those who indulge in it. On the contrary happiness is not evanescent. It is worthwhile because it is lasting. The next thing to consider is in what does happiness reside? Since it is lasting it cannot exist in anything which is unsure, as wealth, beauty of appearance etc. Marcus Tullius Cicero says `A happily life consists in tranquility of mind'. Jean Jacques Rousseu says `Supreme happiness consists in self-content; that we may gain this self-content we are placed upon this earth, and endowed with freedom, we are tempted by our passions, and restrained by conscience. What more could divine power itself have done in our behalf?'[57] Thus happiness lies in living a virtuous and self-contented life. In that respect it is allied to peace, which is the fifth constituent of the inner life. As we have said before the Lord considers, in the *Gita* that self-control (*sādhanā*) leads to wisdom, wisdom to meditation, meditation to peace (*shānti*) and peace to happiness (*ānanda*). This teaching is very much like the Sufi belief. This kind of supreme happiness can have its origin only in the World Soul or God. In Dr Raymond A. Moody's study of after-death experiences of persons declared clinically dead, but who came back to life, he speaks of this World Soul as the Being of Light and its love for the person's soul: `The love and warmth which emanate from this being to the dying person are utterly beyond words... And all during this time, I felt as though I was surrounded by an overpowering love and compassion'.[59] This love is so great that the soul often does not with to return : `However, once the dying person reaches a certain depth in his experience he does not want to come back... As one man put it, most emphatically `I never wanted to leave the presence of this being'.[60] From these accounts it is clear the God is love and love is God and that his love transcends all the love that it of the worldly kind. Hence love in this sense was the belief of great Sufi saints like Jalaudding Rumī, El-Arabi, and Anwari who said `I affirm that I am a Lover'.

Peace and happiness can come to a person only when he finds them in the soul — *yas tv ātmaratir eva syād ātmatriptash ca mānavaḥ* ['One who delights in the Self (Soul) alone and finds contentment and satisfaction (*saṁtushtas*) in it'].[61] This too is what the Bible means when it speaks of 'The peace of God which passeth all understanding'.[62] Such peace cannot be obtained from external things. The pursuit of sensual pleasures cannot bring peace. In fact all effort which is termed 'volition' leads to restlessness, for then we are imposing our will, not accepting. For example sorrows like the death of loved ones. Such things are beyond or control. One may either accept such a sorrow or struggle against it by asking, why? But for the fact of death—that life has gone — it makes no difference. Therefore peace lies in submission to God's will not the imposition of one's own will. As the distinguished Sufi saint Hazat Inayat Khan says:

> 'To attain peace, what one has to do is to seek that rhythm which is in the depth of our being. It is just like the sea; the surface of the sea is ever - moving; and the depth of the sea is still. And so it is with our life. If our life is thrown into the sea of activity, it is on the surface; we still live in, in the profound depths, in that peace which can be found within ourselves. It is this which can bring us the answer to all our problems. If not, when we want to solve one problem there is another difficult problem coming. There is no end to our problems; there is no end to the difficulties of the outer life. And if we get excited over them, we shall never be able to solve them'.[63]

Tulsidasa also expresses a similar thought in the *Rāmacharitmānasa*:

jima saritā sagara maṁha jāhiṁ
jayaapi tābi kāmanā nahiṁ
timi sukha sampati binahiṁ bolaeṁ
dharamasili pahiṁ jāhiṁ subhaeṁ.

[`As rivers go into the sea, even though the sea has no desire for them, so too wealth and prosperity go to a man following the way of dharma of themselves, unasked'][64]

The Sufi creed is not to run away from difficulties but to face them. Human beings are sent on earth to perform the duty which devolves on them according to the position they are placed in. The *Gita* calls this performance of duty one's dharma. One's own dharma means *svadharma* (*sva* meaning 'one's'). *Svadharma* is born with us. It is like one's mother. What one is born unto is not in his hands. As Dr S Radhakrishnan says in his introduction to his translation of the *Gita* the cards one has to play with in a game of cards are dealt with by someone to the players. What cards form a players hand are thus fixed. He has to play with them. But a good player may win even by poor cards, while a bad one may lose it even if he holds the good ones. So too one placed low in life, as for example an officer's oderly, may prove a better man, honest straightforward and kind while the high up, his boss, may turn out to be corrupt, rude and hated by all. Thus one should do his duty in the best possible manner. In the battle of Trafalgar Nelson, the British naval commander put up a flag which read, `England expects every man to do his duty'. In the *Gita* Shri Krishna says: *shreyān svadharmo viguṇaḥ paradharmāt svanushṭhitat* `Better one's own duty, however devoid of merit than another's however well performed'.[65] Further he says `Both the ignorant man and the wise work, but while the former is attached to works, the wise man works for the world's welfare. Nonetheless the man who knows the truth should not unsettle the mind of one who is striving to know it. He should rather encourage him and guide him'.[66] The Sufi belief is much of the same kind. The seeker must have full confidence on the teacher. The *Pīr* or *Murshīd* (the teacher) merely opens the learners's mind. He does not indoctrinate. The seeker should also realize that his mind is clouded by pre-conceived notions which must be got rid of before the Sufi thinking can seep in. As Jalaluddin Rumī says `Open the door of your mind for it has strayed from understanding and is immersed in the poverty of thought and replace such poverty by richness'. Acharya Vinoba Bhavae says `The surface of the water is clear; but throw a stone into it, and at once the mud rises up. Our minds are just like that. At the bottom of the still lake there is knee-deep mud. It is only when an object from without touches it that one can see it'.[67] Works or actions are inevitable for one placed in the world but one have discrimination in their performance. Some, which are bad, should be given up altogether and others should be done, only the fruit renounced. Vinoba Bhave observes:

> `If there is a stain on the body it can be washed off; but if the skin itself is dark in colour what is the good of giving it a coat of whitewash? Let the dark colour remain.
>
> `Once there was a man, who, feeling that there was something inauspicious about his house, left it and went away and settled in another village. That in turn seemed dirty to him, and he went away to the forest. There as he sat under a mango tree a bird's droppings fell on his head. He said "This forest too is unfriendly", and he went and stood by a river. In the river the big fish eating up the small fish filled him with disgust. "The whole creation" he concluded "is unkind. There is no way out except through death". So he came and kindled a fire. Then a gentleman who was passing by said."My brother, why are you preparing to die?". He replied "Because the whole world is inauspicious". The man said, "If this unclean body of yours, this mass of flesh, begins to burn, how it would stink! I live close by. Where could I go? When a single hair burns it smells so awful! And now all this flesh of yours will burn! Just think a little of the stench you will spread". Then the man was bewildered and exclaimed, " If one can neither live in this world nor die in it, what is one to do?"[68]

The Sufi, too, is not in favour of abandoning either the worldly life nor actions. He is mystic but not a relinquisher of works. He realizes that he has various duties to perform, and there is no running away from them. We have a duty towards our children and family, towards our friends and acquaintances, towards the old who deserve our respect and consideration, to our country whose air we have breathed and which has nurtured us, and finally, and in fact primarily, to God our Creator and Sustainer. That ascetism or the performance of torturous austerities is not favoured by Sufis is illustrated by one of the tales of Mulla Nasrudin (some of which we have related before). One day the Mulla came acress a yogi who was sitting in contemplation. When asked why, the yogi said he was trying to obtain harmony with all living creatures. The Mulla said `Well once a fish saved my life, so I think your objective is laudable.' The yogi was impressed and invited the Mulla to join him in contemplation. After some time the yogi said that he had never been in such close communion with living creatures as the Mulla told him about the fish, and wished to know of that amazing experience. Nasrudin said to him `I doubt if it would do you any good to know about it'. But the yogi pressed him to relate it. `Well' said the Mulla `the fish was instrumental in saving my life. I was starving at that time. One getting the fish I ate a little of its flesh each day. It sufficed me for some days as it was a big fish. So it saved me from starving to death'!

Worldly living, however, does not mean that life is meant for eating and drinking and lasciviousness. Life's real porpose is to follow the spiritual path, to live in the world and yet not to be of it. As the Scottish poet Burns says:

> `Give me ane spark of Nature's fire
> That's a' the learning I desire;
> Then, though I trudge through dirt and mire,
> At plough or cart;
> My Muse, though lamely in attire
> May touch the hearth'.

And Chaucer:

`When that Aprille with his shoures sote
The droughte of Marche hath perced to the rote,
And bathed every veyne in swich licour,
Of which vertu engendred is the flour;
When Zephirus eek with his swete breeth
Inspired hath in every holt and heeth
The tendre croppes...'[69]

The Sufi looks for beauty in all things; in nature, song music and poetry for to him as the poet John Keats said `beauty is truth truth beauty'. The Sufi saint and mystic Zu'l Nun al-Misri says:

> `O God, I never hearken to the voices of the beasts or the rustle of the trees, the splashing of waters or the song of birds, the whistling of the wind or the rumble of thunder, but I sense in them a testimony to Thy Unity (*wahdaniya*) and a proof of Thy Incomparableness; that Thou art the All-prevailing, the All-knowing, the All-wise, the All-just, the All-true, and that in Thee is neither overthrow nor ignorance nor folly nor injustice nor lying. O God, I acknowledge Thee in the proof of Thy Handiwork and the evidence of Thy acts; grant me, O God, to seek Thy Satisfaction with my satisfaction and the Delight of a Father in His child, remembering Thee in my love for Thee, with serence tranquillity and firm resolve'.[70]

To be in the world and get busy with whatever avocation one has been destined for and to obtain success in it and reach the top, is not at all frowned upon by a Sufi. Indeed he considers it worth credit and admiration. Work as the Lord says in the *Gita* is essential and inevitable. One cannot even keep alive in the world unless he works — *sharīrāytrā pi ca te na prasidhyed akarmaṇaḥ*.[71] The Lord says even I keepo working `*I* (the Lord) have no duty to perform in all the three worlds, nor anything lacking which I need to obtain, never the less. I am engaged in work. For if I abstained from tirelessly working, people will in all ways follow My example Were I to abandon work, there worlds would perish I would be the cause of the people's fall from morals and of their destruction'.[72] But in what way should one act? Shri Krishna says 'Both the ignorant man and the wise work But while the ignorant man and the wise work But while the ignorant man is attached to works, the wise man works for the world's welfare'.[73] nother observation about work in the *Gita* is particularly relevant in our times in our country. The Lord says 'Whatever a great man does, that in truth, is done by others. Whatever standards he sets the worlds (read our countrymen) follow'.[74] Perhaps our *netas* and leaders, the politicians and scamesters who accumulate illegal wealth, greasing the palm so thick, are ignorant of Shri Krishna's wise observation, or knowing it care a damn. Otherwise our country would not be covered by the heavy smog of corruption. Hazrat Inayat Khan says:

> 'No doubt all things pertaining to the earth have their influence upon a person. It hardens one, it makes one's heart cold and takes away that tender sentiment that one has towards one's dear ones, towards those whom one loves and on whom one depends, towards one's fellowmen. It makes one more greedy and greed makes one unjust. Man becomes more covetous, and his cup of desire is never filled; he is never satisfied. The more that comes the less there seems to be there. Nevertheless, if one does not go through this experience, which is man's test, and one travels by another way, then one has given up a great experience, an experience which really makes the soul noble. A person whom you would otherwise not have understood for ten years, you can understand in a day as soon as there is a question of money. It at once brings out what is hidden in that person'.[75]

It is not necessary to eat a lot of sugar to discover its sweetness or to eat a lot of salt to find out its saltiness Just a few grains placed on the tonque are enough. As a poet says.

> `To see a World in a Grain of Sand,
> And Heaven in a Wild Flower,
> Hold Infinity in the palm of your hand
> And Eternity in an hour'.[76]

Another thing necessary for man is hope. Hope and courage are the beacons of life. An American author and a medical graduate says: `The mind is the natural protector of the body... Every thought tends to reproduce itself and ghastly mental pictures of disease, sensuality and vice of all sorts, produce scrofula and leprosy in the soul, which reproduces them in the body. Anger changes the chemical properties of the saliva to a poison dangerous to life. It is well known that sudden and violent emotions have not only weakened the heart in a few hours, but have caused death and insanity. It has been discovered by scientists that there is a chemical difference between that sudden cold exudation of a person under a deep sense of guilt and the ordinary perspiration; and the state of mind can sometimes be determined by chemical analysis of the perspiration of a criminal which, when brought into contact with selenic acid, produces a distinctive pink colour. It is well known that fear has killed thousands of victims; while, on the other hand, *courage is a great invigorator*'.[77] Hope and good cheer are also necessary for mental health.

> `Know, then, whatever cheerful and serene
> Supports the mind, supports the body, too.
> Hence the most vital movement mortals feel
> Is hope; the balm and life-blood of the soul'.[78]

In his Inferno II Dante says that it is written on the gateway of hell `Abandone hope all ye who enter bere — *lasciate ogni speranza, voi ch'entrate*, and Plautus says:

> `Quick, open wide his gate of hell;
> For I in truth can count it nothing less.

No one comes here who has not lost all hope
Of being good'.[79]

And Alexander Pope says `Hope springs eternal in the human breast'.[80] The way to get rid of the negative quality of hopelessness is to have faith in God. Faith is doubtless difficult to acquire for man does not know about the hereafter. Hazrat Inayat Khan relates that someone went to Ali and said `You tell us about the hereafter and the granting of desire there. What if it not true? Then all our efforts on this earth would be wasted' `Nothing will be wasted' said Ali. `If it were not fulfilled, then you and I would have the same experience. But if it is true that there is a paradise, then you will be the loser and I shall gain, for I have prepared for it and you have scoffed at the idea'.[81] Suppose a man takes a train to a certain place. His wife prepares some *puries* (fried unleavened bread) and cooked vegetables and packs them in a tiffin-box for him to eat on the journey. She knows fully well that there is the railway catering service. But still she puts the eats for him just in case the catering service is not available. So too with the hereafter. If there is no God and an afterlife, as the atheist believes, prayer and worship and devotion will still give us comfort and relief in life's sorrows. But if there is both God and the hereafter, the atheist will always regret that he didn't think of God and will never be able to remedy his omission.

Omar Khayyām, who has been very ably translated by Edward FitzGerald was doubtlessly a Sufi. In his book on the Sufis Idries Shah makes out that FitzGerald's txanslation of Omar's quatrains does not truly follow the original Persian text. However FitzGerald has done for Omar what Boswell did for Dr Johnson. And most certainly his rendering has captured in places the Sufi spirit. As has been said, the Sufi point of view is wide and although it postulates a spiritual way of life, it does not discard worldly activity or the desire to live. Idries Shah has an interesting comment about Khayyām. Three persons came to the eminent Sufi, Khan Jan-Fishan Khan. They were told to study Omar Khayyām's writing and then come and tell him what they thought of it. One of them came and said Omar's work was thought-provoking. The second man said that he concluded Omar was a heretic. The third that some deep mysteries appeared to be hidden in his work which he hoped he would get at by and by. This illustrates the many facets of Khayyām's work and Fitzgerald's is not the only work of his translated from the Persian. Another is *Salaman and Absal*. And it is difficult to imagine that he could translate these works with such great felicity without a knowledge of Persian, for like Sanskrit and Arabic, Persian is not a language one can translate from without any acquaintance with it. Of course the translation could be termed a `transcreation' if so desired, but its merit is indisputable. In his book, *A History of English Literature*, Louis Cazamian says about the quatrains of Omar as translated by FitzGerald.

> `By a unique stroke of fortune, the translation of the medieval Persian quatrains modernized with bold yet delicate skill, moulded and arranged in a personal way, expresses the innermost soul and subtlest essence of nineteenth-century melanchology, which acquiring thus the depth of a far-distant past, seems to spread as well over the whole human destiny. The oriental colour of the setting, exact and yet toned down, together with the inspiring power of the rhythm, is a miracle of refined literary adaptation; and the art which has formed and condensed each pearl in this poetic necklace, which has also polished them and added to their grace the rich lustre of thought, is not unworthy of being compared with that of the greatest artists'.[82]

The diversity and philosophical trend blended with the love sentiment, a Sufi characteristic, may be seen in some of Omar's verses as translated by FitzGerald::

`Myself when young did eagerly frequent
Doctor and Saint, and Saint, and heard great argument

About it and about : but evermore
Came out by the same Door as in I went.'

`There was a Door to which I found no Key:
There was a Veil past which I could not see
Some little Talk a while of me and thee
There was — and then no more of thee and me'.[83]

In the first quatrain quoted above we see the Sufi belief that argument is of no avail in the realization of God. We have quoted the Sufi, Habib-Ajmi, as saying that while others gave argumentative talks and wrote lectures, he was devoting his time in self-purification.[84] Another Sufi said `The beginning of service is meditation and silence, save for the recollection of God'.[85] The second quatrain depicts mysticism. The Sufi belief is that one can attain knowledge of God by meditation and spritualism. This is what FitzGerald implies by `the Door to which there is no Key and the Veil beyond which one cannot see'. The Sufi idea of *latifa*, mention of which has been made earlier in the book, is a mystic one. The *lataif* are the five centres containing the mystic force of *baraka*. Thus Omar's verses as rendered in FitzGerald's English version have certainly captured the Sufi spirit, in some of them at any rate.

According to the Sufi the purpose of creation can be known to God himself. The off-quoted teachings of the Holy Quran are said to be: `Whoever knows himself knows God', `God was and there was naught beside him', `I was a hidden Treasure and I desired to be known, therefore I created that I might be known.[86] Hazrat Inayat Khan says:

> `If a Sufi is asked what was the purpose of this creation he will say that the Knower, the only Knower, wanted to know Himself and there was only one condition of knowing Himself, and that was to make Himself intelligible to His own Being. For Intelligence itself is a

Being, but Intelligence is not known to itself. Intelligence becomes known to itself when there is something intelligible. Therefore the Knower had to manifest Himself thus becoming an object to be known. And by this knowledge the Knower arrives at perfection. It does not mean that the Knower lacked perfection, for all perfection belonged to the Knower; only He became conscious of His perfection. Therefore it is in the consciousness of perfection that lies the purpose of this whole manifestation'.[87]

Regarding creation the Holy Quran says, `And We did not create the heaven and the earth and what is betwixt them for sport. Had We wished to make a diversion, We would have made it from before Ourselves : by no means would We do (it). Nay! We cast the truth against the falsehood, so that it breaks its head, and lo! it vanishes; and woe to you for what you describe'.[88] Thus the Holy Quran says firstly that creation is not the sport of God and secondly that it was done so that truth may triumph over falsehood. The former observation i.e., creation is not God's sport is different from the Hindu view that creation is the *līlā* (sport) of God. When a disciple asked Shri Ramakrishna why there was much suffereving in the world the Swami Said `This world is the *lī lā* of God. It is like a game. In this game there are joy and sorrow, virtue and vice, knowledge and ignorance, good and evil. The game cannot continue is sin and suffering are altogether eliminated'.[89] But the view of the *Gita* is akin to that of the Sufis. Arjuna says to the Lord, `Neither the gods nor the demons, O Lord, know your manifestation. O Supreme Being! O Creator, O Lord of beings, O God of gods! O Father of the universe you alone can know what you are — *svayamevā' tmanā' tmānam vettha*'.[90]

Hindu philosophy also believes that truth shall prevail as the Holy Quran says. In fact the Indian national emblem reads *satyameva jayate* (`truth will triumph'). But then Pilate's famous question to Jesus Christ remains unanswered; for truth is not something external. As Browing says:

> 'Truth is within ourselves; it takes no rise
> From outward things, whate'er you may believe.
> There is an inmost centre in us all
> Where truth abides in fullness'.[91]

And in the same way the American poet, Walt Whitman boldly asserts that all external impressions should be abandoned and only one's own conviction retained:

> 'From this hour I ordain myself loos'd of limits and imaginary lines,
>
> Going where I list, my own master total and absolute,
>
> Listening to others, considering well what they say,
>
> Pausing searching, receiving, contemplating,
>
> Gently, but with undeniable will divesting myself of the hold that would hold me'.

Thus truth is precious but it will not be found in external things, nor it will be found in long discourses. It is the internal concept of an inquiring mind. Besides as Hazrat Inayat Khan says 'There are two things : knowing and being. It is easy to know truth, but most difficult to be truth. It is not in knowing truth that life's purpose is accomplished; life's purpose is accomplished in being truth'.[92] In the same way Buddha says in Dhammapada:

yathāpi ruciram puppham vaṇnavantam agandhakam
evaṁ subhāsitā vācā aphalā hoti akubbato.

> ['Like a beautiful flower full of colour but without scent, are the well-spoken but fruitless words of him who does not act (as he professes to)'].[93]

What really is the aim of religion? The basic purpose is to carry man near to God. To know one's inner soul, and to realize its oneness with God. The Sufi saint, Bayazid of Bistun, says `I went from God to God until they cried from me in me "O thou I".' Once someone went and knocked at Bayazid's door and shouted `Is Bayazid there?' Bayazid said from behind the door `Is anyone here save God?' On another occasion someone asked him his age. He said he was four years old. `How can that be?' said his questioner, pointing to his gray hair and aged body. Bayazid said `Out of my seventy-four years I have been veiled from God for seventy and it was only thereafter that I could know him. The period I was veiled from God do not count. So I am four years old'. Jalaluddin Rumī says `The Beloved is all in all; the lover merely veils Him, the Beloved is all that lives, the lover is a dead thing'. Rumī further says `How can I explain the Friend to one for whom He is no Friend?' This is very much like Miester Eckhart's observation `Why dost thou prate of God? Whatever thou sayest of Him is untrue'. Rumī says `Reason is like an officer who loses his power when the king appears. Then he hides himself. God is the sun, Reason the shadow cast by the sun'. Rumī gives the example of the mother and the baby whom she gives suck to. Does the child ask his mother for proof that he shall savour her milk? The Sufi mystic, Rabia, says `I have no phenomenal existence, for I have ceased to exist and have passed out of self. I exist in God and am altogether His. I live in the shadow of his command'.[94] Shaqiq Balkhi, the Sufi saint, says, `The interpretation of knowledge of God is that thou knowest in thy heart that there is no other who gives and beholds, hurts and soothes. Knowledge of the Self is to know thyself, that thou canst neither hurt nor soothe, that thou hast no power to do anything at all, and likewise to oppose the Self, which means to be submissive to God'.[95] The Sufis believed that spiritualism and wisdom is got by love of God. Maruf al-Karkhi, the Sufi saint, says:

> `Love is not to be learnt from me. It is one of God's gifts and comes of His grace... Sufism is the apprehension of divine realities and renunciation of human possessions... The saints of God are known by three signs, their thought

is of God, their dwelling is with God and their business is in God... The gnostic (*arif*) has no bliss, yet he himself is in every bliss'.[96]

The most important requisite of religion is broadmindedness and toleration. Any religion which does not have this quality is not religion but fanaticism. All religions acknowledge God to be the Supreme Being. The sage, Ramana Maharshi, says:

> 'The meeting point of all religions is that God is everything and everything is God. One must cease calling things "things" and must call them God; and instead of thinking them to be things we must know them to God. Instead of imagining "existence" to be the only thing possible we must realize that this (phenomenal) existence is only the creation of the mind, that "non-existence" is a necessary sequence if you are going to postulate existence.
>
> 'The knowledge of things only shows the existence of an organ to cognize. There are no sounds to the deaf, no sights for the blind, and the mind is merely an organ of conception or of appreciation of certain sides of God'.

Aldous Huxley says that unholiness or in other words ungodlines is a composite phenomenon:

> 'Unholiness arises when we give consent to any rebellion or self-assertion by any part of our being against that totality which it is possible for us to become through union with God. For example, there is the unholiness of the indulged sensuality, of unchecked avarice, envy and anger, of the wantonness of pride and worldly ambition. Even the negative sensuality of ill-health may constitute unholiness, if the mind is permitted to dwell upon the sufferings of its body more than is absolutely necessary of unavoidable. And on the plane of the intellect there is the imbecile unholiness of

> distractions and the busy, purposeful unholiness of curiosity about matters concerning which we are powerless to act on any constructive or remedial way'.[97]

The moment any religion spreads hatred or tries to convert `without a clean heart which is a denial of God and religion'[98] or as Francis Bacon says `tries to propagate itself by wars or sanguinary persecutions, to force consciences'; it ceases to be religious and forfeits the right to be called a religion.

This then is the undeniable achievement and excellence of Sufism. While believing in the Holy Quran it did not advocate its intolerance of other religions. Though not opposed to worldly life, Sufism was prone to ascetism. Before Islam came to Arabia and adjoining regions, ascetic systems like Buddhism, neo-Platonism and so forth existed. The Moslems overran the non-Moslem tribes and considered them to be inferior — infidels or Kafirs, as they called them, and idolaters as they were classified by the Holy Quran. Since idol-worship was mainly a Hindu practice, in effect the Moslem ire as evinced in the Holy Quran (9: 5 - 6) was particularly directed against them. Moslems were forbidden to take the Kafirs as their friends and helpers and the Holy Quran exhorts them to fight them to the finish, so that Islam gets the better of Kufr for good.[99] This oppression of the Arab Moslems made the oppressed seek the shelter of ascetism, though they too accepted Islam. Thus early Sufism was a blend of Islam and ascetism. The earliest writer on Sufism, Abu Nasr Sarraj, who died in A.D. 968, wrote in his book *Kitabul Luma fit-Tasawuf* about it: `As a system it was not evolved by the Sufis, but has been long prevalent among ascetics in the pre-Islamic period'.[100] But as a scholar of Sufism says, the *Kitabul Luma fit Tasawuf* mentions that while the Sufis agree with the Traditationists and Jurists in their beliefs and accept their sciences and consult them in difficult matters of religious law and keep God's commandments; they often leave them behind and `rise to the heights of mystical devotion and ethical self-culture which are exclusively their own'.[101] Al-Hasan al-Basri who died in A.D. 728 is said to be one of the earliest Sufis. He said `A grain of genuine piety is better than a thousand-fold weight of fasting and prayer. Renunciation in fear of hell or paradise is no renunciation. True renunciation is the realization of God and this comes by heart-purification'.[102] Another Sufi of these early times was Ibrahim bin Adham. He was a prince of Balkh who turned an ascetic and wandered about in many places. He became a spiritualist under the guidance of Father Simon, a Christian monk. His famous prayer was `O God, Thou knowest that paradise weighs not with me so much as a gnat's wing. If Thou befriendest me by Thy recollection and sustainest me with Thy love, and makest it easy for me to obey Thee then give paradise to whomsoever Thou wilt'.[103] It is not true that pious Moslems renounced the world and turned mystics by the influence of neo-Platonism, due to fear of God and hell. When the Arabs began to afflict the non-Arab Moslems and others like the Gnostics and Manichiens, they went away to the deserts and perforce adopted the path of renunciation. That was how Sufism took birth.

Thus the greatest achievement of the Sufis was that they removed the fanaticism from Islam. A prominent journalist gives the following instances of such fanaticism and hatred found in textbooks meant for Moslem students in Pakistan, the Moslem homeland:

> `For teaching Pakistani students of class 8 "The advent of Islam in India reformed Hindu society. Sheikh Ali Hujveri, Muinuddin Chishti, Bahauddin Zakria, Bakhtiar Kaki, Baba Farid Shakar Ganj, Nizamuddin Aulia and other holy men won over the people" (Hindus) of India. Their teachings dispelled many superstitions of the Hindus and reformed their bad practices. Thereby Hindu religion of the olden times came to an end' (p., 69 of the textbook for class 8, Social Studies). [All of these-Farid, Aulia, Zakriya, Kaki, Hujwiri and Chishti, belonged, as has been said before, to the school of

Ijadist Sufism who took their inspiration from the bigot Mogul, Aurangzebe, and so were in line with Moslem fanaticism. Thus they did not represent the real Sufi viewpoint].

`The Hindus are cunning, they are ungrateful, say the textbooks, they are consummate conspirators, their conspiracies are what account for the misfortunes which have befallen Pakistan'. *Mutala-a-i-Pakistan*, a textbook of the Allama Iqbal Open University B.A. students says `Hindus are not just cunning conspirators, they are mean murderers; the killings after Partition were all done by these Hindus and Sikhs'. And finally "*Kāf se Kafir*" says the *Quaida* used for teaching the kids Urdu, and the drawing alongside shows a pot-bellied, dhoti-clad pundit with a long *chutia*, "*Zeem se Zā lim*" says the *Quaida* and the drawing alonside shows a bearded Sikh'.[104] The very scholarly but nonetheless not too precise study of Sufism by Idries Shah says: `it was the Sufi teachers who were responsible in great measure for the establishment of what became known as the great Hindu schools of mysticism' and he relies on Auguste Barth, Religions of India which again misrepresents Hinduism. Further Idries Shah says that the *bhakti* movement in Hinduism was `Based to a great extent upon Sufi thought and practice introduced into India after the Islamic conquest'[105] Now that sounds much like what Arun Shourie says about Sufis of the Ijadist school. As has been said Madva, Rāmaṇānd, Kabīr, Mirābaī, Tukārāma, Jñānadeva, Ravidāsā, Chaitanya, Dādū, Rāmānuja, Yamunachārya and so forth were mystics and saints and it was most probably the other way round, that Sufism was influenced by Vaishnavism. At any rate great thoughts and beliefs are not the copyright of any one or of any group of persons. They can come to all independently of one another.

Bhakti in its wider concept existed much before the Christain, Moslem or Sufi civilizations in the *Bhagavadgita* and *Nārada Bhakti Sūtra*. Let us take a look a the age of various civilizations. The excavations of Harappa and Mohenjodaro push back Indian civilizatioon to about 4000 B.C. The excavations made by *Professor Sharma* of the **Allahabad University** show that civilization existed in India 8,000 years ago.[106] Anyway, even discarding this as of academic interest the age of civilizations is said to be as follows:

Egyptian	c. 5000 - 525 B.C.
Indian (Indus Valley)	c. 4000 - 2500 B.C.
Chinese	c. 2000 B.C. - 4th century
Greek	c. 3200 B.C. - A.D. 195
Rome	2000 B.C. - A.D. 170.[107]

And the Islamic civilization and Sufis came much after.

Foreign writers tend to gloss over these facts in a determined but futile effort to belittle Indian civilization. However those who are unprejudiced and openminded, give it its due place. Count Bjornstjerna says: `No nation on earth can vie with the Hindus in respect of the antiquity of their religion... But if it be true that the Hindus more that 3,000 years before Christ, according to Bailley's calculation, had attained a high degree of astronomical and geometrical learning, how many centuries earlier must the commencement of their culture have been, since the human mind advances only step by step on the path of science'.[108] The renowned German scholar Max Müller, says: `If I were to look over the whole world to find out the country most richy endowed with all the wealth, power and beauty that nature can bestow, in some parts a very paradise on earth – in some parts a very paradise on earth — I should point to India. If I were asked under what sky the human mind has most fully developed some of its most choicest gifts, has most deeply pondered on the greatest problems of life, and has found solutions, some of which well deserve the attention of even those who have studied Plato and Kant — I should point to India. And if I were to ask myself from what literature we here in Europe — we who have been nurtured almost exclusive on the thoughts of the Greeks and Romans and of the Semetic races, the Jewish — may draw that corrective which is most wanted in order to make our inner life more perfect, more comprehensive, more universal, in fact more truly human, a life not for this life only but a transfigured and etenal life, again I should point to India'.[109] Colonel Tod says `Where (except in India) can we look for sages whose systems of philosophy were the prototypes of those of Greece: to whose works Plato, Thales and Pythagoras were disciples? Where shall we find astronomers whose knowledge of the planetary system yet excites wonder in Europe as well as the architects and sculptors whose works claim our admiration, and the musicians "who could make the mind oscillate from joy to sorrow, from tears to smiles, with the changes of modes and varied intonation" '.[110] And as for those writers who are so fascinated by the much later Arab thinking, as to observe `Whether nominally of the East or West, we are all heirs in one way or another to the strength and weaknesses of medieval Arab philosophy',[111] the edict of the Indian emperor Ashoka (274 B.C. – 232 B.C.) from whom we have already quoted earlier, and whom David Bury considers one of the most striking personalities in the history of the world, might be an eyeopener.

And the comment of Aldous Huxley who has quoted emperor Ashoka's edict is, `It would be difficult, alas, to find any edict of a Christian king to match Ashoka's. In the West the good old rule, the simple plan, was gloirfication of one's own sect, disparagement and persecution of all others'.[112] Huxley might with justification have added `the Arab and Moslem world' to `the West'. Contrary to some commentators on Sufism, the Sufis made tolerance their watchword, in the spirit of Ashoka's edicts. Therein lies their greatness. With a few exceptions, like the Ijadist Sufis, they were not bigoted. As we have quoted Hazrat Inayat Khan, the Sufi `does not belong to a religion but all religions belong to him'. Many Hindu schools of thought are represented in Sufism, such as Vaishnavism, Vedanta, Krishnaism, Nirguna bhakti and so forth apart from neo-Platonism, mysticism and pantheism. Bullhe Shah believed both in the Hindu doctrine of karma and Krishna-devotion. He says `As soon as I discovered love, I fled from the mosque...'[113] Farid Sani does not believe in the Haj pilgrimage to Mecca : `O Farid, why should you wish to go on Haj to Mecca. The holy Mecca is in your heart. What is needed is that you cast away shame on God's path.[114] Bullhe Shah has much the same idea : `Those undertaking the Haj pilgrimage go to Mecca. But I have both Mecca and the beloved in my heart.[115] In fact the idea of the lover and Beloved was borrowed by Sufis from the Vaishnava concept of *mādhurya bhakti*. The observation of the lover knocking at the door of the Beloved and being admitted inside only when the two become one, of Jalaluddin Rumī, which has been quoted before, is based on the *mādhurya bhāva*. The Sufis thus, even though accepting and professing Islam, gave it a broader interpretation shorn of all fanatacism.

REFERENCES

1. *Kavitā-Kaumudī* part 4 ed. Kripanath Mishra. Prayaga : Hindi Mandir.

2. *The Sufi Message of Hazrat Inayat Khan*. London : Barrie and Rockliffe, 1960. vol. 1, p., 14. [This will be henceforth referred to as `Hazrat Inayat Khan, SB'

3. *Bhagavadgita*, 4 : 7 - 8

4. ibid. 9 : 11

5. William Wordsworth. *Lines composed a few miles above Tintern Abbey*.

6. *The World is Too Much with us*. Ib. xxxiii.

7. *Hazrat Inayat Khan* SB, p., 16 op. cit.
8. *Bhagavadgita*, 6 : 40.
9. Virgil. *Geogics*. III, 242.
10. Euripides *Auge, Fragment* 5.
11. The *First Epistle of John*. i. 8.
12. *Hazrat Inayat Khan, SB*. op. cit. p., 19.
13. W.B Yeats. *When You are Old*.
14. Idries Shah. *The Sufis*. New York : Anchor Books 1964, p., 57 op. cit.
15. *Hazrat Inayat Khan SB*, p., 24.
16. James Branch Cabell. *The Silver Stallion* bk. iv, ch. 17. *Hazrat Inayat Khan* SB. p., 55.
17. *Hazrat Inayat Khan* SB, p., 55.
18. *Bhagavadgita* 2 : 22.
19. Dr Raymond A. Moody Jr. *Life After Life* USA : Bantam Books, 1973, pp., 94-98.
20. *Bhagavadgita*. 4 : 34. Trans.; author's.
21. *The Temple. The Church Porch*, lxxii.
22. *St Matthew* vii, i. 231. *St Luke*. vi. 37.
23. Raymond. A. Moody, Jr. *Life After Life*. USA : Bantam Books, p., 67.
24. *Bhagvadgita* 6 : 33 - 35.
25. *Ramacharitananasa. Aranyakanda* 34 : 4 & 35 : 1 - 2 Gita Press Gorakhpur edition.
26. *Gita*. 4 : 1 - 3.
27. *Hazrat Inayat Khan* SB, p., 97.
28. *Bhagavadgita* 2 : 66.
29. *Sujan - Rasakhann*.
30. *Gita* 13 : 9.
31. *Gita*. 13 : 27.
32. W.G Orr. D.D. *A Sixteenth Century Indian Mystic* London, Lutterworth Press.

33. Paul Brunton. *A Search in Secret India* quoted Tiruvannamal ai : Golden Jubilee Souvenir, 1646, p., 253 op. cit.
34. Prem Lata. *Sri Ramakrishna Paramahamsa*. New Delhi: Sumit Publications, 1991, p 215 - 6. op. cit.
35. Patanjali *Yogasutras*. Ch., 4, Attainments.
36. *Hazrat Inayat Khan* BS, p., 113. op. cit.
37. *Gita*. 16 : 6.
38. Dr Raymond A. Moody Jr. *Life after Life*. USA : Bantam Books, 1975, p., 60.
39. *Talks with Sri Ramana Maharshi*. vol. 2. Sri Ramanasaram, 1955, pp., 440 -441.
40. *Bhagavadgita* 2 :20.
41. *Hazrat Inayat Khan SB*, p., 178 op. cit.
42. Ralph Waldo Emerson. Phi Beta Kappa Address, 18 July 1876.
43. Robert Browining. *Rabbi Ben Ezra*.
44. Socrates, trans; Katheleen Freeman. *Fighting Words*. Beacon Press, 1952.
45. *Kabīr. Sākhī from the Guru Granth Sahib*. Trans; author's. New Delhi Ess Ess Publications 1997.
46. Shankaracharya. *Vivekachuramaṇi*
47. id., *Aparokshanabhiti* 56 - 58.
48. *The Padas of Kabīr*. Trans; author's. New Delhi : Ess Ess Publications 1947.
49. *The Gospel of Sri Ramakrishna. Hama* is the Hindi word for 'I' and *tū* is the Hindi word for 'you', i.e., 'thou'
50. *Bhagavadgita* 5 : 8 - 9.
51. *Īsha Upanishad*. 1 and 12. Trans; author's.
52. Raymond A. Moody, Jr. *Life after Life*. USA : Bantam Books, 1975, pp., 67- 68.
53. Bhagavan Sri Ramana Maharshi *Who am I?* Tiruvannamalai : Sri Ramanasramam, 1955, pp., 6 - 9.
54. *Kabīr Padas from the Guru Granth Sahib*. Trans; Trans' author's. Ess Ess Publications, New Delhi 1997.

55. *The Padas of Kabīr Trans*; author's *A New Look at Kabīr* New Delhi : Ess Ess Publications 1997. (By 'Rāma' Kabīr does not mean Rāma, the avatar of Vishnu, but God — the Formless Absolute *moksha* means `emancipation' and *mantra* `a sacred chant of formula'.
56. Cicero. *De Oratore* III, 25 : 100.
57. J.J. Rousseau : *Emile*, quoted by Adler, *The idea of Freedom*.
58. Aristotle. *Ethica Magna* I. 4, 3.
59. Raymond A. Moody Jr. *Life after Life*. USA : Bantam Books, 1975, pp. 59 & 63.
60. ibid. pp., 77 - 78.
61. *Bhagavadgita*, 3 : 17.
62. *The Epistie of Paul to the Philippinas*, iv. 7.
63. *Hazrat Inayat Khan* S.B. p., 211.
64. *Bālakāṇḍa* 293 (1), (Gita Press Gorakhpur edition).
65. *Bhagavadgita*. 3 : 35.
66. ibid. 3 : 26.
67. Acharya Vinoba Bhave. *Talks on the Gita*. London George Allen.
68. ibid.
69. *Poems of Robert Burns* (Scot language) and Geoffrey Chaucer. *Prologue to the Canterbury Tales* (Old English-Chaucerian).
70. A.J. Arberry. *Sufism*. London 1950, p., 52.
71. *Bhagavadgita* 3 : 8.
72. ibid. 3 : 22 - 24.
73. ibid. 3 : 25.
74. ibid. 3 : 21.
75. *Hazrat Inayat Khan* BS. pp., 21 - 220.
76. William Blake *Auguriesof Innocence*.
77. Quoted in Ralph Waldo Trine. *In Tune with the Infinite*. London : George Bell & Sons, 1905, pp., 46 - 47.
78. id. p., 49.
79. Plautus. *Bacchides*. Act III, Sc. I, I. — (*Lydus*).
80. Pope. *An Essay on Man*.

81. *Hazrat Inayat Khan* BS. p., 228.
82. *A History of English Literature*. Emile Legouis and Louis Cazamian. London: J.M. Dent & Sons Ltd. 1926, p., 1228.
83. FitzGerald. *Omar Khayyām* sxxvi and xxxii.
84. *Outlines of Islamic Culture* A.M.A. Shushtery, p., 348,
85. A.J. Arberry. *Sufism*. London, 1950, p., 37.
86. S.R. Sharda. *Sufi Thought*. New Delhi : Munshiram Manoharlal. 1974, p., 11 op. cit.
87. *Hazrat Inayat Khan BS.*, p., 232.
88. The Holy Quran. Trans; Muhammad Ali. Lahore : Ahmadiyya Anjuman-I-Ishaat-I-Islam, 1928 p., 328. (21 : 17 - 18).
89. *The Gospel of Sri Ramakrishna.*
90. *Bhagavadgita* 10 : 14 - 15. Trans; author's.
91. Robert Browning *Paracelsus*, Part 1.
92. *Hazrat Inayat Khan BS.* p., 240.
93. *Dhammapada*. Tran.; Dr Radhakrishnan.
94. A.J. Arberry. *Sufism* London, 1950, p., 42.
95. ibid. p., 39.
96. R.A. Nicholson. *A Literary History of the Arabs* London, 1923, pp., 385-6.
97. Aldous Huxely. *Seven Meditation.*
98. Mahatma Gandhi *To the Hindus and Mustims*. ed., Anand T. Hingorani 1942, p., 269.
99. *Āl `Imran*(3) 28, 118; *an - Nisā*(4) 144; *al - Māidah*(5) 51, 54, 57, 80; *at-Tawbah*(9) 16, 23; *Al-Qashash*(28) 86;1 *Al-Baqarha*(2) 193; *al-Anfāl*(8) 39; *at Tawbah*(9) 5. Quoted Harsh Narain.
100. *Jizyah and the Spread of Islam.* New Delhi : Voice of India, 1990, p., 3. A.M.A. Shushtery *Outlines of Islamic Culture*, p., 367
101. Abu Nasr as Sarrja, *Kitabul Luma fit-Tasawuf* ed., R.S Nicholoson, p., 9.
102. R.A. Nicholson. *A Leterary History of the Arabs*, p. 227 and R.P. Tiwari. *Sufimat-sādhanā aur Sahitya*. p., 215.
103. A.J. Arberry *Sufism*, London, 1950, p., 37; R.A. Nicholson *A Literary History of the Arabs*, p 232.

104. Arun Shourie. Fifty Years of This. Sunday *Pioneer*, 7 June 1998, p., 14. (Quoting Pakistan's ronowned Historian Prof. K.K. Aziz — *The Pakistani Historians and The Murder of History* Pub., Lahore : Vanguard).
105. Idries Shah. *The Sufis*. USA : Anchor Books, 1964, pp., 402 - 3.
106. P.T.I. 22 December 1978. Paper on Recent Advances in Indo-Pacific Prehistory 1978.
107. *Civilisation, Past and Present*. USA : Scott Foresman and Company 1959.
108. Theogony of the Hindus, p., 37.
109. Professor Max Müllerl, India, *What it can Teach Me*, p., 8.
110. Tod's *Rajasthan*, pp., 608, 609.
111. Idries Shah, *The Sufis*, USA : Anchor Books, 1964, p., 265.
112. Aldous Huxley. *The Perennial Philosophy*. London : Collins, Fontana Books 1958 p., 206.
113. Dr Harnam Singh Shan. *Sufi Kāvya-sangraha*, p., 105.
114. Mohan Singh ed., *Sufian Dā Kalam*. p., 5
115. *Qanun-I-Ishq*, p., 113.

4

Growth and Evolution

When one arrives at the sea, he does not bother about the rivers that pour into it.

Hakim Sanal The Walled Gardent of Truth

As has been said Arabia was the land where first Sufism took root. Except for the districts of Yemen, most of Arabia was a desert with oases in between at some places. The people living there Bedouins. As population grew the requirements of the nomadic Arabs also increased and the result was the formation of caravans which raided the areas round about. An Arab leader was known as a Sheikh. He was selected by a council of his own tibesmen somewhat like our own *panchayat* except that the *sarpanch* and *panches* were by election while the Arab Sheikh was by selection. Each tribe had its own emblem. When one tribe was victorious over another it was a prelude to subjugating the conquered tribe in every possible way and even the religion of the subdued tribe was anathema so that conquest meant conversion. It was not conversion by conviction but by coercion. It was under these circumstances that the Arab Moslems overran the countries connected with the Sufis, namely Iraq, Syria, Egypt, Khrosan, Balkh/Bukhara and Samarqand. The usal choice given to the Sufis was Islam or the sword. Most of them preferred to acknowledge the Prophet as Mohammed, and the Quran as the

Book, and could not die for the sake of religion like Cranmer and Ridley at the stake, or of principles like Socrates. However even after embracing Islam thus, the Sufis turned to mysticism and ascetism, a denial of worldly pleasures and worldly life, as a sort of refuge from the authoritarianism of Islam.

The early Sufis thus were otherworldly believed in purity of the heart, the giving up of wordly desires, prayer complete single-minded love of God, and non-belief in hell or heaven. The Holy Quran speaks both of paradise or *jannat* (Arabic *firdaus*), and hell (*jahannam*). The word *jannat* meaning 'a garden' '(As for) those who believe and do good deeds, their place of entertainment shall be the gardens of Paradise. And abiding there in they shall not desire removal from them', and 'Therein are rives of water that does not alter, and rivers of milk the taste whereof does not change, and rivers of wine delicious to those who drink and rivers of honey clarified; and for them therein are all fruits and protection from their Lord'.[1]

Similarly hell (*jahannam*) is described in great detail. There are seven different names of hell, according to some seven divisions of hell. The word *jahannam* means 'great depth' in Arabic. Then there is *jahīm* meaning 'intensity of fire' (c.f. the Christian 'fire and brimstone'). Next to *jahīm* is *sa'īr* meaning 'the kindling of fire' After this is *saqar* signifying 'scorching heat' and thereafter *hutmah* 'to crush', then *lazā* meaning a flame of fire and lastly, *hāwiyah* meaning 'a bottomless abyss'. In paradise there is neither intense heat nor bitter cold while in hell there are both.[2] All such ideas were repudiated by the Sufis. They were also against materialism and worldiness. One of these early Sufis, Hasan al-Basri says:

> 'Beware of the this world with all wariness; for it is like a snake, smooth to the touch, but its venom is deadly... For this world has neither worth nor weight with God, so slight it is, it weighs not with God as much as a pebble or a single cold of earth...'[3]

Self-restraint, fear of God and submissiveness to him and meditation were enjoined by these early Sufis. Hasan-al-Basri said that one must clean his heart and restrain his desires otherwise he will be taking the path of evil.[4] Ibrahim B. Adham was for meditaion and withdrawing oneself from all except God. He advocated fear of God who only is one's hope and cautioned against disobedience to his will.[5] Shaqiq Balkhi said that God is supreme inasmuch as it is he alone who 'gives and withholds, hurts or heals'. Knowledge of the Self and submissiveness to God are essential.[6] Rabia said that one cannot have individual existence, 'I exist in God and am altogether His. I live in the shadow of His command'. And again, 'I know no cause of my illness except that Paradise was disclosed to me and I yearned after it in my heart; and I think that my Lord was jealous for me and so reproached me and he can make me happy'.[7] These, and others, like the early Sufis were of the ascetic trend which was furthered by their reaction to the oppression of Arab Moslems.

The next stage of early Sufism is the period of mysticism in which the Sufis turned to Greek, Indian and Christian thought. A historian says about the religion of the Greeks

> 'The beliefs concerning the nether world and the fate of the soul after death are essentially linked with the question of the Greek mysteries and the diffusion of the Dionysiac cult... The Greek mystery... differed from the ordinary public cult primarily in its secrecy; that is to say, only the initiated and those prepared for initiation could be admitted; and the preparation included special purification and sometimes the application of certain tests... The religion and the theology that they preached contained many interesting and pregnant ideas... the divine origin of the human soul; its transmigration through a series of rebirths in this world and the next; the belief in eternal happiness and external damnation combined with an idea of purgatory; and the power of

> the human soul to attain through purification and sacrament to complete union with God. It laid its stress on "other-worldliness" and was the first propagandist religion in Europe; for its appeal ignored the barriers of city, caste, family or sex'.[8]

It is with this background that Sufism became esoteric, requiring initiation, preparation purification and even test. The Dervish Orders, therefore, enjoin *baraka* (spiritual transmission) the master, the *Murshīd* to the disciple, *murīd*; the *lataif* the five centres; the doctrine of *tajalli* (iradiation) which is a special communication from the master to diciple; the same being the object of *muraqiuba* which is a kind of preparation for initiation; and *zikr* (Arabic *dhikr*) a kind of repetition to bring home the truth of the teaching. The *Gulistan* ('Rose Garden') of Sheikh Sa'adi of Shiraz insisted on self examination on the part of the aspirant. 'If you don't chide yourself' Sa'adi said 'how will you react favourably when others chide you for something'. According to Sa'adi the would-be disciple must be fit to learn about Sufism. 'How can a sleeping man awake one who is asleep?' he asks. Thus the Greek idea of 'only the initiated and those prepared for initiation' being suitable for the cult seeped into Sufism. The story of the man who came to Bayazid and asked him for a method by which he could come near to an understanding to God, has been told before. The man had not realized his higher Self nor had he got over his ego (called *nafs* in Sufi terminology). If a secret teaching, which Sufism is, following the Greek mysteries; were to be revealed untimely it would do more harm than good as Sa'adi hints in a fable. A girl was so ugly that her father despaired of finding her a husband for no one would marry her because her appearance was so uncouth. So he married her to a blind man. A physician said that he would be able to restore the man's eyesight, but the father, fearing that if his daughter's ugliness was made evident to her husband, he would divorce her, did not let the physician treat her. Sa'adi concludes that 'the husband of an ugly woman had best be blind'! In brief the Greek elements of the creed of mystery, preparedness for initiation and testing before admission to the creed's secrecy, were incorporated in the early Sufi mystics, as was also the Greek element of other-worldliness and love of God. The Greek idea of sacrament entered Sufism. The Christian covenant with God also became part of it. The new ideas of the divine origin of the soul, rebirth and transmigration, eternal happiness and the soul's union with God, were new to the Greeks but had been known to and propounded by Hindu philosophy much before. They are mentioned both in the *Bhagavadgita* and the *Upanishads*. Eternal happiness was known as *akhaṇḍa sukha* and union with God as *moksha*. These concepts–Vedantic and Hindu as well as Greek–also became part of this early Sufism. The prominent Sufis of this period are Maruf al-Karkhi, Abu Sulayman al-Darani, al-Muhasibi and Zu'l Nun al-Misri, all belonging to the ninth century. We have quoted some of the sayings of Zu'l Nun al-Misri before. Some of Maruf al-Karkhi are given as follows:

> 'Love is God's gift to man and follows from his grace... Sufism means knowing divine realities and renouncing worldly possessions ... The agnostic has no bliss, yet is himself every bliss The thoughts of the saints are with God, their dwelling is with God and their business is in God'.[9]

The Sufis of this period conceived God as beauty, goodness and love and considered him to be merciful. The world is God's handiwork and one should not detest it. They believed in God's grace and in predestination. In not believing in free will, the Sufis of this period were of the view that there is no such thing, in the same way as conceived by the sage Sri Ramakrishna, who, when questioned about it by a devotee said:

> 'Everything depends on the will of God. The world is his play. He has created all these different things – great and small, strong and weak, good and bad,

virtuous and wicked. This is all his maya, his sport. You must have observed that the trees in a garden are not of the same kind.

'As long as a man has not realized God he thinks he is free. It is God himself who keeps this error in man. Otherwise sin would have multiplied. Man would not have been afraid of sin, and there would have been no punishment for it.

'But do you know the attitude of one who has realized God? He feels: "I am the machine and Thou, O Lord, art the operator. I am the house and Thou art the dweller. I am the chariot and Thou movest me speak".[10]

These Sufis believed that one should fear God, but gave love of God a higher place than fear of him. It was God who put his wisdom and love in the hearts of men.

As the Sufis say 'Sufism in the essence of all religions.' The departure from the view that Islam is the only worthwhile religion, was naturally not relished by the Moslem fanatics. Foreign writers too, have a queerly prejudiced view of Sufism denying that it had any Vedantic trend. For example one scholar says 'several schools which had been considered to be the product of ancient Hinduism are revealed by scholars to have originated in Sufi teaching'.[11] As has been pointed out, this is not true. Ancient Hinduism existed in remote antiquity, much before there was even a trace of Sufism, Islam, Christianity or even the civilizations of Greece and Rome. Obviously any Vedantic ideas in Sufism or for that matter of any of these civilizations could either be a coincidence of the same truths being realized independently or an incorporation of the ideas of the ancient Hindu beliefs. It could obviously not be other than this. Printing was invented by Gutenberg in about 1440, but before that there were handwritten manuscripts and earlier those written on barks and such materials. But in the very ancient times of the Veda, *Upanishads* and so forth the teaching was by word of mouth faithfully transmitted from teacher to disciple. Thus Professor S. Pigot's view (*Prehistoric India* London, 1961, p., 235) that 'the early Hindu religious literature was written down only in the late eighteenth and early nineteenth centuries, at the instance of such British scholars as Sir William Jones' and that 'ancient documents scarcely exist. The oldest Indian manuscript is thought to be a Buddhist fragment on a birch bark of the late fifth century A.D., from Taxila. The Bakshali manuscript of the same material, seems the next claimant for high antiquity, though this is only of the twelth century':[12] is a misnomer in so far as it states a fact which repudiates revelation and oral transmission of the scriptures. From this point of view the Ten commandments of the Bible communicated by God's voice to Moses at Mount Sinai would have no claim to be scripture and so too the Holy Quran said to be a revelation from the Lord of the Worlds (26 : 192) or a revelation from God, the Mighty, the Wise (39 : 1 etc.), and so on. The Holy Quran was revealed to the Prophet Mohammed (47 : 2), having been sent down upon his heart through the Holy Spirit (26 : 185) on the 25th or 27th night which is known as *lailat ul qadr* (97 : 1) in the Arabic language (44 : 58; 43 : 3)[13]. So too the Vedas of the Hindus (the oldest of whose hymns were dated 2500 B.C. or so) was Shruti meaning 'what was heard', and are said to have been 'revealed orally to the rishis or sages whose names they bear'.[14] Are we therefore to ignore these Christian, Moslem and Hindu scriptures just because they were not in printed form or written on birch barks etc.? The Sufi would never subscribe to such an idea for to him all religions and their scriptures are acceptable, for they are the expressions of the one eternal truth, as, quoting Ishan Kaiser in Speech of the Sages, Idries Shah says:

> 'I am the pagan; I worship at the altar of the Jew; I am the idol of the Yemenite, the actual temple of the fire worshipper; the priest of the Magian; the inner reality of the cross-legged Brahmin meditating; the brush and colour of the arlist; the suppressed, powerful personality

> of the scoffer. One does not supersede the other when a flame is thrown into another flame they join at the point of "flameness". You throw a torch at a candle, and then you say "I have annihilated the candle's flame."[15]

The Arabs had some knowledge about Indians, and in some manner reconized the superiority of Hindu philosoty.[16] They also acquired some knowledge of Indian medicine, mathematics, astronomy and folklore.[17] The renowned Sufi saint Abu Yazid of Bistami absorbed the spiritual teaching of his teacher Abu Ali of Sind.[18] Al-Hallaj himself visited Gujrat and learnt about Hindu philosophy.[19] Abu Yazid propounded the doctrine of *Tauhid* or *Fana* (unity of being). Like the Vedantists he identified himself, i.e., his soul with God. He said 'I am the wine, the drinker of wine and the Saki (cup-bearer). The *Tauhid* doctine became prominent in Sufi thought. But by identifying himself with God, he meant, of course, Allah. This incensed the orthodox Moslems and to escape their wrath he declared himself to be mad, and so taken up with the love of God that he was not in his senses. He also shared the Hindu belief of *moksha*, for he said after liberation has been achieved, the dictates of religion have no further value.[20] Al-Hallaj's saying of *an al-haq* (I am God) is practically the same as the Hindu *aham brahmasmi*.

The orthodox and fanatic Arab Moslems could never stomach such views by Mohammedans themselves. The Abbasi Caliphs started persecuting these Sufis. Zul Nun and Nuri were tortured. Mansur al-Hallaj was executed because 'he discolosed the secrets of God to the uninitiated'. The result was that the Sufi movement was toned down to reconcile it with Islam. The Sufis went underground and could no longer speak out boldly as they feared persecution by the bigoted Arab Moslems. Some like El-Ghazzali, about whom a detailed account has been given before, even though holding on to the liberal Sufi views, managed to keep the extremists at bay by giving a philosophical twist to their liberal doctrines. El-Ghazzali believed in *ittihad* (identity of the soul and God) and *halul* (the doctrine of incarnations), as his writings

Kimiya-i-Saadat and *Miskat al-Anwar* ('Niche for Lights') show. The 'Light' of the latter book is drawn from the Quranic passage Allah is the Light of the heavens and earth. His Light is resembled by a lamp within a niche. The lamp is within a crystal, like a shining star. It is lit from a blessed olive tree, not of the East or the West; of it the oil itself nearly shines, without the effect of any fire. Light upon Light!' This verse of the Quran (*āyat* 24 : 35) as translated above is the version of Idries Shah (*The Sufis*, p., 431). The other version of Muhammad Ali is slightly different, being: 'God is the (giver of the) light in the heavens and the earth; a likeness of His light is as a pillar on which is a lamp, the lamp is in a glass (and) the glass is as it were a brightly shinning star, lit from a blessed olive-tree, neither eastern nor western, the oil whereof almost gives light though fire touch it not - light upon light...'[21] The footnote of the translator makes it out that this light represents Islam which gives light to the east as well as the west, i.e., illuminates the entire world. But Idries Shah's view that it is a 'mystical passage which gives the essence of Sufism, and conceals the nature of the cognition of the extra dimensions of the human consciousness which comes beyond the intellect' is nearer the truth and more acceptable.[22]

The persecution of the Sufis also led to another consequence. Some of them compromised their broadmindedness, which was a prominent feature of Sufi thought, and turned to bigotry. In this they had the support and even instigation of the Mogul rulers, who with lone exceptions, were narror-gauged. The Orders of the Qadiriyas, Suhrawardiyas, Chishtiyas, Naqshbandiyas, Shattariyas, Shahzilliyas and Mevaleviyas were among these. They conformed strictly to the teaching of the Holy Quran and patterned themselves on the Prophet. They could hardly be called Sufis, and were so in name only They went all out to convert persons of other religions to Islam, a practice shunned by genuine Sufis.

A brief period of Sufi resurgence was due to neo-Platonic thought. We have already mentioned about its influence. Traces of this are discernable in some of the Sufis of this period. One of them was Abu Nasar Mohammed of Farabi (A.D. 870-950). According to him the perception of the world by the senses is due to divine knowledge and that beyond cognizance of material things as well as of intellectual experience, is love, by which man is perfected.[23] Ibn Sina incorporated in his thinking the neo-Platonic idea that ultimate reality is eternal beauty reflected in the mirror of the universe. Plato conceived the doctrine of Forms according to which 'Forms' or 'Ideas' are entirely separate from the world one's senses perceive, and are knowable only by the pure intellect. They are the only objects of true knowledge beyond the everchanging appearances we see in the world of sense. The other doctrine of Plato is, as has been said before, the divinity and immortality of the soul, which, in its own right, has always existed, even before it entered the body, and will always exist it its final release from the its chain of incarnations. So too was the belief of the neo-Platonic Sufis. Al-Qushair (d. A.D. 1074) repeats the neo-Platonic idea of creation through agencies in between the shoul and life. God was both transcendent and immanent and it was only the ignorant who thought they were separate from him.[24] We have already spoken of El-Ghazzali who made neo-Platonism the crux of his philosophy and successfully reconciled it with Islamic orthodoxy. Ibn El-Arabi also departed from Moslem narrowness and was because of it called a liar and a heretic and in fact narrowly essaped assassination by a Moslem fanatic. He conceived human beauty to be close to divine reality. His '*Interpreter of Desires*' appeared to be on the surface erotic verse but he managed to satisfy the orthodox Moslems that it had an inner meaning. He propounded the doctrine of Saintship. Ibn Fariz (d. A.D. 1235 advanced the doctrine of the intermediary agency *Nuri-Mohommadi* and Abdul Karim Jili (A.D. 1365-1415) of *Insan Kamil*. Jami, who also belonged to the 15th century, divided Sufis into two separate schools, one *Hama ust* ('He is All') and the other *Hama uz ast* ('All is from Him').

REFERENCES

1. The Holy Quran. Trans.; Muhammad Ali. Lahore: Ahmadiyya

Anjuman-I-Ishaat-I-Islam, 1928, p., 307(18 : 107 - 8) and p., 504 (47 : 15)

2. ibid., pp., lxix - lxx (Introduction).
3. A.J. Arberry *Sufism*. London, 1950, p., 23.
4. R.A. Nicholson. *A Literary History of the Arabs*. London, 1923, p 227.
5. A.J. Arberry. *Sufism* pp. 37 - 38.
6. ibid. p., 39.
7. ibid. p., 42.
8. *Universal History of the World*. ed. J.A. Hammerton, vol. 2. London. The Educational Book Co. Ltd. pp., 1384 and 1386. (Ch., 44 The Religion of the Greeks by Lewis R. Farnell D. Litt.).
9. R.A. Nicholson. A Literary *History of the Arabs*. London, 1923. pp. 385-86.
10. *The Gospel of Sri Ramakrishna*.
11. Idres Shah. *The Sufis* USA : Anchor Books 1964, p., 401.
12. ibid., p., 403 op. cit.
13. The Holy Quran. Trans.; Muhammad Ali Lahore : Ahmadiyya Anjuman-I-Ishaat-I-Islam, 1928, p., ix. Introduction.
14. John Dowson. *A Classical Dictionary of Hindu Mythology. Literature etc*. London : Routtedge and Kegan Paul, 1961, p., 345.
15. Idries Shah. *The Sufis*. USA : Anchor Books, 1964, pp., 51-52. op. cit.
16. R.C. Majumdar. *The History and Culture of the Indian People*. vol. 5. pp., 241 and 448 - 52 and vol. p., 160.
17. Bertrand Russell. *History of Western Philosophy*, p., 444.
18. Lajwanti Ramakrishna, *Punjabi Sufi Poets*, p. xv.
19. A.M.A. Shushtery. *Outlines of Islamic Culture*, p., 352.
20. R.C. Zeahner. *Hindu and Muslim Mysticism*.
21. The Holy Quran. Trans.; Muhammad Ali. Lahore : Anjuman-I-Ishaat-I-Islam, 1928, p., 358.
22. Idres Shah. *The Sufis*. USA : Anchor Books, 1964. p., 431.
23. A.M.A. Shushtery. *Outlines of Islamic Culture*. Bangalore, 1954 pp., 308 and 311.d
24. Tara Chand. *Influence of Islam on Indian Culture*, p., 25.

5

Philosophy and Practice

Rise instantly ab ove time and space.

Brushing the world aside, be a world withing yourself.

Shabistari Secret Garden

The Truly generous man remains steadfast without resisting, praises without pretence to magnanimity and gives unasked.

Maaruf Karkhi

PHILOSOPHY

All religions have five factors in common, rituals, mythology, scriptures, ethics and philosophy. Of these the last two, namely ethics and philosophy, form the core of religions. Philosophy deals with things unknown and unknowable. As Will Durant says: 'Philosophy accepts the hard and hazardous task of dealing with problems not yet open to the methods of science – problems like good and evil, beauty and ugliness, order and freedom, life and death...'[1] The unknown is that which remains unaccountable today and the unknowable is that which has remained beyond comprehension right from the beginning of creation, despite all efforts of man to know it, as for example death, sleep and afterlife. There are many theories and beliefs. For example Hindus believes in karma, thereby explaining away much of the world's suffering and accounting for births and deaths. All these, they say, are because of karma. Thus by his actions man builds his own destiny, and judgment is on the basis of karma. Islam believes in a day of judgment when everyone will be judged – the *yaumul qiyāmah*, *yaumul fasl*, *yaumul hisāb*, *yaumul fat-h*, or *as-sā 'ah* 'The hour'. Thus the dead will rise and be given judgment. Karma is the basis both in Hinduism and Islam. The *Ramayana* says *karam pradhān bisva kari rākahā, jo jasa karai so tasa phala cā khā* ['karma is predominant in the world. As one sows, so he reaps'].[2] The *Upanishad* also has the same idea: 'A man becomes good by good deeds and bad by evil deeds.'[3] The Holy Quran says 'He who has done an atom's weight of good shall see it. And he who has done an atom's weight of evil shall see it' (99 : 7, 8). Christianity also believes in the bodily resurrection of the dead. Despite these religious beliefs much remains unexplained and beyond human understanding. For example why do children and the young die prematurely. The *Upanishad* says 'If you are unable to renounce, live in the world a hundred years performing good works. There is no other way to escape the taint of evil deeds'.[4] But how many can reach that magic figure of a hundred years and why should the young, who as Plautus and Menander and Hypsaeus say, 'are loved of the gods', die young?[5] Over such questions men have been wondering since the beginning of time, but unable to resolve them have to ultimately turn to that unseen, unknown, Infinite and Eternal Being labelled by them under various epithets – Brahmā, Shiva, Vishnu, Allah, Khuda, Jehovah, Deus, Mazda, Redeemer, Jesus Christ and so forth; in one word, God. As Sri Ramakrishna has it:

> 'God laughs on two occasions. He laughs when two brothers divide land between. They put a string across the land and say to each other, "This side is mine, and that side is yours." God laughs and says to Himself "Why this whole universe is Mine and about a little clod they say: this side is mine and that side is yours"!

> 'God laughs again when the physician says to the mother weeping bitterly because of her child's desperate illness: "Don't be afraid, mother. I shall cure your child". The physician does not know that no one can save the child if God wills that he should die'.

In this way unable to solve the mystery of life and death, men ultimately turn to God. Then there is the hereafter, the third boon which Nachiketas asked for from Yama, the god of Death:

> 'When one dies, doubt exists in people's minds
> Whether that is the end of him or some part
> of his (The soul) still exists; about this I'd like to know
> Grant me this knowledge, Yama, as my final boon...
>
> 'Knowing that life ends, however long its span
> And pleasures of the senses last but a moment,
> Who is the mortal who can expect joy from these?
> What worthier boon can be seek from the immortal gods?
>
> 'Tell me, O Yama, of that great hereafter.
> That which remains to us a mystery,
> About which various doubts exist in men's minds,
> It is this alone I wish to know from you'.

Different religions have given various interpretations to life, death and the hereafter, and many researchers have investigated out-of-the-body experiences of people declared clinically dead but who came back to life — Dr Kibler-Ross, Dr Raymond A. Moody Jr., Dr Russell Noyes Jr., Dr Grafield, Albert Heim, Dr R.C.A. Hunter, Dr Robert Crookall and Father Herbert Thurston, among others. But all these are merely guesses. Every religion brings in its now preconceived idea, but none really knows. Sri Ramakrishna says in one of his parables.

> 'Suppose God comes to you as a man and says "I am God". Will you believe it then? After his death Lazarus said to Abraham "Let me go back to the earth and tell

> my friends and relatives that hell and afterlife exist." Abraham replied: "Do you think they will believe you? They will say it is a charlatan who is telling such things"'.[8]

The Sufi does not get involved in the dogma of religious doctrines. To him all religions are acceptable so long as they do not preach hatred or fanaticism. Al-haqq conceives the Real as the 'abyss of Godhead underlying the personal Allah, while the Prophet is taken out of history and regarded as the incarnation of the Logos'.[9] Ansari of Heart says: 'Know that when you learn to lose yourself, you will reach the Beloved. There is no other secret to be learnt, and more than this is not known to me'.[10] And Bayazid of Bistun speaks of the spiritual value of contemplation:

> For twelve years I was the smith of my soul, I put it in the furnace of austerity and burned it in the fire of the combat, I laid it on the anvil of reproach and smote it with the hammer of blame until I made of my soul a mirror. Five years I was the mirror of myself and was ever polishing that mirror with divers acts of worship and piety. Then for a year I gazed in contemplation. On my waist I saw a girdle of pride and vanity and self-conceit and reliance on devotion and approbation of my works. I laboured for five years more until the girdle became worn out and I professed Islam anew. I looked and saw that all created things were dead. I pronounce four *akbirs* over them and returned from the funeral of them all, and without intrusion of creatures, through God's help alone, I attained unto God'.[11]

In this way the three pillars of the edifice of Sufi philosophy are spiritualism, love and mysticism, and its watchword is tolerance. El-Gazzali regarded the mystics to be the ultimate source of knowledge of the soul. They are the ones who save societies from ills and decay. He says 'In the time of the philosophers, as at every other period there existed some of these fervent mystics. God does not deprive this world of them, for they are its sustainers'.[12]

As has been mentioned before, Sufism was a reaction to oppression of Arab Moslems. It was due to this that it took to mysticism and ascetism. The spiritual man can bear suffering to a greater extent than the one inclined to materialism. Conversely suffering itself turns the mind to spiritualism. Besides, the mystic does not care for worldly possessions. Despite Idries Shah's observation of 'the professional Hindu ascetic wedded to a deteriorated tradition'[13] (there can be no 'professional ascetic' for ascetism is not a profession, but merely a way of thinking, nor can there be a 'deteriorated tradition' for traditions develop, they don't deteriorate); despite this remark by this authoritative writer on Sufism, the fact remains that the origin of Sufi philosophy *was* ascetism–ascetism as a consequence of Islamic persecution. Since the oppression of the Arabs continued for long, the Sufis had to adjust themselves to cope with it. This they did by suppressing the ego, as long ago the Hindu Vedantist Shankarācharya had preached, and this became one of the supports of the non-Arab Moslems, the Mawalis (the other two allied ones being the Zimmis and Mamluks). The other refuge from the Arab persecution was the identification of the soul with God, the Hindu-Greek concept. Abu Yazid said that this merging was life's aim. Ibn El-Arabi declared that God and his existence are one and the he is ignorant who sees separation between the two. The love of God was the end for which man strove. The object of man's creation is the acquisition of knowledge. This is also the finding of the research on out-of-the-body experiences of Dr. Raymond A. Moody Jr., who stressed the importance of love, helping others and the acquisition of knowledge (already qoted before).[14] Love and knowledge were also the two quests of the Sufis. Knowledge means knowing God as the Creator and also that of his creation. According to Islamic theology there is the doctrine of *Tawhid* (Unity of Being) which postulates Allah as the only Lord, the Gracious Rabb (Sustainer) Rahman (Beneficent) and Rahīm (Merciful). This Divine Unity summed up in the expression *la ilāha illallāh* refers to Prophet Mohammed, peace be on him. As the Christian teaching. 'Thou shalt have no other gods before me... for I the Lord the God am a jealous God (Exodus. 20 : 3 and 5), the Islamic one too says 'Serve God you have no God other than Him' (Holy Quran 7 : 59, 65, 73, 85) and 'Say, O followers of the Book! come to an equitable proposition between us and you that we shall not serve any but God and that we shall not associate aught with Him and that some of us shall not take others for lords beside God (Holy Quran 3 : 63). Thus in the words of the translator (Muhammad Ali, Lahore: Ahmadiyya Anjuman-I-Ishaat-I-Islam) 'the Holy Quran invites the followers of all religions to come back to that pure teaching as the basis of understanding'! (p., xli Introduction); that is to say, O followers of other religions (barring) Islam leave your faiths and adopt the true one of Islam!

The Sufis, however were not taken in by such conceit. Abu Yazid interpreted *Tawhid* as the identity of the essence of man and God, and other Sufis like Abu Sulayman al-Darani and Zul Nun attributed beauty, goodness and grace to God and these attributes reflected in his creation as we have quoted his saying so before 'in the voices of the beasts, rustle of the trees, splashing of waters, songs of birds, and the whistling of the winds etc.' For the Sufi God is the Supreme Mind and Ultimate Reality and manifests himself in creation through love. In later Sufism sensual objects are also deemed to be God in essence, e.g., Ibn El-Arabi, 'Glory be to God who created things being Himself their essence'.[15]

Similar to the Vedantic belief of a higher Self and a lower, is the Sufi concept of the animal soul (*nafs*) and the rational soul (*rū h*). The *rūh* is the body's spirit or illuminating power of which Junaid says 'Only God knows its essence or nature. All that can be said about is that it is an existence'.[16] Abu Saidal-Kharaz says '*Rūh* is created. The body exists for it, and the mind and reason are associated with it'.[17] *Nafs* is associated with material and carnal living and such desires. It is the *rūh* which overcomes *nafs* and carries the soul God-wards. *Nafs* pulls it down and fetters it. If a man cannot overcome it he gets tied up with the world's sensual pleasures and forgets his real destiny.

The person who loves God hates evil but since he finds it present in the world, he gets reconciled to it. The later Sufis do not believe in anything other than God. The material world proceeds from them like a river from its source. The universe is Reality's essence known as *asma* (names of God) and *sifat* (attributes of God). Another school of Sufis says that the phenomenal world is not real but the reflection of the real world which exists in God's mind as Idea.[18] While with the early Sufis the phenomenal world was an object of hatred and an impediment in reaching God, with the later Sufis it was an aid to knowledge of God.

The doctrine of divine emanation is known to Sufis as that of *wahdatul wajud*. Ibn El-Arabi and Jili considered matter to be God's emanation. We have quoted El-Arabi as saying 'Glory to God who created everything being Himself the essence of all'. This doctrine is that known as *wahdatul wajud*. According to this God manifests himself as *haqiqat ul haqaiq* (the Reality of realities), as the phenomenal world in the form of universal body (*al-jism-al kulli*) and as prime matter and as prime matter (*hayula*). The same is projected in man as body, soul and spirit. The following table will illustrate these divisions:

Haquqat ul haqaiq (Reality of realities)	*al-jism-al-kulli* (universal body)	*hayula* (prime matter)
↓	↓	↓
body	soul	spirit
(mode of the universal body)	(mode of the universal soul)	(mode of the universal reason)

Further reality is manifested in the lower stages without diminution of its higher one. The names of God (*asma*) and his attributes (*sifat*) are essence themselves differentiated in the lower stage of knowledge. External existence is God's own existence. He is present in his creatures as Reality. Divine nature (*al lahut*) is projected into human nature (*al nasut*). In other words man is enveloped by the divine. God is in man and man obliterated in God. This Ibn el-Arabi says, is 'supreme union'. Ibn Arabi says:

> 'There is no existence save his (God's) existence. There is no other and there is no other existence for any other than he... he whom you think to be other than God, he is not other than God, but you do not know him and do not understand that you are seeing him. He is still Ruler as well as the ruled and Creator as well as Created. He is now as He was, as to his creative power and as to His sovereignty, neither requiring a creature nor a subject. When he called into being the things that are, He was already endowed with all His attributes and He is as He was then. In His oneness there is no difference between what is recent and what is original. The recent is the result of His manifestation of Himself and the original is the result of His remaining with Himself... When you know yourself your I-ness vanishes and you know that you and God are one and the same. But thereby one does not become God. The Absolute (*haqq*) remains the Absolute and the individual human (*khalq*) remains *khalq*...[19] If you regard Him through Him, then He regards Himself through Himself, which is the state of unity, but if you regard Him through yourself, then the unity vanishes and there are many'.[20]

In this way the Sufi idea is that creation (*takwin*) is just the manifestation of what was already existing. The eternal passes into external appearance (*zahūr*) The transcendent Absolute is unknowable (as the Vedantic *Brahman*). It is oneness (*ahdiya*) or as Jili calls it, He-ness (*huwiya*). The outward aspect of the One has two aspects, one is that of unity (*jihatul jama*) which is the same as *huwiya* of Jili and the other is of difference (*jihatual farq*) which Jili terms as *aniya* or I-ness.

The Sufis tried to reconcile their teachings with that of the Prophet, peace be on him, through neo-Platonism. The three identical ways of doing so were termed the doctine of *Nur-i-Mohammadi* of Ibn Fariz, the Saintship of Ibn El-Arabi, and *Insan-ul-kamil* of Abdul Karim Jili. As we have mentioned before, when Islamic orthodoxy was bent on persecuing the Sufis they tried to surmount this by bringing their thought as close as possible to it. This was the common object of *Nur-i-Mohammadi*, Saintship and *Insan-ul-Kamil*. The Sufi idea of oneness with God often came too close to the Hindu concept of incarnation. Ibn El-Arabi held that according to one sense 'Mohammed' meant the inhabitant of Mecca and Medina, and in another the 'eternal Mohammed' the term including all the prophets. This oneness is called *haqiqat-el-Mohammedia*. In his Sufi text, The Perfect Man, Jili said 'He is given names and in every age has a name which is appropriate to the guise in which he appears in that age... When he is seen as Mohammed, he is Mohammed, but when he is seen in another form, he is called by the name of that form'.[21] However vehemently one may deny it, this doctrine comes very close to belief in avatar. It was this fear that made these Sufis propound their respective doctrines thus putting the cloak of orthodoxy over the liberality of their beliefs. El-Arabi held all prophets and saints are 'manifestations of the spirit of Mohammed and the Seal of the saints is the perfect manifestation of the spirit of Mohammed. Further he claims "I am the seal of the Saints." '[22] According to Jili, the renowned Sufi saint, the Absolute becomes manifest in three steps–*ahdiya* (oneness) *huwiya* (he-ness) and *aniya* (I-ness) Another way is that of mystic illumination (*tajalli*). The 'perfect man' is the one prized in the universe. He is called by various terms, *qutb* (the pole) *rūh* (essence) *Haqiqat-i-Mohammadi*, *Aqle-awwal* (the highest Intelligence), *Rūh-ul-Quds* (the pure soul), and so forth.

According to Islam love of God means obedience to him. But to Sufis such as El-Ghazzali it is supreme and the end of man. Knowledge is related to love and love is God's gift to man. It is the essence of God, the source of life and existence. Hazrat Inayat Khan says that the whole imagery of Sufi literature contained in the writings of Rumī, Hafiz and Jami is 'The relationship between man as the lover and God as the Beloved'. Further he says:

> 'The one who hates his enemy and loves his friend cannot call God his Beloved, for he does not know God. When love comes to its fullness, then one looks at the friend with affection, on the enemy with forgiveness, on the stranger with sympathy. There is love in all its aspects expressed when love rises to its fullness; and it is the fullness of love which is worth offering to God. It is then that man recognizes in God his Beloved, his ideal; and by that, although he rises above the narrow affection of this world, he is the one who really knows how to love even his friend. It is the lover of God who knows love when he rises to that stage of the fullness of love.'[23] The Sufi mystic Dādū was asked by the emperor Akbar 'What is God's nature? What is His form? What is His substance? What is His colour?' And Dādū is said to have answered 'God's nature is love, God's form is love, God's substance is love, God's colour is love'.[24]

PRACTICE

He who falls asleep on the Road is bound to be deprived of his hat or his head.

Nizami Treasury of Mysteries

The steps or stages (*muqāmāt*) for achieving union with God are narrated in the *Risāla* of al-Qushayrī.[25] According to this there are ten stages:

Tawba (conversion, i.e., turning to God); *mujāhada* (earnest striving, i.e. fighting against lust); *khalwa wa-'uzla* (solitariness and withdrawal); *taqwā* (awe of God);l *wara* (abstention); *zuhd* (renunciation); *samt* (silence); *khawf* (fear); *rajā* (hope); and, *huzn* (sorrow, or repentance of the sins one has committed). Thus the Sufi moves from one stage to another till finally *rīdā* (satisfaction) is reached. Sheikh Shihāb-ud-din Suhrā wardī conceives ten stages, namely repentance, abstinence, piety, poverty, patience, gratitude, fear, hope, contentment and submission to the divine will. But union with God is achieved by nine emotional states (*hāl*). These are love (*muhabbat*); yearning or longing (*shauq*) which is of two kinds *sifat* which yearns for the Beloved's grace, mercy and kindness and of being (*zāt*) which desires union with the Beloved; *gairat* (jealousy), i.e., single-minded service of God; *qurb* (nearness of God), *hayā* shame, i.e., shame at being wanting in sincerity; *uns-o-haibat* (intimacy and awe); *qabz-o-bast* (the heart veiled-*hijāb* and revealed-*kahf*); *fana-o-baqa* (annihilation and subsistence); and, *ittisal* (union with God or the attainment of *wasl*, when there is no distinction between the seeker and God).

True knowledge of God, according to Sufis can be got only by intuition when God's image is mirrored in the heart. But before this happens the heart's mirror on which the dust of wordly desires has settled must be cleared. This dust is called *nafs* (the carnal longings of the soul). This is possible only by detachment, meditation (*muraqabā*) and self-examination (*muhasabā*). This method and progress on the way, or spiritual journey is called *safar* and results in attainment of union with God (*hāl*).

The *safar* is accomplished with the assistance of *tauba*, *wara zuhd, sabr* and so forth which work towards detachment and with their help *nafs* is overcome. Sincerity in thought and action is necessary and also the determination to give up the sinful life and create love for God. This striving is called *anabat*. Gradually the mind is diverted to God and is ultimately united with him. The steps required for achieving this have been given above, i.e., *tauba* or repentance meaning abandonment of wordly life, service of God, advancement on the spiritual path, regret for sins committed and resolving not to commit them in future; *zuhd* abstinence or renunciation, i.e., giving up everything for the sake of God alone; *faqr* or poverty meaning non-possessivenes or equanimity and neither being pleased with the getting of material things nor sorrowing at their loss; what Kabīr expresses in the verse quoted before, namely: *usatati nindā doū bibarajita etc.*[26]

Sabr or patience means withholding the mind from running back to the wordly pleasures and materialism which have been once abandoned, enduring unpleasant and painful things and carrying out difficult tasks uncomplainingly.

Apart from the outward turning away from worldly pleasures there is the inner struggle to purify the mind. This is called *Al-jihād-al-akbarī*. It is performed by meditation on God's glory, self-examination and righting oneself where he has gone astray, reasoning and sincerity in communion with God, truthfulness in its myriad aspects, fear and hope, reliance on God alone, satisfaction with one's own lot, and thankfulness to the Giver.[27]

The Sufi *Murshīd* or *Pīr* is analogous to the Hindu and Sikh guru. He is said to be God's representative on earth. Suhrawardi's says that God reveals the truth to him, and he conveys it to the seeker, disciple or learner called *murīd*. Ibn El-

Arabi claimed that the saints (*auliyas*) are greater even than prophets. Sufism is above all a spiritual teaching. Love is the basis of all Sufi doctrines. Ibn El-Arabi says:

> Love is my religion
> Sometimes I am called on of divine wisdom,
> Or a monk or a sage
> But my Beloved is one
> The one who has no limit.

This love element is also disclosed in Arabi's '*Interpreter of Desires*' which is love poetry of the highest order but in essence spiritual and mystic. *Taubā* is the basis of love and its states are *fanā*, *baqā*, *sadhv* and *mahv*. When the veil between man and God is removed by love the light of faith (*nur-i-yaqīn*) shines. Perfected beauty is then known by the *murid* and yearning for it (*shauq*) awakens in his heart. Other terms for the this proximity of man and God are *uns* (intimacy) and *qurb* (nearness). Absolute communion unveiled and unhindered between man and God is known as *wāsil billah*. This implies removal of the evil (*hijāb*) completely. There are various stages of *wasl* (communion). In the first, God is realized to be the Doer or Agent of all works. Then there comes *uns* and *haibat* which means complete annihilation of the seeker's individuality; thereafter *fanā*, the revealing of knowledge and faith in his heart and finally *haq-ul-yaqīn* in which knowledge gets into every pore of the seeker.[28] But even then the destination is far off and the seeker cannot reach it in his short life.[29] This of course points out that one lifetime is not enough and as we have quoted Raymond A. Moody in *Life after Life*, knowledge is an ongoing process spread through many lifetimes.

The two spiritual states reached by the *murīd* are annihilation and subsistence. Various Sufis have interpreted them in different ways. But basically annihilation (*fanā*) means that the *murīd* or seeker is completely absorbed in God and totally merged in him. *Fanā* is of two kinds-outer (*zāhirī*) or inner *bātini*. In *zāhirī fanā* the seeker is in communion with God through all his senses--hearing, seeing, working and so forth This is much like the *mādhurya* stage (the highest one) of Vaishnava devotion; which has already been narrated before.[30] This is like the state of *bātini fanā* in which says the Sufi, God so overwhelms the seeker that he has no consciousness of his separate existence.[31] This is analogous to the final stage of *mādhurya* Vaishnava devotion.[32]

The Moslem theologians were against celibacy as it was not sanctioned by the Prophet peace be on him, or by the Holy Quran. Suhrawardi, however, enjoined it for two reasons. Firstly it preserves the semen and so does not weaken the new seeker in his spiritual quest and secondly it saves him from worldly necessities essential to family life and protects him from worries so that he can meditate single-mindedly on God. In some Sufi Orders, particularly of Indian origin, seclusion for forty days was undergone during which the Sufi meditates on God and studies the Holy Quran. This period of seclusion was termed *chilla*. As regards music (*sama*), it was shunned by orthodox Sufis, but advocated by others, like Suhrawardi, who believed that it was beneficial in concentrating the mind and producing ecstasy (*wajd*). Suhrawardi said that ordinary people heard music as an entertainment, the novice for *shauq* and *khauf*, the *auliyas* for the bounties of God and the gnostics (*arifs*) for God-knowledge, the perfect for revelation.[33] Those who hear music often shed tears in God's fear and yet others due to joy. Those already perfected are unaffected by it.[34]

REFERENCES

1. Will Durant The Story of Philosophy.
2. *Rāmacharitamānasa Ayodhyākānda*, 218.2 (Gita Press Edn.).
3. *Brihadāranyaka Upanishad*. iii. 2. 13.
4. *Īsha Upanishad* 2.
5. *Plautus. Baechides*, Act IV, Sc. VII., 18 - (*chrysalus*), and *Hypsaeous* (*Stobaeus, Florilegium*, CXX., 13), also Menander. *Dis Exaparation, Fraagment* 4

6. The *Gospel of Sri Ramakrishna.*

7. *Katha Upanishad* 1.20, 28 - 29 (trans.; author's)

8. *The Gospel of Sri Ramakrishna.*

9. Aldous Huxley. *The Perennial Philosophy.* London : Collins 1946, p., 34.

10. ibid. p., 281 op. cit.

11. ibid, pp., 281 - 82 op. cit.

12. ibid. p., 306 op. cit.

13. Idries Shah. *The Sufis.* USA : Anchor Books, 1964, p., 405.

14. Raymond A. Moody, Jr., *Life after Life* USA : Bantam Books, 1975, pp., 67-8.

15. A.E. Affifi. *Mystical Philosophy of Muhyiuddin Ibnal Arabi,* p., 54.

16. Suhrawardi. *Awariful Muarif* Trans; Rashid A. Arshad, p., 507. & A.M.A. Shush tery, *Outlines of Islamic Culture,* p., 358.

17. Suhrawardi *Awariful Muarif,* p., 509.

18. S. Radhakrishnan. *History of Philosophy Eastern* and *Western,* II, pp., 184-86.

19. Margaret Smith. *Readings from the Mystics of Islam.* London, 1950, pp, 99, 100-101.

20. S. Radhakrishnan. *History of Philosophy Eastern and Western* p., 499.

21. Idries Shah. *The Sufis.* USA : Anchor Books, 1964. pp., 160-61. op. cit.

22. S.R. Sharda *Sufi Thought.* New Delhi : Munsharam Manoharlal 1974, p., 34.

23. *The Sufi Message of Hazrat Inayat Khan* London : (vol. 1) Barrie and Rockliff, 1960, p., 72.

24. W.G. Orr. *A Sixteenth Century Indian Mystic.* London : Lutter worth Press.

25. *The Cambridge History of Islam* vol. 2, pp., 615-6.

26. *A New Look at Kabir* Krishna P. Bahadur. New Delhi : Ess Ess Publications, 1997 p., 212.

27. These stages of the struggle are respectively *muraqabā*, *muhasabā*, *fiqr*, *ikhlās*, *sidq̄ khauf* and *razā*, *tawwakul*, *rizā* and *shukra*.
28. *Awariful Muarif* by Umr bin Mohammed Shahbauddin.
29. Suhrawardi Trans.; from Urdu, by Rashid Ahmad Arshad, p., 586. ibid.
30. Dinesh Chandra Sen. *Chaitanya and His Age*.
31. *Awariful Muarif* of Suhrawardi p., 591
32. Dinesh Chandra Sen. *Chaitanya and His Age*. (quoted before).
33. *Awarifūl Muarif* of Suhraward;, p., 250.
34. ibid. p., 245.

Bibliography

Affifi, A.E. *The Mystical Philosophy of Muhyiud-din Ibnul Arabi*, Cambridge, 1939.

al-Hujwiri, Abul Hasan. *Kashf-al-Mahjub*. English trans; R.A. Nicholson, London, 1939.

Arberry, A.J. *Sufism*. London, 1950.

Attar, Farid-ud-din *Tazkaratual Aulia*. English trans.; Bankey Bihari, Lahore, 1961.

Bistami, Abu Yazid *Miraj*. English trans.; by R.C. Zaeher London, 1960.

Cyprian Rise, O.P. *Persian Sufis*. London, 1964.

Davis F.H. Persian Mystics – *Jami*, London, 1918.

Hussain, S.A.Q. Maulvi, *Ibun Arabi* Lahore, 1963.

Ibn Batuta. *The Rehla of Ibn Batuta* English trans.; Mehdi Hussain. Baroda, 1953.

Idries Shah. *The Sufis*. New York : Doubleday, 1964.

Joginder Singh. *Hafiz and Shiraz*. London, 1952.

Junaid, Abul Qasime. *Kita'b Fana*. English trans.; R.C. Zaehner. London, 1960.

Nicholson, *A Literary History of the Arabs*. London, 1923.

Studies in Islamic Mysticism. Cambridge, 1921. *Idea of Personality in Sufism*. London, 1923. *Rumi - Poet and Mystic*. London. 1950.

Nizami, K.A. *Life and Times of Farid-ud-din Ganj-i-Shakar*. Aligarh, 1955.

Rom Landua. *The Philosophy of Ibnul Arabi* London, 1959.

Smith, Margaret. *Readings from the Mystics of Islam* London, 1950.

Subahan, John A. *Sufism, its Saints and Shrines.* Lucknow, 1960.

Titus Burckhardt. *An Introduction to Sufi Doctine.* English trans.; D.M. Mathouson. Lahore. 1959.

Umaruddin, M. *The Ethical Philosophy of Al-Ghazzali.* Aligarh, 1962.

Valiuddin, Mir. *Quranic Sufism.* Delhi. 1959.

Zaehner, R.C. *Hindu and Muslim Mysticism.* London. 1960.